Alexei Khomiakov

Ex Oriente Lux

New Perspectives on Russian Religious Philosophers

SERIES

———————

VOL. 3

Edited by Artur Mrówczyński-Van Allen,
Teresa Obolevitch, and Paweł Rojek

Russian religious philosophy of the nineteenth and twentieth centuries has a great importance for Christian theology and philosophy. Russian thinkers, rooted in the tradition of the Church Fathers, avoided the theological dualism that so deeply penetrates Western thought. Such philosophers and theologians as Peter Chaadaev, Alexei Khomiakov, Vladimir Soloviev, Evgeni Trubetskoy, Pavel Florensky, Sergey Bulgakov, Nikolai Berdyaev, Georges Florovsky, and Aleksei Losev developed unique views on the relationships between religion and culture, science, philosophy, and social life, which, unfortunately, are missing from contemporary Western debates. The pressing task is to include their legacy to the contemporary philosophical and theological discussions.

The series *Ex Oriente Lux* serves as a way to bring Eastern Christian intuitions into the current post-secular philosophical and theological context. Most volumes focus on one Russian thinker and include a selection of essays on his main ideas in historical and contemporary perspectives. The books are prepared by both Western and Russian scholars, thus creating a space for intellectual dialogue.

Previous Volumes

Beyond Modernity: Russian Religious Philosophy and Post-Secularism

Peter Chaadaev: Between the Love of Fatherland and the Love of Truth

Next Volumes

Paweł Rojek, *Theological Philosophy: Theology, Ontology,
and Logic in Russian Religious Philosophy*

Evgeni Trubetskoy: Icon and Philosophy

Alexei Khomiakov

The Mystery of Sobornost'

EDITED BY

Artur Mrówczyński-Van Allen,
Teresa Obolevitch,
and Paweł Rojek

PICKWICK *Publications* · Eugene, Oregon

ALEXEI KHOMIAKOV
The Mystery of Sobornost'

Ex Oriente Lux 3

Pickwick Publications
An Imprint of Wipf and Stock Publishers
199 W. 8th Ave., Suite 3
Eugene, OR 97401

www.wipfandstock.com

PAPERBACK ISBN: 978-1-5326-6155-6
HARDCOVER ISBN: 978-1-5326-6156-3
EBOOK ISBN: 978-1-5326-6157-0

Cataloguing-in-Publication data:

Names: Mrówczyński-Van Allen, Artur, editor. | Obolevitch, Teresa, editor. | Rojek, Paweł, editor.

Title: Alexei Khomiakov : the mystery of sobornost' / edited by Artur Mrówczyński-Van Allen, Teresa Obolevitch, and Paweł Rojek.

Description: Eugene, OR : Pickwick Publications, 2019 | Series: Ex Oriente Lux 3 | Includes bibliographical references.

Identifiers: ISBN 978-1-5326-6155-6 (paperback) | ISBN 978-1-5326-6156-3 (hardcover) | ISBN 978-1-5326-6157-0 (ebook)

Subjects: LCSH: Khomiakov, A. S. (Alekseĭ Stepanovich), 1804–1860. | Orthodox Eastern Church—Doctrines.

Classification: BX597.K5 A50 2019 (print) | BX597.K5 A50 (ebook)

Manufactured in the U.S.A.   06/27/19

Contents

v

Part II: Contexts

Part III: Influences

Contributors

Dmitrii Badalian, Senior Researcher at the National Library of Russia, Saint Petersburg, Russia.

Lucio Florio, Professor at the Argentine Pontifical Catholic University, Buenos Aires, Argentina.

Marek Kita, Professor at the Pontifical University of John Paul II, Krakow, Poland.

Françoise Lesourd, Professor at the Jean Moulin University, Lyon, France.

Marta Łukaszewicz, Assistant Professor at the University of Warsaw, Poland.

Alexei Malinov, Professor at the Saint Petersburg State University, Russia.

Frederick Matern, Independent Researcher, Ottawa, Canada.

Artur Mrówczyński-Van Allen, Professor at the International Center for the Study of the Christian Orient and the Institut of Philosophy "Edith Stein"—International Academy of Philosophy, Granada, Spain.

Teresa Obolevitch, Professor at the Pontifical University of John Paul II, Krakow, Poland.

Zlatica Plašienková, Professor at the Comenius University, Bratislava, Slovakia.

Pawel Rojek, Assistant Professor at the Jagiellonian University in Krakow, Poland.

Peter Rusnák, Professor at the Trnava University, Trnava, Slovakia.

Yulia Shaposhnikova, Professor at the Saint Petersburg State University, Russia.

Lada Shipovalova, Professor at the Saint Petersburg State University, Russia.

Stephanie Solywoda, Director of Stanford Program in Oxford, Oxford, UK.

Boris Tarasov, Professor at the Maxim Gorky Literature Institute, Moscow, Russia.

Elena Tverdislova, Independent Researcher, Tzur Hadassah, Israel.

Jennie D. Wojtusik, Assistant Professor at the University of Texas, Austin, USA.

INTRODUCTION

Alexei Khomiakov[1]

Thinking from Inside the Church

ARTUR MRÓWCZYŃSKI-VAN ALLEN

TERESA OBOLEVITCH

PAWEŁ ROJEK

Alexei Khomiakov (1804–1860) saw the European aristocracy declining before his eyes. Having emerged in the turmoil between Enlightenment thought and the conservative reaction, this aristocracy was becoming the stage for the fight between bourgeois liberalism and the radical democratic and socialist movements, between the nationalist and pro-independence trends and the large empires' policies of repression and expansion. The Catholic Church in the West ceased to play the role assigned to it by the self-styled conservatives, who were still submerged in fruitless nostalgia—at best, it served, like the Protestant Churches did, as formal justification of the new moral structures for the modern alchemists of the nation states. The Orthodox Church in Russia began to once again reflect on its identity while the world it knew was tragically collapsing. The rule of the tsars, the kaisers, and the emperors, which had become a bastion of conservatism, no longer represented an alternative. In the first half of the nineteenth century, Khomiakov, aware of this and with inspiring clairvoyance in the face of the increasingly obvious signs of this decline, sought answers in the Church's tradition of community identity, allowing Nikolai Berdyaev to write: "among the Slavophiles, was the genius of freedom, among the traditionalists, was

1. This publication was generously supported by a grant from the National Science Center, Poland (No. 2014/15/B/HS1/01620).

the genius of authority."[2] This freedom in thinking from within the Church, from within the free Church, means that today this retired cavalry officer offers us a superb locus for reflection.

In our opinion, it is very significant that in keeping with Chaadaev's assessment, today Alexei Khomiakov's thought is still considered a "retrospective utopia"[3] instead of being offered the place it deserves based on its own merit: a place alongside his contemporary Alexis de Tocqueville, in recognition of the Russian thinker as one of the great precursors of critical thought on the dangers of modern political ideas—ideas that, with increasingly more evidence, are revealed as utopian.

Therefore, in keeping with Berdyaev, we must underscore that "this particularly needs to be stressed, that *Sobornost'*, as a community within love, was not for Khomiakov a mere philosophical idea, a borrowing from Western thought, but was the rather a religious fact, taken from the living experience of the Eastern Church."[4]

Consequently, the second decade of the twenty-first century, which is especially rich in events of great importance to the Church, gives us a privileged position from which to try to outline a contemporary view of issues that are key to modern man—and, therefore, fundamental to theology, philosophy, and literature. The specific nature of Russian religious philosophy allows us to build a more complete interpretation of the contemporary world by avoiding the increasingly obvious tricks of modern positivist thought, and to explore the theological and philosophical intuitions of Russian thinkers, which with the passing of time seem to be ever more current and on the mark. This attitude towards the legacy of Russian thought allows us to reaffirm the importance of research on the history thereof. At the same time, it makes it possible for us to try to overcome a certain complex that reduces such studies to a type of "exotic philosophical archeology" within academic theological/philosophical circles, even in Russia. Philosophy cannot exist without the "history of philosophy," but when it is reduced to mere investigations of the past, it ceases to be philosophy (the same occurs with theology). This idea underlies the selection of essays collected in this second book of the *Ex Oriente Lux* series and dedicated to Alexei Khomiakov's personality and thought and to the idea of *sobornost'* in our current context.

As we have already indicated in the Introduction to the prior book in the series, *Peter Chaadaev: Between the Love of Fatherland and the Love*

2. Berdyaev, *Aleksei Stepanovich Khomiakov*, 90.

3. See Walicki, "Russian Social Thought," 10; Popov, "Khomiakov," 14.

4. Cf. Berdyaev, *Aleksei Stepanovich Khomiakov*, 92.

of Truth,[5] we can identify, as specific for Peter Chaadaev and for posterior Russian thought, the development of anthropological and historiosophical aspects into an ecclesiological narrative (which is the case, for example, both for Marxists and Slavophiles). This ecclesiological aspect of Russian thought reveals its existential roots and vocation, because "we are called upon to resolve most of the problems in the social order, to accomplish most of the ideas which arose in the old societies, to make a pronouncement about those very grave questions which preoccupy humanity."[6] As Vasilii Zenkovsky highlights:

> Eighteenth- and nineteenth-century Russian humanism—in its moral or aestheticizing form—grew from this *theurgical* root, from the religious need to "serve the ideal of justice." This same theurgical motif found expression in the occult searchings of the Russian freemasons, and in the mystical flurry of various spiritual movements during the reign of Alexander I; it was also expressed with exceptional force in Chaadayev.[7]

His understanding of Russia's future as a space open to the intervention of God's will was deeply rooted, as Zenkovsky emphasizes, in a "Christocentric conception of history,"[8] a "conception of history," for example later ingrown by Alexei Khomiakov in an ecclesiological principle of *sobornost'*.[9]

For this Russian thinker, one of the founders of the Slavophile school of thought, belief in the Church's—and Christian thought's—organic relationship with the society that has been given to us, is an assertion as self-evident as the need to nourish ourselves from the legacy of age-old ecclesiastic experience. Khomiakov was thus able to unreservedly offer an alternative to the also-Christian schools of thought colonized by modernity and shackled in the sterile fields of neo-Scholasticism, Kantianism, liberalism, and capitalism, even overcoming the limits of the deserts of Christian thought mangled by modernity and buried under the names of conservatism, traditionalism, values, etc. The Slavophile proposal of "integral life" entails the need for ontological, epistemological, anthropological, and historiosophical exploration, which, rooted in the experience of *sobornost'*—communion—allows Khomiakov to explore ways to overcome the colonization by modernity, which is something that the Church continues to need today as well. The life of the Church community thus emerges as a true alternative, full of life and

5. Mrówczyński-Van Allen et al., "Critique of Adamic Reason."

6. Berdyaev, *Meaning of History*, 109.

7. Zenkovsky, *History of Russian Philosophy*, 1:55–56.

8. Zenkovsky, *History of Russian Philosophy*, 1:157.

9. Mrówczyński-Van Allen et al., "Critique of Adamic Reason."

hope—and not just as one element of individualized, alienated, and frag-mented post-Enlightenment society. Thanks to this position, Khomiakov was able to emphatically affirm,

> The communion in love is not only useful, but fully necessary in order to grasp truth; the comprehension of truth is founded upon love and is impossible without it. Truth, inaccessible for any individual method of thought, is accessible only to the sum of methods of though tied by love. This trait sharply distinguishes Orthodox teaching from all others: from Latinism, which rests on external authority; and from Protestantism, which liberates the personality in the deserts of rationalistic abstraction.[10]

The pathologies that Khomiakov attributes to the Latin Church and to Protestantism—namely, authority and individualism alienated in the desert of the abstraction of reason, no less alienated and fragmented—are today the fundamental characteristics of modern states, of the societies in which we live, and to a large extent, of the alternatives that are brought forth in an attempt to counter them, too, whether they be new anarchist and anti-system schools of thought or nationalistic or imperialist claims; that may also be presented as Christian, whether Catholic, Protestant, or Orthodox. For Khomiakov, the Church is not merely an institution or a doctrine, but rather a living body of truth and love, imbued with the spirit of *sobornost'*. Understood in this way, the Church is also a social and political community and organization. The importance of this view of the nature of the Church became evident during the dramatic years 1917–1918, when the Local Council of the Russian Ortho-dox Church was convened and held. This Local Council, *Sobor*, turned out to be absolutely essential to the life of the Russian Orthodox Church under the control of the Bolshevik party and in the face of the assault of Communist ideas—a life that fundamentally depended on the Russian Orthodox Church's capacity to safeguard its identity.

Alexei Khomiakov's works therefore still figure today as a provocation that helps us once again take on the challenge of rescuing Christian thought from modern colonization, of taking it back from the desert of enlightened abstraction so that it can offer modern man a true alternative, a space for love and truth, the living experience of the Church. His person and thought present us with this challenge, which shapes the objectives of this book and the essays collected in it: namely, furthering knowledge of the work of this Russian thinker, advancing studies of his sources and his influence on the development of Russian thought, and exploring the surprising topicality of his philosophical/theological proposal—because the entire life of this

10. Khomiakov, "On the 'Fragments,'" 313.

"doctor of the Church"[11] figures before us as a profound reflection in light of God's generosity. It figures as a reflection before God, who creates mankind; before God who is the master of history and invites man to, in his freedom, participate in it; before God, who incarnates in Christ this invitation and dedication to humanity in the form of the Church.

In keeping with the entire series, our intention here is to offer Western readers a selection of works that we hope will serve as aids to rediscovering Khomiakov's thought (and the eventual consequences thereof) in the modern context. We would like to do so free from the typical complexes imposed on Christian thought in our era. Our readers will decide if we have been able to achieve this objective. As with this Introduction, which faithfully reflects the idea brought to bear in the series as a whole, we hope that we have been able to put the figure of Alexei Khomiakov into a living and contemporary context without imposing formal or interpretational restrictions and structures. He is a fundamental figure in Russian thought specifically, and through it, in Christian thought more globally. We also hope that this book will serve as the next step on the path towards recovering the Church's reflection on its own identity as *sobornost'*, as the Community that is the living body of Christ, that it will be the next step forward towards recovering the capacity for thought from within the Church.

Bibliography

Berdyaev, Nicolas. *Aleksei Stepanovich Khomiakov*. Translated by Fr. Stephen Janos. Mohrsville, PA: FRSJ, 2017.

———. *The Meaning of History*. New Jersey: Transaction, 2009.

Khomiakov, Alexei. "On the 'Fragments' Discovered among I. V. Kireevsky's Papers." Translated by Boris Jakim and Robert Bird. In *On Spiritual Unity. A Slavophile Reader*, edited by Boris Jakim and Robert Bird, 295–313. Hudson, NY: Lindisfarne, 1998.

Mrówczyński-Van Allen, Artur, et al. "The Critique of Adamic Reason: Peter Chaadaev and the Beginning of the Russian Religious Philosophy." In *Peter Chaadaev: Between the Love of Fatherland and the Love of Truth*, edited by Artur Mrówczyński-Van Allen, et al., ix–xv. Eugene, OR: Pickwick, 2017.

Popov, Andrey. "A. S. Khomiakov i yego socialnaya utopiya." In *Filosofskie i bogoslovskie proizvedeniya*, by Alexei S. Khomiakov, 3–26. Moscow: Knigovek, 2013.

Samarin, Yuriy. "Predislovie k pervomu izdaniyu." In *Polnoe sobranie sochineniy Alekseya Stepanovicha Khomiakova*, by Alexei Khomiakov, i–xxxvii. Vol. 2. Moscow: Universitetskaya tipografiya, 1886.

Walicki, Andrzej. "Russian Social Thought. An Introduction to the Intellectual. History of Nineteenth-Century Russia." *Russian Review* 36.1 (1977) 1–45.

Zenkovsky, Vasily. *A History of Russian Philosophy*. Vol. 2. Translated by George L. Kline. London: Routledge, 2006.

11. Samarin, "Predislovie," xxxvi.

PART I

Ideas

1

Looking for *Sobornost'*

Khomiakov's Ecclesiology as an Alternative to the Schmitt-Peterson Debate[1]

ARTUR MRÓWCZYŃSKI-VAN ALLEN

I

The century that separates us from 1917 has afforded us enough perspective to calmly look back at that era and reinforce our awareness that our times are a direct legacy of those events. And if we inevitably associate the year 1917 with the date of the Russian Revolution, it would seem fair to begin our examination of that era by reflecting on the experience and history of our sister Church, the Russian Orthodox Church. Our interest is further justified by the fact that we will be exploring the history of a Church in the midst of rebirth, a process of rebirth that began in the first few decades of the nineteenth century and was powerful enough to bring the Russian Orthodox Church to its encounter with history, prepared for mature reflection on its own nature and vocation and ready to give the strongest possible testimony of its faithfulness to Christ and to his people. In this context, therefore, it is not an exaggeration to state that for members of the Russian Orthodox faith, the year 1917 was marked not only by the tragic events of Russian and world history, but also by an event whose transcendence is difficult to overstate. I am referring to the "Pomestnyy Sobor Rossiyskoy Pravoslavnoy Cerkvi" that is, the Local Council of the Russian Orthodox Church, which was held in Moscow between 1917 and 1918.

1. This publication was generously supported by a grant from the National Science Center, Poland (No. 2014/15/B/HS1/01620).

In this work, I will first provide a short outline of the historical context that led the Russian Orthodox Church to convene the *Sobor* or Council in the year 1917. I will then turn to a discussion of Alexei Khomiakov's concept of *sobornost'*, briefly situating it in the context of the Schmitt-Peterson debate that continues to determine how the Church is understood in the Western world and for which the legacy of Russian Christian thought can (and should) offer us an alternative, surprisingly current view deeply rooted in Church Tradition. In this way I hope to offer an approach to the history of the Russian Orthodox Church and above all to its experience and way of understanding the world one hundred years after two events that were pivotal in its recent history: the Local Council of the Russian Orthodox Church and the Russian Revolution.[2]

II

In order to begin to understand the meaning of the 1917 events, we must first look back to 1453, the year in which the capital of the Byzantine Empire fell and Moscow was able to style itself as the heir and keeper of its tradition. In 1472, the Grand Prince of All Rus', Ivan III, wed Sophia Palaiologina, niece of the last *basileus*, Constantine XI, thereby joining the Rurik dynasty with the Byzantine imperial family, and, in Moscow, opening the doors to the ideas of empire, the "Third Rome," and the Muscovite patriarchy. In the year 1589, the Patriarch of Constantinople, Jeremias II, named Job, the Metropolitan of Moscow, to the position of Patriarch, thereby establishing the Moscow Patriarchate.

We must also recall that this Moscow Patriarchate, established in 1589, was de facto eliminated in 1700 by Tsar Peter I (Peter the Great). That was the year that Patriarch Adrian died; he had defended the freedom of the Church against secular power, and Peter I did not allow a successor to be elected. The Church was thus brought under the authority of the imperial power. In 1721, the *Ecclesiastical Regulations* were promulgated, in connection with

---

2. We should recall that the term "Russian Revolution" encompasses the events that occurred in Russia in the context of two revolutions. The first was the February Revolution (March 8–12, 1917, according to the Gregorian calendar, and February 23–27, 1917, according to the Julian calendar), which led to the abdication of Tsar Nicholas II and the creation of the Provisional Government. The second was the October Revolution (November 7, 1917, according to the Gregorian calendar, and October 25, 1917, according to the Julian calendar), which began with the Bolshevik coup d'état and sparked a cruel civil war resulting in the establishment of the Communist dictatorship and what today is known as the Soviet Union (Union of Soviet Socialist Republics, 1922–1991).

the reforms to modernize Russia advanced by Peter I. These regulations, following Prussian-Protestant models, incorporated the Russian Orthodox Church, rather than the Patriarchate, into the administrative structures of the Russian Empire. The government of the Orthodox Church was granted to the *Most Holy Governing Synod*, made up of ecclesiastical representatives (the Metropolitans of Saint Petersburg, Moscow, and Kiev among them) and officers of the imperial government. The most powerful position in the *Synod*, the *oberprocuror* (Chief Procurator), was held by a high-level secular (and sometimes military) officer appointed by the tsar.

However, despite the evident lack of formal and institutional freedom, this era in the history of the Russian Orthodox Church give birth to an impressive inner life, made extraordinarily apparent, above all from the nineteenth century onward, in a colossal theological, philosophical, and cultural explosion. The Russian Church, having been under the authority of the absolutist power for two centuries, thus came into the strength and vitality necessary to proclaim its freedom, even in the most challenging of times. This declaration of freedom had a very specific framework: the "Pomestnyy Sobor Rossiyskoy Pravoslavnoy Tserkvi," or Local Council of the Russian Orthodox Church, which took place from 1917 to 1918.

But the path to this Council began much earlier, and was simultaneously marked by such complexity (typical of the history of any people and of their local Church) and richness, that we are forced to choose only one aspect to discuss here, an aspect that had an exceptional impact on this transcendental moment in the history of the Russian Orthodox Church. The extent to which the idea of *sobornost'* put forth by Alexei Khomiakov (13 May 1804 to 5 October 1860), one of the founders of the Slavophile school of thought, did or did not directly impact the *Sobor's* decisions and work, can definitely be (and is) debated. But what is unquestionable is that all of the *Sobor* participants were familiar with it, and in one way or another, participated in it, insofar as they formed part of the Church and shared the same way of understanding themselves as a Church. Therefore, the practical, formal decisions made at the Council, which established how the life of the Church was organized, clearly stemmed from the ecclesiology of *sobornost'*. And the Russian Orthodox Church, closing the doors on one phase of its life with a reform that came out of its reflections on its own nature, was reborn with strength, prepared for what would occur over the following seventy years.

III

The idea of *sobornost'* thus appears in our work with a specific importance, for which reason I will sketch a brief outline below of its meaning and the context into which Alexei Khomiakov's thought places it, in an effort to disprove the accusation that it is an "obscure and vague"[3] term. We have transcribed the term from the original Russian neologism *sobornost'*, in order to avoid certain difficulties in finding an exact translation, and at the same time preserve the richness and validity of its specific nature as a theological and philosophical concept with its own value.

In Russian, the Slavic *sobor* is, in principle, a synonym for the Greek word *súnodos*, synodos. Although the Slavic noun *sobor* basically means "assembly," or even "council" or "cathedral," within the Slavophile school of thought the semantic evolution of the term *sobornost'* has resulted in a vastly different meaning. Today, the Russian Orthodox Church uses the term *synod* for the permanent council headed by the Patriarch of Moscow: the Holy Synod (*Svyashchennyy Sinod*). The Holy Synod is currently the standing administrative governing body of the Church. The Council of Bishops (*Arkhiyereyskiy Sobor*), convened every four years, is the supreme body responsible for the most important decisions on matters of faith, liturgy, and morality: in essence, on the life of the Church. From this formal, institutional, and practical partitioning of the organization of the Church, we can intuit the ecclesiology involved. We can also understand the complexity involved in translating the term *sobornost'*, and that our efforts at simplification would lead us to fail to convey its meaning. Moreover, as John Zizioulas indicates in a brief reflection, *sobornost'* is an idea that stems from the translation of the Greek word *katholikos* as *sobornaya* in the Slavic religion, and processes similar to those of Western theology were involved in that development.[4] To continue with Zizioulas's thought, *sobornost'* is also a Church whose

> nature is revealed and realistically apprehended *here and now* in the Eucharist. The Eucharist understood primarily not as a *thing* and an objectified means of grace but as an *act* and a *synaxis* of the local Church, *a 'catholic' act of a 'catholic' Church*, can, therefore, be of importance in any attempt to understand the catholicity of the Church.[5]

---

3. As defined by a jesuit, Ivan Gargarin. See Khomiakov, "Letter to the Editor," 135.

4. Zizioulas, *Being as Communion*, 143.

5. Zizioulas, *Being as Communion*, 145.

Likewise, the Church includes and constitutes the entire community: bishops, presbyters, and laypeople. It should also be noted that the presence of the idea of *sobornost'* in contemporary Western theology is in fact no longer a novelty, above all thanks to the editor of Khomiakov's works in France, the Dominican theologian Ives Congar, who suggested translating the term *sobornost'* not as *conciliarité* (conciliarity) but as *collegialité* (collegiality).

Khomiakov himself, in an exchange of letters with the most famous Russian Jesuit convert to Catholicism, Prince Ivan Gagarin, in defense of the tradition that credited Methodius and Cyril with translating the Creed to Slavic, argued for using the word *sobornaya* instead of the Greek *katholikos*:

> It is they who chose the word *sobornyi* to render the Greek term *katholikos*; and so it is by the word *sobornyi* that one can judge about the meaning they attributed to *katholikos*. . . . It is therefore evident that, in the thought of the two great servants of God sent by Greece to the Slavs, the word *katholikos* came not from *kath'ola* but from *katha'olon*. *Kata* often means "according to" (*kata Loukan, kata Ioannes*—"according to Luke," "according to John"). The Catholic Church is the Catholic Church *that is according to all*, or *according to the unity of all*, the Church of free unanimity, of perfect unanimity, the Church in which there are no more nationalities, no more Greeks or barbarians; in which there are no more differences in conditions, no more masters and slaves. This is the Church prophesied by the Old Testament and realized by the New. This finally, is the Church as St. Paul defined her.
>
> Was it a profound knowledge of the character of the Church, a knowledge drawn from the very sources of the truth in Eastern schools that dictated the choice of the word *sobornyi* to translate "katholikos" of the Creed? Or was it a yet loftier inspiration sent by the One who alone is the truth and the life? This question I do not dare answer. But I do dare to emphasize that the word *sobornyi* contains a profession of faith.[6]

So for Alexei Khomiakov, belief in the Church and Christian thought's organic relationship with the society in which we live was an affirmation as obvious as the need to draw from the legacy of age-old ecclesiastic experience. Khomiakov was thus able to uninhibitedly offer an alternative to the thought, above all Christian, that he felt had been influenced by modernity. It is impossible to overemphasize Khomiakov's importance to Russian theology, philosophy, and ultimately, culture. Quite rightly, this retired cavalry officer is among the most important Russian lay Christian thinkers of the

6. Khomiakov, "Letter to the Editor," 138–39.

nineteenth century (along with Nikolai Gogol, Fyodor Dostoevsky, and Vladimir Soloviev), of whom the dean of the Faculty of Theology at St. Tikhon's Orthodox University in Moscow, Father Pavel Khondzinsky, speaks in his recently published monograph *Church is not Academia. Non-academic Russian Theology of the Ninteenth Century.*[7] As Father Khondzinsky sets forth, these "non-academic" theologians—and among them, Khomiakov in particular—were extremely influential in the development of Trinitarian and Eucharistic ecclesiology, understood within the vast complexity of the life of the community, or, in a manner of speaking, of society in all its dimensions. His importance, as this present-day Russian theologian concludes, means that he is truly indispensable for today's Church as well.[8] It should not come as a surprise that Khomiakov's friends and disciples considered him a "teacher of the Church."[9]

This way of understanding ecclesiology within all the aspects of the life of the community, and community life from the ecclesiological perspective, is decisive. The Slavophile proposal of "integral life" entails the need for ontological, epistemological, anthropological, and historiosophical exploration, which, rooted in the experience of *sobornost'*—communion—allows Khomiakov to explore ways to overcome the colonization by modernity, which is something that the Church continues to need today, as, for example, Father Khondzisky's work testifies. In this way, the existence of the Church community emerges as a true alternative, full of life and hope, and not just as one element of individualized, alienated, and fragmented post-Enlightenment society. Thanks to this position, Khomiakov was able to emphatically affirm:

> The communion in love is not only useful, but fully necessary for the apprehension of truth, and the apprehension of truth is dependent upon it and impossible without it. That which is inaccessible for an individual's pondering of truth becomes accessible only by conjoined thought, united by love. This feature sharply differentiates the Orthodox teaching from all the other: from Latinism, standing upon an external authority, and from Protestantism, relegating the person to freedom within the wastelands of abstraction in judgmental reason.[10]

It is easy to verify that the pathologies that Khomiakov attributes to the Latin Church and to Protestantism—authority and individualism,

---

7. Khondzinskiy, *Tserkov' ne yest' akademiya.*

8. Khondzinskiy, *Tserkov' ne yest' akademiya*, 462–63.

9. Samarin, "Theological Writings," 183.

10. Khomiakov quoted in Berdyaev, *Aleksei Stepanovich Khomiakov*, 92.

alienated in the desert of the abstraction of a no less alienated and frag-mented reason—are today the fundamental characteristics of the societies in which we live and that form our modern states, and to a large extent, of the alternatives that are brought forth in an attempt to counter them as well, whether new anarchist and anti-system schools of thought or nationalistic or imperialist, progressive or conservative arguments—whether or not they are also presented as Christian-Catholic, Protestant, or Orthodox.

In this context, what is of particular interest in Khomiakov's thought is that, for him, the Church is not simply a more or less traditional institution or a rather abstract doctrine, but is a living body of truth and love, impregnated with the spirit of *sobornost'* and that understood in this way, the Church is also a fully social organization. Even more: it is the fully social organization par excellence, as it includes all dimensions of community life.

IV

The issue that is the core of Khomiakov's legacy—ecclesiology in its relation-ship with the modern world—has, some decades later, become a central issue in the West as well. There are, broadly speaking, two schools of thought on this topic: one represented by Carl Schmitt and another by Erik Peterson. Schmitt's position, which ultimately subordinates the Church into the role of providing metaphysical and ethical-legal resources for the administration of power, has been eclipsed in the past few lustrums by the Petersonian perspec-tive, which points out the dynamic of the practical timidity of the Church's presence in the social and political spheres, from which the discourse of the civil society and modern state's supposed neutrality has been gleaned. Conse-quently, today we find ourselves with a situation in which the Church either tries to appear like it has nothing to say in the affairs of the *polis*, or it lets itself be manipulated by the various political currents, trusting in Christians to, *on their own accord*—but thus as alienated individuals—join the competition among the organizations fighting for power.

In my opinion, Khomiakov's understanding of the Church offers a way to break the impasse created by the apparent lack of options in view of the reductionist Schmitt-Peterson dyad. Not without reason, Khomiakov's com-prehensive conception of ecclesiology has been fundamental to the Russian Orthodox Church's rediscovery of its identity, free from the conditions im-posed by the modern state,[11] even in its Communist dictatorship form.

---

11. We should note here that the expression "modern state" is a pleonasm, insofar as the idea of "state" comes from modern thought.

To a large extent, Schmitt's political theology was a development that Khomiakov roundly criticized under the name of "Authority." For Schmitt, authority was fundamental, and was built on the concept of "Sovereign." Khomiakov correctly pointed out the process by which excessive "Authority," of which he accused the Church of Rome, had been transferred to the state. In my opinion, a short quote from Khomiakov's famous response to the Swiss theologian Rodolphe Vinet very accurately defines Schmitt's position: "Land and materials are the domain of the state[12]—its weapon is the physical sword."[13]

And further on:

A this-worldly State took the place of the Christian Church.[14]
The singe living law of unity in God was displaced by private

---

12. In the French original, "L'État" (Khomiakov, *Quelques mots*, 9). In the Russian edition, "*gosudarstvo*" (Khomiakov, "Neskol'ko slov," 32).

In the context of our work, this lexical question is by no means trivial, and it must be addressed, albeit briefly. The Russian word *gosudarstvo* derives from the Old Russian *gosudar*, the governing prince of Old Rus', which was in turn joined with the word *gospodar* to form *gospodarstvo*, which we can translate as estate, property, farm. We can thus see the semantic relationship among the words *gosu-darstvo*, *gos-podarstvo*, and *gos-pod'*, short for *gos-podin*. The Paleoslavic word present in the Slavic languages as *gospodin* or *hospodin* is translated from the Greek *kúrios*, and has, in different contexts, the various meanings of master, host, and even husband. The relationship with the Latin word *hospes* is also usually noted. Khomiakov himself, in a short work published by the Imperial Academy of Sciences in 1855, *Comparison of Russian and Sanskrit vocabulary*, presents, in two entries, some etymological clues to the words *go-spodin* and *go-sudar*, with a somewhat different approach. He points out the relationship between the root "go," which comes from Sanskrit and indicates a person who others see as great, worthy of praise. See Khomiakov, *Zapiski o vsemirnoy istorii*, 5:537–38, 546.

At any rate, the etymology and semantics of the word *gosudarstvo* are not associated with the meaning of the word "state," although in modern Russian, as in so many other cases, it is used as the direct translation. Perhaps the closest English translation, would be to, starting with Latin, understand *gosudarstvo* as *dominium* and *gosudar* or *gospodin* as *dominus*, and, therefore, *dominium* and "master."

However, although Khomiakov himself uses the word *gosudarstvo* very carefully in accordance with the historical context he is describing (as we can see in his historio-sophical works, *Notes on Universal History*, where he defines *gosudarstvo* as a society/political community (Khomiakov, *Zapiski o vsemirnoy istorii*, 5:16), it is true that in his texts written in French, he uses the word *l'état* (sometimes with a capital letter and other times in lowercase) when he is describing *gosudarstvo* in Russian, and he uses the French word *souverain* when he refers to the emperor as *gosudar'*. Accordingly, in order to best convey Khomiakov's thought and intention, when translating the quotes into English in this work we have also consulted the French sources as necessary.

13. Khomiakov, "Neskol'ko slov," 32.

14. In the French edition, "Un état terrestre avait remplacé l'Eglise du Christ" (Khomiakov, *Quelques mots*, 28).

laws, bearing in themselves the imprint of utilitarianism and juridical concerns.[15]

As far as I know, in Europe today, only in Poland does Schmitt's political theology have some intellectual political relevance. In the other schools of Christian political thought, Erik Peterson's influence is evident. Therefore, I will now briefly explain the central point of Peterson's thought. In so doing, I hope that we will be able to verify that, despite Peterson's stated opposition to Schmitt's political theology, his way of thinking leads to the very same consequences. I also hope that we will be able to see that the Schmitt-Peterson option, characteristic, to a large extent, of contemporary Catholic political thought, is, in practice, illusory. Subsequently, I will try to ascertain the extent to which Khomiakov's idea of *sobornost'* can soundly guide us toward escaping the trap of seeing the Schmitt-Peterson option as the only possible one.

Peterson's famous interpretation of a passage in the third oration of one of the most classic works of patristics, *The Five Theological Orations* of Saint Gregory of Nazianzus, which aims to demonstrate the impossibility of maintaining a monotheistic political discourse in the Christian perspective, also, as a result, closes off society's political arena to the Church. This profound criticism of the monotheism of Schmitt's political theology, whose central point is a rather biased interpretation of the Cappadocian father, consequently removes the Church from the relationships that form the community, the society—and allows the modern state to take its place. Peterson affirmed, in reality freely interpreting Saint Gregory, that

> Christians . . . confessed the Monarchy of God. To be sure, not the Monarchy of a single person . . . but the Monarchy of the triune God. *This conception of unity had no correspondence in the created order.*[16]

In this way, the German theologian not only "liquidated" Schmitt's political theology, but also confined ecclesiology to a place far from the entire realm of community life, denying its fundamental relational, Trinitarian nature[17] and, therefore, making room for the state's soteriological ambitions. Thus, in practice, the Petersonian alienation of the Church from the *politeia* has the same consequences as Schmitt's thought. The quote from Khomiakov that we cited above to describe the consequences of Schmitt's

15. Khomiakov, "Western Confessions," 49; *Quelques mots*, 28.

16. Peterson, "Monotheism as a Political Problem," 103 (emphasis mine).

17. More on this topic in Mrówczyński-Van Allen, "Beyond Political Theology"; "Posle zapada i vostoka."

thought, somewhat expanded, also serves to define the effects of Peterson's "non-political theology":

> Rationalism grew up in the form of arbitrary definitions ... it placed between God and man a balance of obligations and merits, weighing sins against prayers, crimes against meritorious exploits; it set up transferences from one man to another, legitimized the barter of illusory merits; in short, it brought the whole machinery of the banking house into the treasury of faith.[18]

In this context, moving beyond the surface of interfaith criticism, the exercise of finding, in Khomiakov's thought, the elements to help recover, with an explicitly Trinitarian ecclesiology, the awareness of the Church as the very seed of society, of community, of the *polis*, makes it possible, in the first place, to understand the extent to which his influence marked the ecclesiology of the *Sobor* in 1917–1918. Secondly, it allows us to see the extent to which, through the decisions made at that time, the Russian Orthodox Church was able to bequeath us a type of concrete testimony of freedom in the years of Communist persecution. And thirdly, it allows us to verify the extent to which this retired cavalry officer and "teacher of the Church" catalyzed, to an extent that is difficult to overstate, the process of redefining the awareness of the Church's identity in twentieth-century Russia—the awareness of the ecclesiastical community's particular identity, of *sobornost'*, which means the unity, the community that is born on freedom and love and that brings all men together with each other and with God. This unity can only spring forth from within a community of freedom and cannot be mandated by state laws. In order to establish this distinction, as well as the line between the state and the people, we must start with a very clear awareness of the Church as a community, as a living body, as a city that does not relinquish earthly life. In the circumstances surrounding the Orthodox Church in Russia throughout most of the twentieth century, choosing either of the two options in the Schmitt-Peterson dyad meant losing freedom or renouncing truth, as they existed in the specific community; it meant either nationalization or alienation—two poles of the same, likewise bipolar process: the secularization of the Church and the sacralization of the state. That is to say, the totalitarian process, the process by which the community is destroyed through individualization and alienation.

Therefore, the question of whether Christians' lives are "individual"[19] or, on the contrary, part of a collective, shared growth, is a fundamental one,

18. Khomiakov, "Western Confessions," 49.

19. The concept that appears in the Slavophiles' discussion—for example, in the letters between Aksakov and Khomiakov—is "particularism" (*partikulyarizm* in Russian);

and it was key to the development of Slavophile thought as well. The correspondence among Aleksandr Koshelev, Ivan Aksakov, and Aleksei Khomiakov in the autumn of 1852 allowed them to develop a view of the Christian people as a free, living community, a community alive in love and free from slavery, free from the fragmentation and alienation that are nourished by "egoism that goes beyond the tomb."[20] In perhaps his best-known work, *The Church is One*, Khomiakov defined the Church as follows:

> The Church, even upon earth, lives, not an earthly, human life, but a life of grace which is divine. Wherefore not only each of her members, but she herself as a whole, solemnly calls herself Holy. Her visible manifestation is contained in the sacraments, but her inward life in the gifts of the Holy Spirit, in faith, hope, and love. . . . She lives not under a law of bondage, but under a law of liberty. She neither acknowledges any authority over her, except her own, nor any tribunal but the tribunal of faith.[21]

This way of understanding the Church makes it possible to understand Khomiakov's *sobornost'*, as described by Nikolai Berdyaev:

> Khomiakov, like all the Slavophiles, perceived society as an organism, rather than as a mechanism. There is an organic societal *Sobornost'*, an organic collectivism, rather than mechanistic, beyond which lies concealed the churchly *Sobornost'*. Only a Christian sociality is organic in the genuine sense of the word; a societal order, having lost its faith, decays and is transformed into a mechanism.[22]

As Berdyaev described it, "the ideal of an organic Christian societal order, an ideal opposed to every sort of mechanism, to every formalism"[23] lived within Khomiakov. And thanks to living the Church this way, Khomiakov was able to understand that the relationship within the free community that defines, constitutes, and builds it, is one of love: "This is a relationship based upon mutual love, and without the love they have sort of justification, they would become moribund and decay onto despotism."[24] Despotism, or totalitarianism, as we define it today, is the state danger to which the

---

however, in our opinion, it is the English word "individualism" that best transmits the meaning intended by the Russian authors in question.

20. Khomiakov, "Pis'mo," 337.

21. Khomiakov, "Church Is One."

22. Berdyaev, *Aleksei Stepanovich Khomiakov*, 138.

23. Berdyaev, *Aleksei Stepanovich Khomiakov*, 138.

24. Berdyaev, *Aleksei Stepanovich Khomiakov*, 139.

Church submits, giving up what today we call "civil society," or becoming the instrument of a caesaropapist or theocratic idea. Khomiakov also recognizes these dangers and can identify them, because, as another Slavophile, Yuri Samarin, wrote, "Khomiakov represented an original manifestation of total freedom in religious consciousness, one nearly unprecedented in our land,"[25] "Khomiakov *lived in the Church.*"[26]

Khomiakov, looking out from within the Church, critically analyzed the Protestant Churches, the Catholic Church, and the state as well. For him, the separation between what is understood as the state and the people/nation leads to a proposal that can overcome one of the fundamental elements of the Schmitt-Peterson alternative. These two German thinkers identified the state as the people/nation. But for Khomiakov, the Church was the people, the *sobornost'*. For Khomiakov, once again quoting Samarin:

> The Church is not a doctrine, not a system, and not an institution. The Church is a living organism, an organism of truth and love, or more precisely: *truth and love as an organism.*[27]

And this organism is not abstract, is not an idea; it is a people, a body; it is the Church. It is most likely Khomiakov's experience of life within the Church that makes understanding him today problematic and somewhat difficult. Perhaps because of that, Berdyaev mistakenly affirmed that "A central question about the relationship of the Church and the state was . . . not resolved by Khomiakov, although he did more than the other Slavophils for the teaching about the Church."[28]

But in fact, we would be more than justified in affirming that Khomiakov did respond in depth to the question of "Church/state" relations by explaining the Church's social, communital, political, and organic nature, keeping his response within the union of his ecclesiology and his historiosophy. Specifically, he posits his response and thought from within the Church, understood as the community body par excellence. This means that he cannot concede the state its alleged organic character, even though that is modernity's principal and foundational aspiration.

The very fact that Khomiakov differentiates between the society and the state (*gosudarstvo*) demonstrates that he does not identify the state with the nation or with society—this identification emerged in the nineteenth century and has been dominant since the twentieth—that is to say, with all

25. Samarin, "Theological Writings," 165.

26. Samarin, "Theological Writings," 162.

27. Samarin, "Theological Writings," 171.

28. Berdyaev, *Aleksei Stepanovich Khomiakov*, 144.

the ways in which the state appropriates the communities. The *gosudar* is not the sovereign in the Schmittian sense, given that his legitimacy derives from his unity with the community and not from his extraordinary *decisionist* capacity. The society is not the state. The people do not identify with the state, but neither do they reject, in line with Peterson's thought, its legitimacy for forming a political community, a *polis*. Khomiakov writes that

> the people entrusted to their chosen one all the power with which they themselves had been invested, in all its forms. By right of this election the sovereign became the head of the people in ecclesiastical matters as well as in matters of civil governments, I repeat—became head of the people in ecclesiastical matters, and only in this sense head of the territorial Church. The people did not and were not able to transfer to the sovereign a right which they did not possess.[29]

He explains what he had stated a few paragraphs earlier:

> we acknowledge not head of the Church, either clerical or temporal. Christ is her head and she knows no other.[30]

Furthermore, only a free people can legitimate a sovereign, and this freedom also includes freedom of religion, even for the emperor. What would happen if the sovereign made some kind of "mistake"? In that case, responds Khomiakov, he would continue to be emperor within the legitimacy granted him by the people, "the only thing that happen is that there would be one less Christian in her [the Church's] bosom."[31]

It does not matter that to us, this interpretation might seem to be an idealized view of history and politics. What matters is Khomiakov's clear interpretation of the nature of legitimate power. This legitimacy, in his opinion, was only possible because of the *acte de souveraineté*, in virtue of the *souveraineté du peuple*, which is the *souveraineté suprême*.[32]

But the people can only be qualified to perform the *acte de souveraineté* if organically they are one, if they form an ontological and gnoseological unit. Khomiakov sought to resolve this issue as follows:

> But in order that this may come to pass, the life of every individual must be in full accord with the life of all, so that there will be no disunity either within the individual or in society.

29. Khomiakov, "Western Confessions," 34.

30. Khomiakov, "Western Confessions," 33.

31. Khomiakov, "Western Confessions," 36.

32. Khomiakov, *Zapiski o vsemirnoy istorii*, 8:200–201.

Individual thought can be powerful and fruitful only when there
has been a strong development of common thinking; and that
can take place only when learned men are bound with the rest
of the body of society through the bonds to the main body of
society by ties of rational love and when the intellectual powers
of every individual are revivified by the intellectual and spiritual
lifeblood circulating in his people.[33]

This assertion illustrates an idea that was fundamental to the Slavophiles, and the principle of "integral knowledge" is necessary in order to
understand its meaning since, as Berdyaev sets forth:

The idea of an integral knowing, based upon an organic fullness
of life,—is the departing point of Slavophil and Russian philosophy. Following upon Khomiakov and Kireevsky, the original
and creative philosophical thought with us has always posited
itself the task of discerning not an abstract, intellectual truth,
but rather truth as both pathway and life.[34]

The quote from the Gospel according to Saint John, "I am the way
and the truth and the life" (John 14:6), seems to be particularly present in
Khomiakov's thought. For the Church, "life and truth are one"[35] because
"the truth of faith is given to the union of all and to their mutual love in
Jesus Christ."[36] With the philosophy based on that "definition" of truth, the
fundamental rejection of Kant and Hegel seems to be a given. Despite German philosophy's profound influence in shaping Russian philosophy, the
latter became the critic, and to a large extent, the response to the former. For
Khomiakov, Hegel's logic meant "inspiriting of abstract being (*Einvergeisti-
gung des Seyns*)."[37] He wrote:

That which is had to be completely discarded. Concept itself, in
its fullest abstractness, was to resurrect everything from its own
depths. Rationalism, or the logical understanding, was to find
its final crown and divine blessing in the new creation of the
entire world. This was the enormous task that the German mind
set itself in Hegel, and one can only admire the boldness with
which he undertook its resolution.[38]

33. Khomiakov, "On Humboldt," 229.

34. Berdyaev, *Aleksei Stepanovich Khomiakov*, 83.

35. Khomiakov, "Western Confessions," 54–55.

36. Khomiakov, "Some Remarks," 68.

37. Khomiakov, "On the 'Fragments,'" 299.

38. Khomiakov, "On the 'Fragments,'" 298.

But for Khomiakov, as we have already seen, Christ and the Church, which is his body, are not abstract beings. Therefore, knowledge of truth (and, therefore, of theology and philosophy) is tied to experience, to the practice of Logos in life. In this way, the Russian thinker was able to overcome the influence of the Socialist and conservative variations of German idealism. In the traditionalists is the genius of authority, summarized Berdyaev. In Khomiakov, the genius of freedom.[39] This is the difference between the law and love. This is the difference between a society of slaves and *sobornost'*; this is the difference between the state and the Church. Therefore, continuing with Berdyaev, we must underscore that "this particularly must needs be stressed, that *Sobornost'*, as a community within love, was not for Khomiakov a mere philosophical idea, a borrowing from Western thought, but was the rather a religious fact, taken from the living experience of the Eastern Church."[40]

Khomiakov was thus able to famously write:

> The Church is not an authority, just as God is not an authority and Christ is not an authority, since authority is something external to us. The Church is not an authority, I say, but the truth—and at the same time the inner life of the Christian.[41]

Alexis de Tocqueville shared this idea of "authority," as the editor of his complete works indicated in a footnote.[42] Because, as Khomiakov explains in his best-known work, *The Church is One*, the law of the Church "is not a law of bondage or of hireling service, laboring for wages, but a law of the adoption of sons, and of love which is free."[43]

V

This way of understanding the Church, formulated by Khomiakov, already held weight in the first attempts to convene the *Sobor* in 1905, although the initial steps towards the *Sobor* can be found in the meetings organized by some bishops in the last few decades of the nineteenth century and

---

39. Cf. Berdyaev, *Aleksei Stepanovich Khomiakov*, 90.

40. Berdyaev, *Aleksei Stepanovich Khomiakov*, 92.

41. Khomiakov, "Western Confessions," 50.

42. "Very few Western (and also Orthodox) writers understand this difference; but among them it is mostly well-received. From America, he wrote the following to one of his friends: 'It is clear that many Protestants, in desperation, abandon the search for truth and once again deliver themselves to the yoke of authority'" (Tocqueville, *Oeuvres et correspondance*, 312, editor's note; cf. Khomiakov, "Western Confessions," 50).

43. Khomiakov, "Church Is One."

dedicated to analyzing the Russian Orthodox Church's missionary vocation. We must also therefore take into account the deeply missionary character of the 1917–1918 *Sobor*, in which the mission was already understood as the "Church's dialogue with the world."[44]

The Local Council of the Russian Orthodox Church was solemnly opened on August 15, 1917, in the Moscow Cathedral of the Dormition, in the Kremlin. It lasted for over a year, until September 7, 1918, the date on which the so-called synodal period ended and the patriarchate was returned to Moscow. On November 21, 1917, the XVI Patriarch of Moscow and All Russia, Tikhon (Vasilii Belavin, November 21, 1917 to April 7, 1925) was enthroned. He would be canonized in 1989. The *Sobor* had more than 564 participants, including 227 priests from among the hierarchy and the clergy, plus 299 laypeople.

The historical events in which Russia was immersed did not, obviously, remain on the sidelines of the *Sobor*'s work. Rather, the Council very thoughtfully addressed issues like the war with Germany, the Russian declaration of the Republic, the fall of the provisional government, the Communist October Revolution, the dissolution of the Constituent Assembly, the proclamation of the Decree on the Separation of Church and State, and the beginning of the Civil War. Although the sounds of the revolutionary storm literally reached to where the Council was being held at the Eparchial House in central Moscow, the participants' attention focused above all on questions vital to the Church. Neither did the Bolsheviks directly interfere in the work. However, not long after the *Sobor* was concluded, the building was expropriated from the Orthodox Church and converted for a time into the headquarters of the Communist Education Academy. Today it holds the facilities of St. Tikhon's Orthodox University.

The issues that were of particular import to the *Sobor* participants can be identified by comparing the number of individuals in each work group. It is no coincidence that, of the nineteen committees or work groups formed to perform the Council's work, the largest seven were directly related to the clear awareness of the urgent need for "a synodal organization of the life of the Church and of liberation from state protection,"[45] which in practice meant redefining the Church's identity itself: the identity of a free organic reality. It is therefore significant that the largest groups were dedicated to the "organization of the parish" (166 members), followed by "higher ecclesiastical government" (138 members), then liturgy, diocesan structure, educational and pastoral institutions, etc., down to the work group on the "legal

44. Kraveckiy, *Tserkovnaya missiya*, 10.

45. Kraveckiy, *Tserkovnaya missiya*, 10.

position of the Russian Church in the state," with 94 members. From the perspective offered by a century of time gone by, it is difficult to not point out, at a minimum, that this order of the efforts put in to building the Russian Church reflects, to a large extent, Khomiakov's ecclesiology and, above all, how he prepared the Russian Church for the great test to which history was already putting it.

In the declaration *On the Relationship of the Church and the State*, written by Sergei Bulgakov at the request of the *Sobor*'s Committee VII,[46] and presented by the author on November 13, 1917, the imperative of the separation of the Church and the state, understood as the exclusion of the Church from public life, was compared with the desire for the "sun to not shine and fire to not heat." The Russian theologian continued: "The Church, by virtue of the internal law of its existence, cannot renounce its vocation to illuminate and transform all of human life, to impregnate with its light."[47]

But he likewise made it clear that the Church does not commit to any particular form of government:

> Now, when due to the will of Providence the tsarist autocracy has collapsed and new forms of government are taking its place, the Orthodox Church has no particular opinion about them from the point of view of their political expediency, but invariably continues to subscribe to an understanding of power under which all governance must be a Christian act of service.[48]

Having already emigrated, Bulgakov wrote, reaffirming his 1917 position and continuing along the path of Khomiakov's thought:

> The Church in accepting juridical separation from Caesar, from the state, and in seeing it as liberation, does not renounce its influence over the *whole* of life. The ideal of the transformation of the state by the interior energies of the Church remains in all its force and without any restriction, and the very time of the separation of Church and state; for that separation remains exterior and not interior. The Church's methods of influence change; the work is no longer done outside, from above, but from within, from below, from the people and by the people.[49]

46. Committee in charge of the question, "The Russian Church's legal position in the state."

47. Bulgakov, *Sobranie opredeleniy*, 14.

48. Bulgakov, *Sobranie opredeleniy*, 14–15.

49. Bulgakov, *Orthodox Church*, 189.

This affirmation of the freedom of the life of the Church, evidenced in the *Sobor*'s work, starting with the organization of parish community life, passing through the restoration of the patriarchate, and concluding with the self-affirmation of freedom *vis-à-vis* the state (in that exact order), has made the Church's existence possible, even when it was underground, during Communist rule. Despite the new regime's endless attempts to destroy the life of the parish community, to break or exploit its communion with the episcopal order and the Patriarch, that community's ability, generated "from within," to live the unity of the Christian people, has allowed it to resist persecution by the state. *Sobornost'* has won out over the state, because, as we have already seen, "the Church is a living organism, an organism of truth and love, or more precisely: *truth and love as an organism.*"[50]

During the Council a serious, profound debate was held on the creation of the Church's metropolitan structure, the position of the parish clergy, the autonomous organization of the life of the community that forms the parish, and the active participation of laypeople, both men and women.

As Natalia Krivosheeva, researcher at the Orthodox University of Moscow, underscores, for the 1917–1918 Council,

> *sobornost'* was obviously a leitmotiv, the principal inspiring idea. The *Sobor* participants associated the future of the Russian Church precisely with the idea of *sobornost'*.[51]

The longest text to emerge from the *Sobor*, the "Parish Decree," passed on April 20, 1918,[52] reaffirmed the Church's unity pursuant to the hierarchical principle and, at the same time, ensured the parishes' organizational and community autonomy. The Decree's introduction ends with the affirmation that the parish, "the little Church," must be understood just as the entire Church is a body whose head is Jesus Christ, and as such it participates in the fullness of all of Christian life and activity. A parish is defined as follows:

> In the Orthodox Church, a parish is defined as the community of Orthodox Christians, made up of clergy and laypeople from a specific area who come together around a church, as part of a diocese and united in the canonical management of their diocesan bishop, under the leadership of an appointed resident priest.[53]

In this way, the principle of *sobornost'* was implemented in practice with the establishment of parishes, largely autonomous in their management, in

50. Samarin, "Theological Writings," 171.

51. Krivosheyeva, "Pomestnyy Sobor," 65.

52. Bulgakov, *Sobranie opredeleniy*, 13–41.

53. Bulgakov, *Sobranie opredeleniy*, 13.

both the administrative and ecclesiological senses. This was how the Church was understood, and it became the space where the ecclesiastic community sought to defend itself over various periods of the Soviet regime's persecution against Christians.

As historian Dimitry Pospielovsky wrote, with the Local Council in 1917–1918, the Russian Orthodox Church entered the storm of the twentieth century as a "dynamic living organism." Khomiakov's idea of *sobornost'* and the *Sobor* itself marked the history of that era in a profound, complex way, but we are still far from understanding it adequately. For example, it is difficult to discern to what extent the one—and only—statistic from the Soviet era, with all the obvious conditioning factors, is relevant, and how to interpret it. This statistic, from 1937, states that at that time, 57.6 percent of the population of the communist state called themselves Christian believers.[54] Over the decades of persecution, several developments took place in the life of the Russian Orthodox Church: the Civil War, the great terror, the Second World War, the so-called destalinization; they all marked, in their own significant ways, the entire Soviet society. The seventies brought a significant generational change. Many young people, who were discovering Christianity and approaching the Church, did so thanks to literature. They first discovered the Church in books.[55] Intellectually they were much better prepared than Christians from earlier generations who had survived, but they did not know the living experience of the faith. Sergey Averintsev, an exceptional Russian historian, philologist, and writer, describes how in that era, a grandmother once said to [Averintsev's] wife, "You're young and you'll probably know: when is Easter this year?"[56] She wasn't asking a theological or institutional question, but rather the date Easter would be celebrated. It is hard to find another question that would be more important or relevant than this one. And it is hard to imagine another scene that would better define *sobornost'*, a scene that would better illustrate the history of the Russian Orthodox Church from 1917.

VI

Berdyaev ends chapter VI of his book on Khomiakov by stating that Slavophile thought on the nature of the state has been refuted by life itself.[57] Life today would seem to demonstrate that Khomiakov's intuitions were

54. Kraveckiy, *Tserkovnaya missiya*, 551.

55. Kraveckiy, *Tserkovnaya missiya*, 571.

56. Kraveckiy, *Tserkovnaya missiya*, 571.

57. Cf. Berdyaev, *Aleksei Stepanovich Khomiakov*, 146.

surprisingly accurate and ahead of his time. Although they are not aware of it, many modern Western philosophers and theologians (Nisbet, Kassierer, Cavanaugh, McIntyre, Milbank) explore the same paths that Khomiakov traveled a hundred years earlier. The Russian thinker was aware of the trap of caesaropapism in Byzantium's history, reinterpreted in Schmitt's political theology (characteristic of the current vanguards of conservatism), and in the same way could see the dangers of what today we call the Petersonian dynamic of the Church's abandonment of the public arena, the polis (characteristic of the rearguards of liberalism). Alexei Khomiakov deserves mention alongside his contemporary Alexis de Tocqueville as one of the great precursors of critical thought on the dangers of modern political ideas. And, ahead of Schmitt and Peterson, as a master of a free and liberating ecclesiology.

However, we should highlight a fundamental difference between de Tocqueville and Khomiakov. The Russian thinker was able to see where the answer lay to the totalitarian character of the modern state, to the state idol. And he knew how to explain this answer in his work; setting it out in the experience of *sobornost'*, he knew how to respond, with the only answer: the Church.

> The Church that serenely sees how century after century, wave after wave, the storms of historic upheavals, the currents of human passion and thought, crash around the rock, on which she safely sits. This rock is Christ.[58]

Khomiakov seems to offer us a way out of the tricky Schmitt-Peterson alternative. That is why perhaps this answer, constituting the ecclesiological freedom of *sobornost'*, also made it possible that, even though the *Sobor* had to close on September 20, 1917, without it we could not possibly understand not only the recent history of the Russian Orthodox Church, but also, perhaps, the future of the universal Church. The joint declaration signed in the Italian city of Chieti on September 21 of last year, in which the words *sínodos* (Greek), *concilium* (Latin), and *sobor* (Russian) appear together, is an unequivocal sign of this shared future.[59] Because, as Father Alexander Schmemann explained,

> *Sobor* is not *government* in the legal sense of the word, since there cannot be any government of the Church—the Body of

58. Khomiakov, "Eshche neskol'ko slov," 255.

59. The Fourteenth Plenary Session of the Joint Commission for Theological Dialogue between the Orthodox Church and the Roman Catholic Church, "Synodality and Primacy During the First Millennium: Towards a Common Understanding in Service to the Unity of the Church" (in Russian "Sobornost' i pervenstvo v pervom tysyacheletii: na puti k obshchemu ponimaniyu dlya sluzheniya yedinstvu Tserkvi").

Christ. *Sobor* is the testimony on the identity of all the Churches as the Church of God: in faith, in life, in love.[60]

A testimony that, in an extraordinary way, was given by the participants of the 1917–1918 *Sobor*, of the Local Council of the Russian Orthodox Church in 1917–1918. A testimony made by more than half of the participants, by those who today we know were jailed, tortured, sent to work camps, and murdered during the Communist state's years of terror. A testimony made by the definitive *Sobor* at its peak, by the *Sobor* of the Church's confessors and martyrs.

Bibliography

Berdyaev, Nicolas. *Aleksei Stepanovich Khomiakov*. Translated by Fr. Stephen Janos. Mohrsville, PA: Fr. Stephen J. Janos, 2017.

Bulgakov, Sergius. *The Orthodox Church*. Translated by Elizabeth S. Gram. London: Centenary, 1935.

———. *Sobranie opredeleniy i postanovleniy Svyashchennogo Sobora Pravoslavnoy Rossiyskoy Tserkvi 1917–1918 gg.* Vol. 4. Moscow: Izdatel'stvo Novospasskogo monastyrya, 1994.

Khomiakov, Alexei S. "The Church is One." In *On Spiritual Unity: A Slavophile Reader*, edited by Robert Bird and Boris Jakim, 29–53. Hudson, NY: Lindisfarne, 1998.

———. "Eshche neskol'ko slov pravoslavnogo Khristianina o zapadnykh veroispovedaniyakh po povodu raznykh sochineniy Latinskikh i protestantskikh o predmetakh very." In *Polnoe sobranie sochineniy Alekseya Stepanovicha Khomiakova*, by Alexei S. Khomiakov, 169–258. Vol. 2. Moscow: Tipo-litografiya T-va I. N. Kushnerov, 1904.

———. "Letter to the Editor of *l'Union Chrétienne* on the Occasion of a Discourse by Father Gagarin, Jesuit." In *On Spiritual Unity: A Slavophile Reader*, edited by Robert Bird and Boris Jakim, 135–39. Hudson, NY: Lindisfaene, 1998.

———. "Neskol'ko slov pravoslavnogo khristianina o zapadnykh veroispovedaniyakh. Po povodu broshyury g. Loransi." In *Polnoe sobranie sochineniy Alekseya Stepanovicha Khomiakova*, by Alexei S. Khomiakov, 27–92. Vol. 2. Moscow: Universitetskaya tipografiya, 1900.

———. "On the 'Fragments' Discovered among I. V. Kireevsky's Papers." Translated by Boris Jakim and Robert Bird. In *On Spiritual Unity: A Slavophile Reader*, edited and translated by Boris Jakim and Robert Bird, 295–313. Hudson, NY: Lindisfarne, 1998.

———. "On Humboldt." In *Russian Intellectual History: An Anthology*, edited by Marc Raeff, 209–29. Atlantic Highlands, NJ: Humanities, 1978.

———. "On the Western Confessions of Faith." Translated by Ashleigh E. Moorhouse. In *Ultimate Questions: An Anthology of Modern Russian Religious Thought*, edited by Alexander Schmemann, 31–69. New York: St. Vladimir's Seminary Press, 1977.

———. "Pis'mo k I. S. Aksakovu." In *Polnoe sobranie sochineniy Alekseya Stepanovicha Khomiakova*, by Alexei S. Khomiakov, 329–38. Vol. 2. Moscow: Tipo-litografiya T-va I. N. Kushnerov, 1904.

60. Schmemann, "Primacy," 48.

————. *Quelques mots par un chrétien orthodoxe sur les communions occidentales. A l'occasion d'une brochure de M. Laurentine.* Paris: Ch. Meyerueis, 1853.

————. "Some Remarks by an Orthodox Christian Concerning the Western Communions, on the Occasion of Several Latin and Protestant Religious Publications (Excerpts)." In *On Spiritual Unity: A Slavophile Reader*, edited by Robert Bird and Boris Jakim, 63–116. Translated by Boris Jakim. Hudson, NY: Lindisfarne, 1998.

————. *Zapiski o vsemirnoy istorii.* Vols. 5–6 of *Polnoe sobranie sochineniy Alekseya Stepanovicha Khomiakova.* Moscow: Tipolitografiya T-va I. N. Kushnerov, 1904.

————. *Zapiski o vsemirnoy istorii.* Vols. 7–8 of *Polnoe sobranie sochineniy Alekseya Stepanovicha Khomiakova.* Moscow: Universitetskaya tipografiya, 1900.

Khondzinskiy, Pavel. *Tserkov' ne yest' akademiya. Russkoe vneakademicheskoe bogoslovie XIX veka.* Moscow: Izdatel'stvo PSTGU, 2016.

Kraveckiy, Aleksandr. *Tserkovnaya missiya v epokhu peremen (mezhdu propoved'yu i dialogom). Pomestnyy Sobor 1917–1918 gg. i predsobornyy period.* Moscow: Tsentr "Dukhovnaya biblioteka," 2012.

Krivosheyeva, Natalia. "Pomestnyy Sobor 1917–1918 gg.: vozvrashchenie k idei sobornosti v Russkoy Tserkvi." In *Berdyanskie chteniya. Iz varyag v greki: vozvrashchenie k istokam. III Mezhdunarodnaya nauchno-prakticheskaya konferentsiya. 8–10 sentyabrya 2009 g.,* 64–87. Simferopol: Izdatel'stvo "Nizhnyaya Orianda," 2010.

Mrówczyński-Van Allen, Artur. "Beyond Political Theology and its Liquidation. From Theopolitical Monotheism to Trinitarianism." *Modern Theology* 33.4 (2017) 570–93.

————. "Posle zapada i vostoka. Ikona i russkoe teopoliticheskoe voobrazhenie." *Vestnik PSTGU. Seriya I: Bogoslovie. Filosofiya. Religiovedenie* 69 (2017) 33–47.

Peterson, Erik. "Monotheism as a Political Problem: A Contribution to the History of Political Theology in the Roman Empire." In *Theological Tractates,* by Erik Peterson, 68–105. Translated by Michael J. Hollerich. Stanford: Stanford University Press, 2011.

Samarin, Yury. "On the Theological Writings of Aleksei Khomiakov." In *On Spiritual Unity: A Slavophile Reader,* edited by Robert Bird and Boris Jakim, 161–83. Hudson, NY: Lindisfarne, 1998.

Schmemann, Alexander. "The Idea of Primacy in Orthodox Ecclesiology." In *The Primacy of Peter,* edited by John Meyendorff, et al., 30–56. London: Faith, 1963.

Tocqueville, Alexis de. *Oeuvres et correspondance inedites d' Alexis de Tocqueville.* Vol. 1. Paris: Michel Lévy Frères, 1861.

Zizioulas, John D. *Being as Communion: Studies in Personhood and the Church.* Crestwood, NY: St. Vladimir's Seminary Press, 1997.

2

Faith and Science in the Thought of Khomiakov[1]

TERESA OBOLEVITCH

Critique of Western Solutions

In the activity of Alexei Khomiakov and other Slavophiles one can observe some paradoxes: on the one hand, it emerged under the tremendous impact of European philosophy; on the other, it was a reaction to the westernization of the Russian tradition.[2] Indeed, they were well-versed in German idealism, especially in the philosophy of Hegel and Schelling, whom they knew in person.[3] Although their opponents, the Westernizers, accused them of "scientific emptiness,"[4] the Slavophiles supported the humanities (especially history) as well as natural and exact sciences. Suffice it to say that Khomiakov, who graduated from the faculty of mathematics of the Moscow University—according to his contemporaries—was "interested in everything, had an extensive knowledge in all fields and there was no subject alien to him"[5] and, consequently, was perceived as "a systematic dialectician, with great talents."[6] In this context one can mention his invention

---

1. This publication was generously supported by a grant from the National Science Center, Poland (No. 2014/15/B/HS1/01620).

2. See Noble et al., *Orthodox Theology*, 89.

3. See Kireevskiy, "Rech' Shellinga"; Lyaskovskiy, "Brat'ya Kireevskie," 355–57; Christoff, *I. V. Kireevsky*, 43–46, 58; Lipich, "Slavyanofil'stvo i zapadnichestvo," 9–15.

4. See Vicunich, *Science*, 267.

5. Koshelev, *Alexei Stepanovich Khomiakov*, 43.

6. Stojanović, "First Slavophils," 564.

of the steam engine "Moskovka" which he patented and sent to the World Exhibition in London in 1851.[7] Generally speaking,

> they never abandoned scientific and philosophical modes of discourse, even when they employed the language of faith, as such an abandonment would have placed their arguments outside the linguistic contours of their day. Instead, Khomiakov and Kireevskii sought to align philosophy and science with their own spiritual autobiographies, which were imbued with religious experiences shaped by Orthodoxy.[8]

In spite of their great respect for science, the Slavophiles "devoted much time to attack Western Enlightenment ... both in its rational and empirical form" and postulated a solution in the shape of a Russian counterpart that was supposed to be a spiritual Enlightenment.[9] For Khomiakov, true education consisted not so much in training in science as in rational illumination and clarification of the spiritual component of the person as well as the entire nation. In other words, science as such is just one aspect of education and should be completed with a religious element.

The first half of the nineteenth century was a period of the domination of positivism as well as a recovery of the monastic tradition in Russia, according to which the purpose of human life consists not in "informing the intellect," but "training the soul, not *máthesis* but *áskesis*."[10] The Slavophiles embraced this tradition and popularized *Philokalia*,[11] the outstanding anthology of Patristic mystico-ascetical texts (translated into Russian, as mentioned above, by St. Theophane the Recluse). At the same time, in a manner similar to the adherents of Russian academic philosophy,[12] they tried "somehow to employ that tradition in such a way that it might generate a theoretical, truth-telling power comparable to that of Western intellectual tradition, but not based on it."[13]

---

7. See Khomiakov, *Description*; Riasanovsky, "Khomiakov's Religious Though," 88; Christoff, "Industrial Problem," 143–44.

8. Michelson, "Slavophile Religious Thought," 259.

9. See Rabow-Edling, *Slavophile Thought*, 87.

10. Nichols, "Metropolitan Filaret," 325.

11. See Coates, "Philokalia," 676, 687–94; Hughes, "Mysticism and Knowledge," 18–22; Gvozdev, "Svyatootecheskie korni antropologii."

12. See Andreev, *Dukhovnaya Akademiya*; Fedotova, "Bogoslovskoe nasledie"; Evfimiy (Moiseev), "Dukhovnaya Akademiya"; Tsvyk, "Dukhovno-akademicheskaya filosofiya."

13. Nichols, "Metropolitan Filaret," 325.

The Slavophiles, especially in the primary stage of their activity, adhered to Schelling's idea about the necessity of "positive, living knowledge."[14] However, they were convinced that German thought could not be transplanted onto Russian soil and postulated creation of a new, original Slavic philosophical system. Starting with the argument that the Western culture had lost its Christian roots, they criticized the disparity between religion and everyday life; secularization on the one hand and the true or irremovable limitation of scientific investigation on the other.

Khomiakov's criticism of the "inappropriate" attitude of the Western model of the relationship between science and religion was a consequence of their disapproval of the European civilization as such. According to them, in the Western tradition (known in Russia from the time of Peter I, who attempted the "secularization" of the Russian culture) science and religion were divorced. The Western Church would interfere in the issues of science and did not leave room for its independent development.

By contrast, Orthodoxy was perceived by the Slavophiles—too enthusiastically and inaccurately—as a place of non-conflicting coexistence of faith and science. Khomiakov's position may serve as an illustrious example of the conviction about the potential, harmonious correlation between science and religion. He affirmed that positive sciences did not appear to fully resonate with the historical evidence of the Holy Scripture or with its dogmatic system.

> Every science should report its contemporary conclusions correctly and openly, without humiliating lies, without ridiculous exaggeration, without reticence which could be easily exposed. There is no doubt that the data of some positive sciences, such as geology, a factual science such as history or a speculative science such as philosophy do not seem to be in accordance with the historical testimony of Holy Scripture or its dogmatic system. . . . Sciences have not complited their development and we are still far from reaching their final conclusions. Similarly, we have not achieved a complete understanding of Holy Scripture. There should be doubts and alleged disagreement; but only by addressing them boldly and appealing to further scientific development of can faith show its firmness and steadiness.[15]

Khomiakov did not strive for the unification of Christian truths and scientific data. Quite the opposite, he was convinced that by forcing other

14. See Kireevskiy, "Devyatnadtsatyy vek," 15.

15. Khomiakov, "Ob obshchestvennom vospitanii v Rossii," 357. Yury Samarin concurred with this statement. See Samarin, "Predislovie," xv.

sciences to lie or be silent, faith undermines not their authority but its own. In doing so, Khomiakov expressed his aspiration concerned with the freedom of scientific research that was supposed to be in the Orthodox culture. For instance, he wanted to attack the censorship in Russia after the revolutions of 1848. Nevertheless, this standpoint was often in contradiction with the other remarks of the Slavophiles. For them, faith was the premise and result of all human knowledge, including science. As Khomiakov perceptively pointed out in his unfinished letter, which was posthumously published,

> I gave the name *faith* to that faculty of reason which apprehends actual (real) data and makes them available for analysis and awareness by the understanding [*Verstand*]. Only in this area do the data still have the fullness of their character and the marks of their origin. . . . The blind student of optics of whom I spoke knows the laws of light which is inaccessible to him, but he accepts them as phenomena on faith in other men senses, just as the man who can see has faith in his own senses, and the artist in his own creation.[16]

As we can see, in the above-cited letter Khomiakov treated faith as an initial phase of each process of cognition, not in a specifically religious sense, but rather as an affirmation of the subject of knowledge. At the same time, the Slavophiles considered faith to be "a higher stage" of knowledge inasmuch as it covers not only a number of rational convictions (e.g., mathematical truths), but also convictions that transcendent reason (e.g., faith in God).[17] "Faith is an utter limit of human knowledge, whatever form it takes: it determines the entire sphere of thought."[18] Viewed as such, faith has universal epistemological significance and acts as a guiding principle. Its preceding point is an intimate recognition of the subject, "inner" or "leaving knowledge."[19]

The Slavophiles adamantly insisted that the one-sided development of education in Europe had culminated in modern atheism. At the same time, as it has been noted, the Slavophiles struggled against rationalism (considered "the greatest threat to inner wholeness" or integrity[20]), but not against rationality or reason as such. They did not

16. Khomiakov, "Recent Developments," 251–52.
17. See Kireevskiy, "Dnevnik. 1852–1854," 272.
18. Khomiakov, *Zapiski o vsemirnoy istorii*, 6: 250.
19. Khomiakov, "On the 'Fragments,'" 312.
20. Walicki, *Slavophile Controversy*, 150.

sought to eliminate the study of the natural sciences in Russia, nor did they endeavour to subordinate it to strict religious control: their aim was to show that Russia's national genius and "world mission" derived their strength from the Russian "religious mind" untouched by and only slightly cognizant of the world of reason and science. They appreciated the power of scientific experiment and theory, but they thought the wisdom of the saints infinitely more powerful as well as more congenial to the Russian mind.[21]

The Slavophiles insisted that the Orthodox legacy, where faith interconnects with reason, could serve as an archetype for European education. It is no wonder then that the Slavophiles proposed, as a solution to this situation, an attempt to defend the traditional Byzantine and Slavic way of philosophizing that considered reason (and science) in the broader perspective of the so-called integral life and where the priority belongs to the faculty of faith.

Postulate of Integral Life

The Slavophiles were highly skeptical about the current state of Russian philosophy and theology, as it had grown to be remote from its Patristic sources. They did not diminish the role of reason, but only intended to establish the proper correlation between faith and knowledge, intuitive, empirical and discursive principles. In order to return to an adequate system of cognition, the advocates of this movement postulated recovering the chief position of faith as a state of the entire human being which "is able to embrace the whole of life."[22] According to Khomiakov:

> Faith is always the consequence of revelation recognized as revelation, it is a perceiving of an invisible fact manifested in some visible fact; faith is not *belief* or logical conviction based on conclusions, but much more. It is not the act of one perceptive faculty separated from others, but the act of all the powers of reason grasped and captivated in all its depth by the living truth of the revealed fact. Faith is not known only or sensed only, but is known and sensed together, so to speak; in a word, it is not knowledge alone but knowledge and life.[23]

21. Vicunich, *Science*, 389.

22. Letter of Khomiakov to Samarin from March 1, 1849 (Khomiakov, *Pis'ma*, 276). See also Nizhnikov, "Vera v tvorchestve."

23. Khomiakov, "Western Confessions," 56.

The Slavophiles' project of "integral knowledge" rooted in the Patristic tradition consisted of the coordination and concentration of all human capabilities, the wholeness of the human personality. It is not about simple integrity of faith and reason. The point is that the very process of cognition rises up to a higher level in accordance with faith so that the New Testament postulate of "the renewal of mind" (Rom 12:2) would be fulfilled.[24]

This kind of Christian thinking and philosophy would be "the sum and the common foundation of all sciences and the conductor of thought between the sciences and faith."[25] There is no need to *adjust* worldly knowledge to religion, since the Christian faith should be a *foundation* of each kind of cognition. In this respect Khomiakov asserted that the controversies between scientific knowledge and religion that took place in history curiously stimulated the development of science. As an example, he pointed to paleontological discoveries considered to be a "weapon" against the Bible and urged scientists to continue their work even if their initial motivation was to give up.[26] According to this interpretation, it is science that ought to face up to the Christian truths and not the other way round.

Science as such and, in consequence, freedom of science is not dangerous for believers. What is more, science could be an instrument of Christian culture and education, because this knowledge implies the hypothesis which transcends the empirical data. "Science should expand the field of human knowledge and enrich man by its data and conclusions"[27]; it "makes clear our notions . . . reveals the mysteries of the divine world."[28] Yet, science is just one of the manifestations of true enlightenment and education, the way to the truth, but not the truth itself.[29] Whereas the Westernizers (particularly Alexander Herzen) treated science as a remedy for the idealistic philosophy of German Romanticism, the Slavophiles found it to be a merely formal ability that does not reflect the whole of reality. In other words, science is just a *plan* of a building but *not the building* itself. In this depiction, Khomiakov, in his letters of 1844 and 1845 addressed to William Palmer, an Anglican theologian and a Fellow of Magdalen College, Oxford, claimed that "Germany has in reality no religion at all but the idolatry of science."[30] As we can

24. See Obolevitch, "*Locus Philosophicus*," 11.

25. Kireyevsky, "Necessity and Possibility," 262.

26. Khomiakov, *Zapiski o vsemirnoy istorii*, 5: 30.

27. Khomiakov, "Foreigners' Opinions of Russia," 169.

28. Khomiakov, "K serbam poslanie iz Moskvy," 388.

29. Khomiakov, "O vozmozhnosti Russkoy khudozhestvennoy shkoly," 76.

30. Khomiakov, *Russia and the English Church*, 6; cf. Khomiakov, *Russia and the English Church*, 17.

see, the Slavophiles contended that absolutization of scientific knowledge (as it takes place in positivism) leads to a false interpretation of the world. Additionally, science—contrary to "believing reason" or "knowledge"—has no moral value, and so is inferior to the latter.[31]

At the same time, the members of the Slavophile movement demanded free teaching of secular disciplines and improvement of education at all levels including universities.

> Serious and challenging science quenches passion and leads man to reasonable humility; only an empty and superficial science annoys pride . . . in final classes of university courses science cannot be too deep and comprehensive: it needs freedom of opinion and doubt, without which it would lose everybody's respect and esteem; it needs frank boldness that in the best way prevents secret impudence. . . . Science . . . needs freedom of opinion as well as freedom of doubt, without which it loses its estimation and dignity.[32]

Khomiakov added: "where science enjoys freedom and respect for the sake of itself it bears fruit and greatly contributes to the common good, but where it is treated as a hired servant it is powerless and does not bear any fruit."[33]

Their project of integral knowledge had both an apparently polemic and apologetic character. First of all, it was an opposition to the "abstract" (for instance, overestimated, autonomic, isolated, separated from the other powers of cognition, therefore partial and perverted) principle of reason that was presented in the West.

The conception of the Slavophiles, following Patristic thought, was directed against the fragmentation of cognition and the whole of human life.

> The truth of reason, if it is to be truth, must also be both a moral and an aesthetic truth. From this it follows that for the realization of truth, the spirit must have other qualifications which are not rationalistic. Our intellectual power is also conditioned by the moral side of our life. . . . Truth needs the entire man, and reason that is out of harmony with religion is as powerless a vehicle of truth as faith that denies reason.[34]

31. Gershenzon, "Ivan Vasil'evich Kireevskiy," 436.

32. Khomiakov, "Ob obshchestvennom vospitanii v Rossii," 369–70.

33. Khomiakov, "K serbam poslanie iz Moskvy," 407.

34. Stojanović, "First Slavophils," 578.

To crown it all, knowledge is not of a private character, but belongs to the whole of the Church community, that is conciliarity or catholicity (*sobornost'*).[35] "The medium of the knowledge of the truth is not the individual but the Church; truth that is not attainable by the individual is attainable by an assembly of persons bound together by love."[36] To some degree, it resembles the concept of "epistemology of interpretation" by Charles Sanders Peirce (1839–1914) and Josiah Royce (1855–1916),[37] according to which cognition is not an individual but a social process.

These philosophers did not so much intend to harmonise faith and reason, theology and science, as to establish a new order for the whole of life itself (in diverse aspects, such as reasoning and cognition education, religious practices, etc.) that would be in accordance with Christian Revelation and the principles of faith. The Slavophiles did not intend to highlight the pure transrationalism that, taken in itself, could be as abstract as pure rationalism.[38] They rather sought unity of faith and reason in the realm of the so-called living knowledge and "believing reason" that is natural reason permeated by the Christian truths and acting in accordance with them. The task was not to exclude or suppress science or any rational activity but provide integrity of different human capabilities in their "free" cooperation, in order to "gather together the separate parts of the soul into one force, to search out that inner heart of being where reason and will, feeling and conscience, the beautiful and the true, the wonderful and the desired, the just and the merciful, and all the capacity of mind converge into one living unity."[39] In fact, the liberty of scientific investigation proclaimed by the Slavophiles was just a declaration far removed from reality. According to this project, science is not a neutral field and should be determined by Biblical truths. The Slavophiles' aim was not to distinguish between methods of science and theology, but to show that scientific knowledge does not guarantee truth and needs be supplemented with a religious attitude.

Khomiakov recognized that science has an international character: "in the field of abstract and applied sciences all of the educated world constitutes a whole union,"[40] and yet, each country conveys scientific truths in its own

35. On the various meanings of the Russian word *Sobornost'*, see Christoff, *A. S. Xomjakov*, 139–40, 145–47; Sabev, "Nature and Mission," 262–63; van Rossum, "A. S. Khomiakov," 76–77; Vogt, "Church as Community," 407–10.

36. Stojanović, "First Slavophils," 570.

37. Gavin, "Community as Process," 120–21, 123–25.

38. See Sudakov, *Filosofiya tsel'noy zhizni*, 84.

39. Kireevsky, "Fragments," 285.

40. Khomiakov, "Pis'mo v Peterburg," 115.

manner.[41] Indeed, the Slavophiles underlined the leading role of the very "Slavic" comprehension of philosophy in order to "subordinate the entire meaning of Western civilization to the dominance of Orthodox Christian conviction by developing a law of indigenous thinking,"[42] since "this higher principle of knowledge is preserved within the Orthodox Church"[43] as a repository of the requested *sobornost'*. For this reason their statement was—to a certain extent—of a nationalistic (contrary to the cosmopolitan views of the Westernizers) dimension.

Russia has its own word to say about philosophy and science that should be founded on "living" faith, unlike "formal faith" (that is, formally "proved") in scholasticism,[44] because "in seeking to arrive at the truth of speculation, Eastern thinkers were primarily concerned with the proper inner condition of the thinking spirit, while Western thinkers were more interested in the external coherence of concepts."[45] As the opponents of the Slavophiles noticed, they had built a fictional model of Western education—a sort of a "chemical formula" that could be transformed arbitrarily, instead of real facts.[46] Indeed, their critics hit an imaginary situation according to which science and religion in the West remained in permanent conflict, whereas in Eastern Christendom it had a place where it enjoyed a fruitful cooperation already on the epistemological level in the shape of "believing reason" and "integral knowledge," which are a description or even metaphors of the existential aspirations of believers rather than a very state of cognition. The Slavophiles had a tendency "to treat reason and faith as essentially a single entity, with rationality (discursive reason) and faith ('higher' or 'believing' reason)."[47] It must be stressed that Khomiakov and other Slavophiles were "among the first Russian intellectuals to pay attention to the heritage of the Holy Fathers"[48] so that Khomiakov himself was considered by another Slavophile, Yuri Samarin, to be "a teacher of the Church."[49]

41. Khomiakov, "Razgovor v Podmoskovnoy," 219.

42. Kireevsky, "Fragments," 280.

43. Kireevsky, "Fragments," 282.

44. See Kireevsky, "Reply to A. S. Khomiakov," 83.

45. Kireevsky, "European Culture," 213.

46. See Pisarev, "Russkiy Don Kikhot," 241.

47. Coates, "Philokalia," 694; "'Light of the Truth,'" 161.

48. Dushin, "St. Gregory Palamas," 117; cf. Christoff, *I. V. Kireevsky*, 143–74.

49. Samarin, "Theological Writings," 183.

Bibliography

Andreev, Fedor. *Moskovskaya Dukhovnaya Akademiya i slavyanofily.* Sergiev Posad: Tipografiya Svyato-Troickoy Seriievoy Lavry, 1915.

Christoff, Peter K. *A. S. Xomjakov.* Vol. 1 of *An Introduction to Nineteenth-Century Russian Slavophilism. A Study of Ideas.* The Hague: Mouton, 1961.

———. *I. V. Kireevsky.* Vol. 2 of *An Introduction to Nineteenth-Century Russian Slavophilism. A Study of Ideas.* Paris: Mouton, 1972.

———. "Khomiakov on the Agricultural and Industrial Problem in Russia." In *Essays in Russian History: A Collection Dedicated to George Vernadsky,* edited by Alan D. Ferguson and Alfred Levin, 131–59. Hamden, Connecticut: Archon, 1964.

Coates, Ruth. "'The Light of the Truth': Russia's Two Enlightenments, with Reference to Pavel Florenskii." In *Thinking Orthodox in Modern Russia: Culture, History, Context,* edited by Patrick Lally Michelson and Judith Deutsch Kornblatt, 151–74. Madison, WI: University of Wisconsin Press, 2014.

———. "Russia's Two Enlightenments: The Philokalia and the Accommodation of Reason in Ivan Kireevskii and Pavel Florenskii." *The Slavonic and East European Review* 91.4 (2013) 675–702.

Dushin, Oleg E. "St. Gregory Palamas in Russian Thought: Spiritual Practice versus Rationality." In *Triune God. Incomprehensible but Knowable—the Philosophical and Theological Significance of St. Gregory Palamas for Contemporary Philosophy and Theology,* edited by Athanasopoulos Constantinos, 114–23, Newcastle: Cambridge Scholars, 2015.

Evfimiy (Moiseev). "Moskovskaya Dukhovnaya Akademiya i slavyanofily." In *A. S. Khomiakov—myslitel', poet, publitsist,* edited by Boris N. Tarasov, 361–74. Vol. 1. Moscow: Yazyki slavyanskikh kul'tur, 2007.

Fedotova, Irina A. "Bogoslovskoe nasledie A. S. Khomiakova i pravoslavnaya akademicheskaya mysl' vtoroy poloviny XIX veka." *Veche. Zhurnal russkoy filosofii i kul'tury* 8 (1997) 64–72.

Gavin, William J. "Royce and Khomiakov on Community as Process." *Studies in Soviet Thought* 15.2 (1975) 119–28.

Gershenzon, Mikhail O. "Ivan Vasil'evich Kireevskiy." In *Polnoe sobranie sochineniy,* edited by Ivan V. Kireevskiy and Petr V. Kireevskiy, 415–46. Vol. 4. Kaluga: Grif, 2006.

Gvozdev, Andrey V. "Svyatootecheskie korni antropologii i gnoseologii I. V. Kireevskogo." *Vestnik Pravoslavnogo Svyato-Tikhonovskogo gumanitarnogo universiteta. Seriya I: Bogoslovie, filosofiya* 15 (2006) 142–67.

Hughes, Michael. "Mysticism and Knowledge in the Philosophical Thought of Ivan Kireevsky." *Mystics Quarterly* 30.1–2 (2004) 15–27.

Khomiakov, Alexei S. *Description of the "Moskovka," a New Rotator Steam Engine.* London: I. I. Guillaume, 1851.

———. "Foreigners' Opinions of Russia." In *A. S. Khomiakov's "Foreigners' Opinions of Russia": A Translation and Historical Commentary,* by Joseph Leon Wieczynski, 135–80. PhD Dissertation. Washington: Georgetown University, 1966.

———. "K serbam poslanie iz Moskvy." In *Polnoe sobranie sochineniy Alekseya Stepanovicha Khomiakova,* by Alexei S. Khomiakov, 377–408. Vol. 1. Moscow: Universitetskaya tipografiya, 1900.

———. "O vozmozhnosti Russkoy khudozhestvennoy shkoly." In *Polnoe sobranie sochineniy Alekseya Stepanovicha Khomiakova,* by Alexei S. Khomiakov, 73–101. Vol. 1. Moscow: Universitetskaya tipografiya, 1900.

———. "Ob obshchestvennom vospitanii v Rossii." In *Polnoe sobranie sochineniy Alekseya Stepanovicha Khomiakova*, by Alexei S. Khomiakov, 350–74. Vol. 1. Moscow: Universitetskaya tipografiya, 1900.

———. "On Recent Developments in Philosophy: Letter to Y. F. Samarin." In *Russian Philosophy*, edited by James Edie, et al., 221–69. Vol. 1. Translated by Vladimir Pastuhov and Mary-Barbara Zelden. Chicago: Quadrangle, 1965.

———. "On the 'Fragments' Discovered among I. V. Kireevsky's Papers." In *On Spiritual Unity: A Slavophile Reader*, edited and translated by Boris Jakim and Robert Bird, 295–313. Hudson, NY: Lindisfarne, 1998.

———. "On the Western Confessions of Faith." In *Ultimate Questions. An Anthology of Modern Russian Religious Thought*, edited by Alexander Schmemann, 31–69. Translated by Ashleigh E. Moorhouse. Crestwood, NY: St. Vladimir's Seminary Press, 1977.

———. *Pis'ma*. Vol. 8 of *Polnoe sobranie sochineniy Alekseya Stepanovicha Khomiakova*. Moscow: Tipo-litografiya T-va I. N. Kushnerov, 1900.

———. "Pis'mo v Peterburg po povodu zheleznoy dorogi." In *Polnoe sobranie sochineniy Alekseya Stepanovicha Khomiakova*, by Alexei S. Khomiakov, 104–18. Vol. 3. Moscow: Universitetskaya tipografiya, 1900.

———. "Razgovor v Podmoskovnoy." In *Polnoe sobranie sochineniy Alekseya Stepanovicha Khomiakova*, by Alexei S. Khomiakov, 202–30. Vol. 3. Moscow: Universitetskaya tipografiya, 1900.

———. *Russia and the English Church During the Last Fifty Years. Containing a Correspondence Between Mr. William Palmer Fellow of Magdalen College, Oxford, and M. Khomiakov, in the Years 1844–1854*. Edited by William John Birkbeck. Vol. 1. London: Rivington, Percival, 1895.

———. *Zapiski o vsemirnoy istorii*. Vols. 5–6 of *Polnoe sobranie sochineniy Alekseya Stepanovicha Khomiakova*, by Alexei S. Khomiakov. Moscow: Tipo-litografiya T-va I. N. Kushnerov, 1904.

Kireevskiy, Ivan V. "Devyatnadtsatyy vek." In *Polnoe sobranie sochineniy*, by Ivan V. Kireevskiy and Petr V. Kireevskiy, 7–46. Vol. 1. Kaluga: Grif, 2006.

———. "Dnevnik. 1852–1854." In *Polnoe sobranie sochineniy*, by Ivan V. Kireevskiy and Petr V. Kireevskiy, 266–302. Vol. 3. Kaluga: Grif, 2006.

———. "Rech' Shellinga." In *Polnoe sobranie sochineniy*, by Ivan V. Kireevskiy and Petr V. Kireevskiy, 108–21. Vol. 2. Kaluga: Grif, 2006.

Kireevsky, Ivan. "Fragments." In *On Spiritual Unity: A Slavophile Reader*, edited and translated by Boris Jakim and Robert Bird, 275–91. Hudson, NY: Lindisfarne, 1998.

———. "On the Nature of European Culture and on its Relationship to Russian Culture. Letter to Count E. E. Komarovsky." In *On Spiritual Unity: A Slavophile Reader*, edited and translated by Boris Jakim and Robert Bird, 189–232. Hudson, NY: Lindisfarne, 1998.

———. "On the Necessity and Possibility of New Principles in Philosophy." In *On Spiritual Unity: A Slavophile Reader*, edited and translated by Boris Jakim and Robert Bird, 233–73. Hudson, NY: Lindisfarne, 1998.

———. "A Reply to A. S. Khomiakov." In *A Documentary History of Russian Thought: From the Enlightenment to Marxism*, edited by William J. Leatherbarrow and Derek C. Offord, 79–87. Ann Arbor, MI: Ardis, 1987.

Koshelev, Vyacheslav. *Alexei Stepanovich Khomiakov, zhizneopisanie v dokumentakh, v rassuzhdeniyakh i razyskaniyakh*. Moscow: Novoe literaturnoe obozrenie, 2000.

Lipich, Tamara I. "Slavyanofil'stvo i zapadnichestvo: kontseptual'naya oppozitsiya doktrinam klassicheskoy nemetskoy idealisticheskoy filosofii?" *Nauchnye vedomosti. Seriya Filosofiya. Sotsiologiya. Pravo* 14 (2010) 5–16.

Lyaskovskiy, Valeriy N. "Brat'ya Kireevskie." In *Polnoe sobranie sochineniy*, by Ivan V. Kireevskiy and Petr V. Kireevskiy, 332–414. Vol. 4. Kaluga: Grif, 2006.

Michelson, Patrick Lally. "Slavophile Religious Thought and the Dilemma of Russian Modernity, 1830–1860." *Modern Intellectual History* 7.2 (2010) 239–67.

Nichols, Robert L. "Metropolitan Filaret and the Slavophiles." *St. Vladimir's Theological Quarterly* 4 (1993) 315–30.

Nizhnikov, Sergey A. "Vera v tvorchestve A. S. Khomiakova." In *A. S. Khomiakov—myslitel', poet, publitsist*, edited by Boris N. Tarasov, 349–54. Vol. 1. Moscow: Yazyki slavyanskikh kul'tur, 2007.

Noble, Ivana, et al. *The Ways of Orthodox Theology in the West*. Crestwood, NY: St. Vladimir's Seminary Press, 2015.

Obolevitch, Teresa. "Faith as the Locus Philosophicus of Russian Thought." In *Faith and Reason in Russian Thought*, edited by Teresa Obolevitch and Paweł Rojek, 7–23. Krakow: Copernicus Center, 2015.

Pisarev, Dmitriy I. "Russkiy Don Kikhot." In *Polnoe sobranie sochineniy*, by Ivan V. Kireevskiy and Petr V. Kireevskiy, 236–62. Vol. 4. Kaluga: Grif, 2006.

Rabow-Edling, Susanna. *Slavophile Thought and the Politic of Cultural Nationalism*. New York: State University of New York Press, 2006.

Riasanovsky, Nicholas V. "A. S. Khomiakov's Religious Though." *St. Vladimir's Theological Quarterly* 23.2 (1979) 87–100.

Rossum, Joost van. "A. S. Khomiakov and Orthodox Ecclesiology." *St. Vladimir's Theological Quarterly* 35 (1991) 67–82.

Sabev, Todor. "The Nature and Mission of Councils in the Light of the Theology of Sobornost." *Ecumenical Review* 45.3 (1993) 261–70.

Samarin, Yuriy. "Predislovie k pervomu izdaniyu." In *Polnoe sobranie sochineniy Alekseya Stepanovicha Khomiakova*, by Alexei S. Khomiakov, i–xxxvii. Vol. 2. Moscow: Universitetskaya tipografiya, 1886.

Stojanović, J. D. "The First Slavophils: Homyakov and Kireyevsky." *The Slavonic and East European Review* 18.6 (1928) 561–78.

Sudakov, Andrey K. *Filosofiya tsel'noy zhizni. Mirosozertsanie I. V. Kireevskogo*. Moscow: Kanon+, 2012.

Tsvyk, Irina V. "A. S. Khomiakov i dukhovno-akademicheskaya filosofiya." In *A. S. Khomiakov—myslitel', poet, publitsist*, edited by Boris N. Tarasov, 375–78. Vol. 1. Moscow: Yazyki slavyanskikh kul'tur, 2007.

Vicinich, Alexander. *Science in Russian Culture: History to 1860*. Stanford, CA: Stanford University Press, 1963.

Vogt, Peter. "The Church as Community of Love according to Alexis S. Khomiakov." *St. Vladimir's Theological Quarterly* 48.4 (2004) 393–413.

Walicki, Andrzej. *The Slavophile Controversy. History of a Conservative Utopia in Nineteenth-Century Russian Thought*. Translated by Hilda Andrews-Rusiecka. Notre Dame: University of Notre Dame Press, 1989.

3

Khomiakov's Church and Pope Francis's Church

The Future Fate of the Idea of Conciliarity

MAREK KITA

Although the term *sobornost'* (conciliarity) and the idea described by it entered ecclesiological discourse via Alexei Khomiakov in the nineteenth century, it has always been a reference to reality by all means primary and fundamental for the proper experience of Christianity—perceiving the Church and being it in a truly neo-testamentary way. Hence, irrespective of the occurrence or not of this Slavic denotation of catholicity—interpreted as the charismatic unanimousness of mutually loving people[1]—the idea of the harmonious combination of unity with freedom, joint participation with subordination, remains a constant motif of renewal projects in ecclesiastical life in both East and West. The essential convergence with varied distribution of accents results simply from the unity of sources to which we attempt to return, namely the Revelation of Trinity (being One) and the Grace of Pentecost (where a multitude of languages conjoin in the symphony of the Spirit).

---

1. According to the liturgical acclamation before the *Credo* cited by Khomiakov: "Let us love one another, that with oneness of mind we may confess . . . Father, Son, and Holy Spirit: Trinity, one in essence and undivided" (John, Chrysostom, "Divine Liturgy"). The acclamation is mentioned by the Russian thinker in his polemic treaties addressed to Western readers. See Khomiakov, "Western Confessions," 69; "Some Remarks," 116.

The Difficult Recovery of the Conciliar Spirit

The fate of Khomiakov's idea of conciliarity is very peculiar; the concept was initially controversial from the point of view of the official theology of its author's confessional community—as it is known, Khomiakov's ecclesiological works published abroad were banned in Russia and published there only nineteen years after the thinker's death. Even then, however, the Orthodox Church authorities made the publisher include a note in the publication warning that it contained theological inconsistencies due to the lack of proper education on the part of the author.[2] It was feared that the doctrine presenting the authentic (namely Eastern, naturally) Church as a mystical-social "organism" of living truth would gain a voice in the community (with the people of God as the guardian of whole truth), would let some traits of democracy into the ecclesial system.[3] Also, Pavel Florensky, another, but later, representative of "seeking theology," saw in the idea of conciliarity (against the intentions and declarations of Khomiakov) simply "honed Protestantism."[4]

Yet, over the years, conciliarity began to gain ground exactly for its hallmark of Eastern Orthodoxy—although theologians affirming it took care to harmonize the vision of the "incessant council" resulting from the universal anointment of worshippers with the Spirit of charismatic knowledge on God's issues (cf. 1 John 2:20) with the awareness of the indefeasible role of the Church hierarchy in having divine mandate. It is emphasized that conciliarity is not about negating bishops' prerogatives, and that the universal reception—necessary for determining an authentic interpretation of a faith tradition—of decrees by official synods does not have the nature of formal approval of these decisions in the way of social consultations: the faithful do not "express" their agreement with the synod of bishops but "experience" it.[5] Charismatic *consensus fidelium* is the "common desire to be conformed to the Truth" which is "the perpetuated *totus Christus*."[6] From the onset, the doctrine of conciliarity, worked out in the context of

---

2. See Walicki, *Rosja, katolicyzm*, 71–72.

3. See Ware, *Orthodox Church*, 258. Incidentally, the concept, according to which "the *guardian* of the faith . . . is the whole people of God" was taken by Khomiakov from the famous Letter of the Orthodox Patriarchs of 1848, a reply to the epistle of Pope Pius IX, in which the Pope appealed to "the Easterns" to recognize the highest Apostolic See of St. Peter's. See Ware, *Orthodox Church*, 255.

4. See Walicki, *Rosja, katolicyzm*, 73. Florensky formulated this opinion in "Around Khomiakov," a brochure published in 1916.

5. See Ware, *Orthodox Church*, 257.

6. Evdokimov, *Orthodoxy*, 168.

a polemicizing Orthodox apology, had common sources with a promising current of Catholic thought, as it resembles the teachings of the Catholic theologian of Tubingen, Johann Adam Möhler (1796–1838),[7] perhaps even inspiring Khomiakov. This theologian with Romantic leanings described his faith family as the true Church begotten from Christ, "God's life in history," and a living organism developing thanks to the presence of the Holy Spirit and acting in it.[8] Such a view of ecclesiology was based on patristic notions, namely the thought of St. Irenaeus and St. Cyprian, as well as Origen.[9] Khomiakov's version of teaching on the living truth existing in a living People subsequently inspired, despite its polemical tinge, a number of thinkers in the Eastern Orthodox current open to dialogue with other confessions: the authors representing the Russian philosophical-religious renaissance of the beginning of the twentieth century, who popularized his ideas in a slightly modified form, namely as interpreted in the ecumenical spirit.[10] Eventually, conciliarity (not necessarily under this name) became to some extent an inspiration for the similarly ecumenically oriented theology of the Roman Catholic Church. The Catholicism of the *Vatican II*, experiencing a great renewal of its ecclesiology, owes a lot to the intuition of charismatic collegiality, and a classic of this renewal (and one of the most important theological experts of the last Western council), the Dominican Yves Congar, openly admitted contacts with representatives and the legacy of Russian Orthodox theology—including an acquaintance with the Slavophile tradition and Khomiakov's ideas.[11] According to Congar, who also drew from the abovementioned Möhler's work, the Church is primarily the People of God, although this category remains connected with another likewise fundamental category of Christ's Body[12] (which precludes anti-hierarchical egalitarianism). The ecclesiology of the Second Vatican Council, by no means renouncing the position of Petrine primacy, bolsters both the collegiality of episcopacy (third chapter of the *Lumen gentium* constitution) as well as the communality of the "royal priesthood" (1 Pet 2:9) of all christened and with co-responsibility for the whole flock for the advance in comprehending the Revelation. Chapter two of the *Lumen gentium* dogmatic constitution includes a vision of the church which is far from a

---

7. See Walicki, *Rosja, katolicyzm*, 67–68.

8. See Illanes and Saranyana, *Historia de la Teología*, 285–86.

9. See Puyo, *Interroge le Père Congar*, 48.

10. See Walicki, *Rosja, katolicyzm*, 78.

11. See Puyo, *Interroge le Père Congar*, 50–51, 74, 76–77.

12. See Skowronek, "Promotor reformy w Kościele," 80; Illanes and Saranyana, *Historia de la Teología*, 331.

clerical pyramid with the Pope at the top, and the *Dei verbum* constitution (item 8) clearly bolsters *sensus fidelium*—by mentioning "contemplation and inquiry by the faithful," in the first place in the context of "pursuit of God's truth" (cf. John 16:13), and only secondly in the experiences of mystics and teaching of the bishops.[13]

Contemporarily, it seems that, despite exposing the idea of conciliarity in Eastern Orthodox theology, the ecclesial practice of particular autocephalous churches still does not meet the ideal of collectiveness (which was soberly pointed out by Oliver Clement at the end of his life)[14]—whereas the theology and life of the Catholic Church struggles for ecclesiology and the spirituality of "communion" (which was claimed by St. John Paul II in his Apostolic Letter *Novo millennio ineunte*). The pontificate of the Polish pope, with all its undeniable refulgence, was a time favorable neither for effectively experiencing the bishops' collegiality nor for the full acknowledgement of the subjectivity of the laity. The unease raised in the Vatican by various crises resulted in a tendency towards recentralization,[15] and grassroots initiatives of the faithful used to be ignored or even *a priori* excluded, even if they remained within the bounds of allowed discussion and did not touch upon dogmatic issues.[16]

Pope and the People Bless Each Other

Pope Francis's pontificate began with a recollection, in his very first speech after the conclave,[17] of the old Christian vision of the correlation between the hierarchic service of a bishop and his continuance in brotherly community with the People. He also symptomatically referred to the earliest patristic tradition concerning the role of Rome in the Catholic Church. The speech from the balcony of St. Peter's Basilica was, with all its concision and simplicity of form, a deep exposition of the personal theology of the post to be taken up by the speaker. The new Pope, consistently avoiding this pompous title and calling himself simply "the Bishop of Rome," repeated the expression from the second century on Rome's "primacy of love."[18] Adept in Ignatius of Loyola's spirituality (who taught identification with the "poor and humble

13. See Kita, "Szanse i zagrożenia," 144–45.

14. See Clément, *Mémoires d'espérance*, 192.

15. See Clément, *Rome autrement*, 89–90; Clément, *Mémoires d'espérance*, 136.

16. See the opinions of Dzidek and Bortnowska, "Kościół Jana Pawła II," 28–32.

17. See Francis, "First Speech as Pontiff."

18. Kelly, *Early Christian Doctrines*, 191.

Christ"),[19] Francis spoke then in the language of another Ignatius, the Bishop of Antioch also called Theophorus—clearly referring to his *Epistola ad Romanos*: Francis, alongside the ancient bishop martyr, ascribed the abovementioned "presiding over the Church universal" to the whole "Church of Rome" as he saw in this service "a common way of a bishop and the people." The words and gesture of Francis's blessing, given directly afterwards, were a particularly strong accent of the pontifical expose. Before giving the blessing, the Pope asked the gathered to pray for him, and bowed in silence, accepting the blessing from those whom he was to bless.

In reaction to this scene one could paraphrase the shout of the Chalcedonian Council's fathers "It is Peter who says this through Francis!" Naturally, this is not about the "Prince of the Apostles" from the triumphant narrative, but about Peter from the New Testament—the one who did not allow Cornelius to fall at his feet (cf. Acts 10:25–26) and who had to give an account before the community of his ministry (cf. Acts 11:2–4) and who, in the Council of Jerusalem, participated in a discussion based on partnership (cf. Acts 15:6–29). Not the *Pontifex maximus* but *servus servorum Dei*, and not "the monarch of the world Church" but the first in the collegium of brethren and the animator of their unity, "servant of communion" (to use Brother Roger of Taizé's expression) emerged. By taking the office of the first among bishops in such a manner, the son of the Latin "poor Church" more than symbolically met the desires once expressed by Olivier Clément, who formulated (in reaction to an invitation by John Paul II from the *Ut unum sint* encyclical (95–96) a friendly-critical interpretation of the primacy of the successors of Peter from the point of view of Eastern Orthodoxy.[20]

In view of the above, it is not so surprising that the Patriarch of Constantinople was present in person at the solemn inauguration of the Roman pontificate (for the first time since the unhappy schism nine centuries ago). The first Sunday address before the Angelus was another distinctive expression of Francis's brotherly relations both to other bishops and to the laity.[21] Commenting on the episode of the adulterous woman (cf. John 8:1–11) and praising God's mercy (which was also to become his keynote speech), the Pope cited two authorities: Cardinal Kasper Walter, whose book on this issue he recommended, and an anonymous elderly lady from Buenos Aires, whom he described as wise as if she had "studied at the Gregorian University."

---

19. Cf. Ignatius of Loyola, *Spiritual Exercises*, 50–56, 72–76 (paragraphs 91–98, 136–47).

20. See Clément, *Rome autrement*, 109.

21. See Francis, "First Angelus Address."

"We Must Walk Together"

Not long after the start of Francis's ministry, a booklet containing an extensive interview carried out with the new Pope by a Jesuit, Antonio Spadaro (editor in chief of *La Civiltà Cattolica* fortnightly) was published. It recorded a dialogue in which the Pope spoke openly about personal spirituality and theology. Recollecting the period when he was Argentina's provincial superior of the Society of Jesus, Francis repented his authoritarianism at that time, at odds with the Jesuit principle of consultation with a subordinates before issuing a decision.[22] He admitted that the authoritarian and quick way of making decisions caused him many problems and led him to be seen as ultra-conservative, which he was not. Simultaneously, he stated that, having drawn God's lesson from the effects of those "faults and sins," he always cared for regular consultation with auxiliary bishops during his later period as Archbishop of Buenos Aires, and several times also with the pastoral council of the archdiocese—experiencing the benefits of discussions that allowed for wiser decisions. He transferred this style of administration to the Apostolic See by establishing a council of eight (and later nine) cardinals as advisory group, and also by postulating a less rigid and more genuine dialogue formula for consistories and synods. This Jesuit habit, adapted to Papal practice, recalls the words of St. Cyprian: "I have decided to undertake nothing without your advice and the agreement of the people."[23]

As regards the ecclesial "people," in the quoted interview by Spadaro, Francis answers the question about Ignatius's idea "thinking with the Church (or: "feeling with the Church," *sentire cum Ecclesia*) by citing, after the Second Vatican Council, the idea of "holy, faithful people of God,"[24] on the journey through history as Israel led out of bondage. Francis says that, for him, *sentire cum Ecclesia* is the consciousness of being one of that people and acknowledging that: "all the faithful, considered as a whole, are infallible in matters of belief, and the people display this *infallibilitas in credendo*, this infallibility in believing, through a supernatural sense of the faith of all the people walking together."[25] In this context, the Pope speaks of "the dialogue among the people and the bishops and the Pope," taking place in the spirit of fidelity to a common feeling of faith (*sensus fidei* of the whole community on a pilgrimage through history; this supernatural "instinct" reflects *infallibilitas in credendo*). For Francis, "thinking with the

---

22. See Spadaro, "Interview with Pope Francis."

23. St. Cyprian cited in Evdokimov, *Orthodoxy*, 167.

24. Cf. *Lumen gentium*, §12.

25. Spadaro, "Interview with Pope Francis."

Church" is by no means limited to sticking only to its hierarchical part, but, on the other hand, is not religious populism either. St. Ignatius's expression "holy Mother the hierarchical Church" is explained by the Pope as the whole of the Church (perhaps it could be expressed as the "conciliar whole"), ordered by a hierarchy of responsibility, namely "pastors and people together." An analogy can be seen with the assertion of Evdokimov, that Eastern Orthodoxy is neither about anarchic egalitarianism nor a clerical caste system.[26] Francis relates Ignatius's term of the "militant Church" (*Ecclesia militans*) to daily patience and perseverance in sustaining drawbacks and the struggle to move forward (which is reflected by the neo-testamentary term *hypomonē*)[27] displayed by the simple faithful. The sanctity of the Church, expressed by this patience, means that

> this Church with which we should be thinking is the home of all, not a small chapel that can hold only a small group of selected people. We must not reduce the bosom of the universal church to a nest protecting our mediocrity.[28]

Such a universal and universalist Church would be "mother and shepherdess,"[29] a community breeding mercy and cherishing it, where ministers are not officials but good Samaritans. According to Francis's vision, reiterated in the *Evangelii gaudium* encyclical:

> The bishops, particularly, must be able to support the movements of God among their people with patience, so that no one is left behind. But they must also be able to accompany the flock that has a flair for finding new paths.[30]

In the encyclical, in a more nuanced form of this recommendation to bishops (more greatly accentuating their mission as spiritual guides), the Pope stresses, apart from the "ecclesiology of communion," his affirmation of the supernatural sense of faith reflected in the collegiate sense of the faithful (*sensus fidelium*). It mentions the bishop's role as the one who "will sometimes go before his people, pointing the way and keeping their hope vibrant. At other times, he will simply be in their midst with his unassuming and merciful presence. At yet other times, he will have to walk

---

26. Cf. Evdokimov, *Ages of the Spiritual Life*, 230.

27. See Luke 8:15; 21:19; Rom 2:7; 5:3–4; 8:25; 15:4–5; 2 Cor 1:6; 6:4; 12:12; Col 1:11; 1 Thess 1:3; 2 Thess 1:4; 3:5; 1 Tim 6:11; 2 Tim 3:10; Titus 2:2; Heb 10:36; 12:1; Jas 1:3–4; 5:2, 11; Pet 1:6; Rev 1:9; 2:2–3, 19; 3:10; 13:10; 14:12.

28. Spadaro, "Interview with Pope Francis."

29. Spadaro, "Interview with Pope Francis."

30. Spadaro, "Interview with Pope Francis."

after them, helping those who lag behind and—above all—allowing the
flock to strike out on new paths."[31] The quoted conversation of the Pope
with Antonio Sparado also contains highlights of "synodality" (the evident
equivalent of *sobornost'* in Eastern Orthodox nomenclature), the imperative of which is explained by the Pope, in line with its Greek etymology, as
the united peregrination of all God's people: "we must walk together: the
people, the bishops and the Pope."[32] To the Pope, synodality is necessary
at various levels of ecclesial life; the synodal (*vel* conciliar) current should
permeate all decisions and actions. With this, according to his desire for
"real, not ceremonial consultation," he suggests the necessity for changes
in the way formal synods of bishops are held because "the current method
is not dynamic."[33] Also in this context, direct references to the "tradition
of synodality" and "episcopal collegiality" in Eastern Orthodox brethren
are made. The pope expresses the hope that "The joint effort of reflection,
looking at how the church was governed in the early centuries, before the
breakup between East and West, will bear fruit in due time."[34]

Marked by *Aparecida*

Jorge Mario Bergoglio—first as auxiliary bishop and then as Buenos Aires
ordinary—witnessed and was involved in the clash of the concept of "af-
fective collegiality," forced by the Vatican and based uniquely on trustful
solidarity with the Pope, with the idea of "effective collegiality," which is
real participation in decision-making about the Church.[35] A particularly
poignant instance of this confrontation was at the Fourth General Conference of The Latin American Episcopal Council (*Consejo Episcopal Latino-
americano*, CELAM).[36] This regional assembly of the National Conference
of Bishops of the whole continent had been established three decades earlier
with the blessing of Pope Pius XII, and was the first collegial structure of
management within the Roman Catholic Church on this scale. CELAM,
integrating local experiences and reflections, became a proponent and
moderator of a native Catholicism with a specific identity and unique theology. In the 1980s, when Liberation Theology was in serious crisis and
concern for the unity of the Church dictated John Paul II's arbitrary style of

31. *Evangelii gaudium*, §31.

32. Spadaro, "Interview with Pope Francis."

33. See Spadaro, "Interview with Pope Francis."

34. Spadaro, "Interview with Pope Francis."

35. See Ivereigh, *Great Reformer*, 277.

36. See Ivereigh, *Great Reformer*, 234–36.

leadership, the autonomy of this organization was exposed to curtailment. During this general assembly, a number of deep interventions in the process of preparation and the course of proceedings were carried out. The Roman Curia changed the working document that had been prepared by the Latins with its own version, exchanged most of the members of the board of theology experts, and entrusted the chairmanship of the council (right after its official opening by the Pope) to the nuncio. It was only through a trick that the South-Latin bishops managed to publish a final declaration that was independently prepared (though with all its autonomy, very conservative) instead of the one that the Vatican attempted to foist on them.

In this time full of tensions, the freshly consecrated Bishop Bergolio befriended and shared views with a Uruguayan lay Catholic intellectual, a philosopher named Albert Methol Ferré, who was an influential expert of CELAM.[37] Both men's thinking was permeated with ideas of the "theology of the people" (*teología del pueblo*)—an alternative to Liberation Theology, which had a Marxist tinge.[38] Having such forthright opinions, and feeling strong disapprobation to the mentality of the Roman Curia,[39] the Jesuit bishop simultaneously a truly respected John Paul II for his deep spirituality and righteous character,[40] and must have enjoyed his essential confidence, which was expressed by the Pope's signing of a nomination for Bergolio's succession as bishop.[41] Striving for Church reform, which on many occasions means making enemies among those who defend the *status quo*, Bergoglio avoided moves that would attract differences of opinions to severe divisions. As a Jesuit superior, he taught his confreres to overcome futile controversies, distinguish between their abstract ideas and God's will, as well as to remember that their only true opponent is the opponent of God's plan,[42] namely the Evil Spirit (cf. Eph 6:12). Later, as Archbishop of Buenos Aires and member of the College of Cardinals, regardless of his contacts and undeniable similarity of opinions with the group of St. Gallen[43]—a circle of reform-oriented cardinals which included, i.e., Carlo Maria Martini, Godfried Danneels and Karl Lehmann—he refrained from all actions that would mark him as a member of some crusading faction. During the Synod of Bishops in Rome in 2001, when 20 percent of addresses referred

37. See Ivereigh, *Great Reformer*, 233–36.

38. See Metalli, "Methol Ferré."

39. See Ivereigh, *Great Reformer*, 265.

40. See Ivereigh, *Great Reformer*, 274–80, 284–86.

41. See Ivereigh, *Great Reformer*, 230–32.

42. See Ivereigh, *Great Reformer*, 115–16.

43. See Ivereigh, *Great Reformer*, 257.

to bothersome centralism, but when the representative of the Papal Curia exerted pressure to ignore these voices, Cardinal Bergoglio was in charge of relating the final proceedings. When asked by journalists about collegiality, he showed a mixture of a dove's innocence with the shrewdness of a snake (cf. Matt 10:16). His reply that deeper discussion on this issue was beyond the scope of this Synod and should be undertaken on another occasion after relevant preparation does not sound revolutionary, yet discretely suggests the necessity to deal with the issue in more favorable circumstances and without Curial auspices.

Assertive Latin bishops eventually saw a major breakthrough with the Fifth General Assembly of CELAM at the Marian shrine in Aparecida,[44] Brazil, in 2007. Despite the designs of the Curia, again trying to dominate the preparations and the course of proceedings, the ally and protector of real autonomy of this assembly was Benedict XVI himself, namely Joseph Ratzinger, who had previously defended centralistic moves by the Apostolic See as Prefect of the Congregation for the Doctrine of the Faith. But this time he gave local bishops and theologians free rein: nothing was imposed from the top, and Pope Benedict (who, like his predecessor, came to inaugurate the council) greenlighted the final document—according to the suggestion of its redactor, Cardinal Bergoglio—as "an act of the magisterium [official teaching] of the Latin-American Church."[45] This was a tremendous change in comparison to the previous Vatican line, according to which there could be no more than one preaching subject in the Church. The truly synodal experience of the Aparecida conference, along with the abovementioned document, remain important for Pope Francis.[46] When accepting the Polish bishops, who in 2014 came *ad limina Apostolorum*, the Pope animatedly discussed (upon the request of Bishop Grzegorz Ryś) the main advantages of the Aparecida teachings—accentuating for example the adoption of a pupils' perspective (who faithfully allowed Christ to transform their perception of reality) and close ties between organized theological reflection and joint prayer with the crowds of common pilgrims (every day began with Eucharist in the shrine hosting the conference). Thanks to this, enticements to ideologize the message of Gospel or to distinguish some allegedly omniscient elite were avoided. Besides, the Conclusions, in the context of remarks on spiritual formation of the faithful, mention popular piety as one of the spaces of encounter with Jesus Christ (after prayerful reading of the

44. See Ivereigh, *Great Reformer*, 295–98.

45. See Ivereigh, *Great Reformer*, 297.

46. See Ryś, "Rozmawiając z Franciszkiem," 7–9.

Bible, namely *lectio divina*, and Sunday liturgical celebration).[47] Chapters 258–265 of the discussed text express the Argentinian theology of the people to a great extent.[48] Though the authors admit that popular piety requires evangelization and purification, chapter 263 clearly states that:

> We cannot deprecate popular spirituality, or consider it a secondary mode of Christian life, for that would be to forget the primacy of the action of the Spirit and God's free initiative of love. Popular piety contains and expresses a powerful sense of transcendence, a spontaneous ability to find support in God and a true experience of theological love. It is also an expression of supernatural wisdom, because the wisdom of love does not depend directly on the enlightenment of the mind, but on the internal action of grace.[49]

The Pope's Struggle for Synodality

The work method of Synod of Bishops in 2014–2015, devoted to issues of family, became a telling witness of the realization of Francis's desire to restore "effective collegiality" in the Church,[50] and also of real "synodality."[51] The system of wide-ranging consultations with the faithful of local Churches that he launched, as well as his making a point of freedom and openness of discussion during the consistory of cardinals and two sessions involving delegations of episcopates and invited experts, were to make the Synod a real forum for the exchange of ideas and of mutual, humble discernment of God's will. Openness, the free expression of the grassroots perspective, exhortation of the hierarchs themselves to be similarly audacious, to show *parrēsia* (cf. 2 Cor 3:12) worthy of people internally free thanks to relying on God—served to create a space for the Holy Spirit, which "blows where it wishes" (cf. John 3:8). Before opening the Synodal assembly, Francis said a prayer for the gift of listening for the Synod Fathers: to listen in the manner of God, so that they may hear, with him, the cry of the people; to listen to the people, until they breathe the will to which God calls us.

As we know, the course of the Synod outraged conservative factions, and many people expressed concern with the presentation of antagonizing

47. See CELAM, "Aparecida Document," 88–90.

48. See Ivereigh, *Great Reformer*, 299.

49. CELAM, "Aparecida Document," 89.

50. See "Lettera del Santo Padre."

51. See Ivereigh, *Great Reformer*, 373–91.

bishops which brings confusion to the Church. But Francis, in his conversation with the Argentinian journalist Elisabetta Piaqué, stated that he was not "afraid of following this trail, the road of the Synod . . . because it is the road that God has asked us to follow."[52] He also added that his presence at the Synod (holding debates *sub Petro et cum Petro*, acknowledging Peter's primacy and in connection with him) was to guarantee orthodoxy and the freedom of each participant in their trustful searches—which he repeated later in his general audience.[53] Continuing the responsibility to "strengthen your brothers" (cf. Luke 22:32), the Pope from the end of the earth not only transplants to the Vatican and propagates on a global scale the Latin experience of collegiality, but also decidedly preaches that collegiality is a principle in Church life. In his address, in 2015, for the fiftieth anniversary of institution of the Synod of Bishops, Francis, cited Saint John Chrysostom, saying that "Church and Synod are synonymous," and stated that "Synodality is a constitutive element of the Church."[54] In the perspective of "journeying together" on the road of faith (*syn-hodos*, in Greek: "road taken together"):

> A synodal Church is a Church which listens, which realizes that listening "is more than simply hearing" (12). It is a mutual listening in which everyone has something to learn. The faithful people, the college of bishops, the Bishop of Rome: all listening to each other, and all listening to the Holy Spirit, the "Spirit of truth" (John 14:17), in order to know what he "says to the Churches" (Rev 2:7).[55]

Hence, we have lived to see a situation hard to envisage in the times when Khomiakov proclaimed to the world his interpretation of "Catholicity" from credo as radical "synodality." There, in the Catholic Church, the advocate of "episcopal collegiality within an entirely synodal Church"[56] proves to be the Pope himself, and his natural opponents seem to be traditionalists with their ultramontane orientation. In the context of dialogue with Eastern Orthodoxy—which is clearly articulated in the quoted speech by Francis[57]—we can see here the desirable "conversion of papacy" (Peter in the Gospel was to strengthen the others after having conversed himself, cf. Luke 22:32). The pope, in the perspective of synodality (*sobornost'*) "is not, by himself, above the Church; but within it as one of the baptized, and

52. Piqué, "Reach Out."
53. See Papa Francesco, "Udienza."
54. See Francis, "Ceremony."
55. Francis, "Ceremony."
56. See Francis, "Ceremony."
57. See Francis, "Ceremony."

within the College of Bishops as a Bishop among Bishops, called at the same time—as Successor of Peter—to lead the Church of Rome which presides in charity over all the Churches."[58] Visibly, the idea of primacy is maintained in its essence, but changed in form into a more adequate one. The Pope may "strengthen brothers" as disciples of Christ and children of God only after having himself become converted to the attitude of being their co-disciple and brother. He therefore does not act as lord over their faith, but as co-author of their joy (cf. 2 Cor 1:24).

Translated by Katarzyna Popowicz

Bibliography

Bortnowska, Halina, et al. "Kościół Jana Pawła II—Kościół Benedykta XVI." *Znak* 608.1 (2006) 18–43.

Clément, Olivier. *Mémoires d'espérance*. Paris: Desclée de Brouwer, 2003.

———. *Rome autrement. Une réflexion orthodoxe sur la papauté*. Paris: Desclée de Brouwer, 1997.

Evdokimov, Paul. *Ages of the Spiritual Life*. Translated by Michael Plekon and Alexis Vinogradov. Crestwood, NY: St. Vladimir's Seminary Press, 1998.

———. *Orthodoxy*. Translated by Jeremy Hummerstone and Callan Slipper. Hyde Park, NY: New City, 2011.

Francis. "Ceremony Commemorating the Fiftieth Anniversary of the Institution of the Synod of Bishops." October 17, 2015. http://w2.vatican.va/content/francesco/en/speeches/2015/october/documents/papa-francesco_20151017_50-anniversario-sinodo.html.

———. "First Angelus Address." March 17, 2013. http://www.catholicworldreport.com/2013/03/17/full-text-pope-francis-first-angelus-address.

———. "First Speech as Pontiff." March 13, 2013. http://www.npr.org/2013/03/13/174224173/transcript-pope-francis-first-speech-as-pontiff.

———. "Lettera del Santo Padre Francesco al. Segretario Generale del Sinodo dei Vescovi, Em.mo Card. Lorenzo Baldisseri in occasione dell'elevazione alla dignità episcopale del Sotto-Segretario, Rev.do Mons. Fabio Fabene." April 1, 2014. http://w2.vatican.va/content/francesco/it/letters/2014/documents/papa-francesco_20140401_cardinale-baldisseri.html.

———. "Udienza, Al Sinodo Presenza del Papa 'Garanzia Per Tutti.'" December 10, 2014. https://agensir.it/quotidiano/2014/12/10/papa-francesco-udienza-al-sinodo-presenza-del-papa-garanzia-per-tutti.

Ignatius of Loyola. *The Spiritual Exercises*. Translated by Lewis Delmage. New York: Joseph F. Wagner, 1968.

Illanes, José Luis, and Josep Ignasi Saranyana. *Historia de la Teología*. Madrid: Biblioteca de Autores Cristianos, 1995.

Ivereigh, Austen. *The Great Reformer: Francis and the Making of a Radical Pope*. New York: Henry Holt, 2014.

58. Francis, "Ceremony."

John Chrysostom. "The Divine Liturgy of Saint John Chrysostom." *Greek Orthodox Archdiocese of America.* https://www.goarch.org/-/the-divine-liturgy-of-saint-john-chrysostom.

Kelly, John Norman Davidson. *Early Christian Doctrines.* London: Adams & Charles Black, 1968.

Khomiakov, Alexei S. "Some Remarks by an Orthodox Christian Concerning the Western Communions, on the Occasion of a Letter Published by the Archbishop of Paris." In *On Spiritual Unity: A Slavophile Reader,* edited by Robert Bird and Boris Jakim, 63–116. Hudson, NY: Lindisfarne, 1998.

———. "On the Western Confessions of Faith." Translated by Ashleigh E. Moorhouse. In *Ultimate Questions. An Anthology of Modern Russian Religious Thought,* edited by Alexander Schmemann, 31–69. Crestwood, NY: St. Vladimir's Seminary Press, 1977.

Kita, Marek. "Szanse i zagrożenia związane z uwzględnianiem *sensus fidelium* we współczesnej praktyce sprawowania Magisterium." In *Wiara—wiarygodność,* edited by Damian Wąsek, 143–59. Krakow: WN UPJPII, 2004.

Latin American Episcopal Conference CELAM. "The Aparecida Document." May 13–31, 2007. https://pl.scribd.com/document/257681153/General-Conference-of-the-Bishops-of-Latin-America-and-the-Caribbean-concluding-document.

Metalli, Alver. "Methol Ferré, il filosofo di Bergoglio." *Avvenire,* March 20, 2014. https://www.avvenire.it/agora/pagine/filosofo.

Piqué, Elisabetta. "'We Must Reach Out': Pope Francis speaks about the Curia, the Synod on the Family, and the year ahead." *America: The Jesuit Review* 212.1 (2015). https://www.americamagazine.org/issue/we-must-reach-out.

Puyo, Jean. *Jean Puyo Interroge le Père Congar: "Une vie pour la vérité."* Paris: Le Centurion, 1975.

Ryś, Grzegorz. "Rozmawiając z Franciszkiem o dokumencie z Aparecidy." In *Aparecida. V Ogólna Konferencja Episkopatów Ameryki Łacińskiej i Karaibów. Dokument końcowy: Jesteśmy uczniami i misjonarzami Jezusa Chrystusa, aby nasze narody miały w Nim życie,* 7–9. Translated by Krzysztof Zabawa and Krzysztof Łukoszczyk. Gubin: Wydawnictwo Przystanek Jezus, 2014.

Skowronek, Alfons. "Promotor reformy w Kościele." In *Leksykon wielkich teologów XX–XXI wieku,* edited by Józef Majewski, Jarosław Makowski, 73–80. Warsaw: Biblioteka "Więzi," 2003.

Spadaro, Antonio. "Interview with Pope Francis." https://w2.vatican.va/content/francesco/en/speeches/2013/september/documents/papa-francesco_20130921_intervista-spadaro.html.

Walicki, Andrzej. *Rosja, katolicyzm i sprawa polska.* Warsaw: Prószyński i S-ka, 2003.

Ware, Timothy. *The Orthodox Church: An Introduction to Eastern Christianity.* New York: Penguin, 2015.

4

Khomiakov, Sacrifice, and the Dialogic Roots of Russian Kenosis

STEPHANIE SOLYWODA

I n the Slavophile-Westernizer debate in the mid-nineteenth century, the Slavophiles set forth what, in their opinion, was unique and laudable about the Russian experience. A great deal of what they eulogized was the Russian Orthodox Christian experience. One hundred years later, in *The Russian Religious Mind,* Fedotov identified the importance of kenosis, "self-emptying," as a particular trait of Russian Orthodoxy.[1] Strikingly, despite the scrutiny of the theological and practical aspects of Orthodoxy in Russia, the Slavophiles did not use the term kenosis. Yet, Fedotov was not wrong and examples of the "kenotic mood" are important parts of Slavophile thought. Khomiakov is a thinker-subject inseparable from his thought-object: *Sobornost'.* Is kenosis apparent in Khomiakov's work, especially about *sobornost'*? If it is not there, then either Fedotov is incorrect when he identifies this ideal as particular to Russian thought, or Khomiakov overlooked something very significant in his own speculations about the unique contributions of Russian thought. If kenosis is there, how does Khomiakov articulate it? And what does his attention to the kenotic aspects of *sobornost'* tell us about his thought, and contribute to our present day understanding of the relevance, or even popularity, of this idea?

The foundation of *kenosis* as a theological concept is in Philippians, where it is written that Christ "*emptied* himself, taking the form of a bond-servant, and being made in the likeness of men" (Phil 2:7). The term kenosis comes from the Greek for "emptying." This passage is surely significant to all Christologies, but it is only in the kenotic doctrine that a special relevance

1. See Fedotov, *Russian Religious Mind,* 94–132.

51

is made of the "self-emptying" action and nature of Christ. Kenotic Christology can be scrutinized for its theological implications, but it can also be questioned prima facie (i.e., is the emptying taking place in this passage really present or relevant). Since Khomiakov does not engage with either of these questions himself, it is important here to first characterize the kenotic ideal put forward by Fedotov and other groups of kenotic theologians, primarily in the Lutheran theology of Thomasius, a contemporary of Khomiakov's, and in Anglican thought after him. It is especially important to clarify the difference between the kenosis identified by Fedotov on the one hand and both of the protestant kenotic theologies on the other. They focus on the life of Christ and his psychological personality (in other words, on what Christ could have thought or knew) whereas Fedotov draws attention to the imitation of divine humility in others—especially in the lives of saints. Although this is a difference, the two foci are fundamentally connected: if it is not clear what happened when God emptied himself in order to be made man, then it is also not clear what the saints could be said to be imitating. Nevertheless, particular aspects of Slavophile thought do problematize finding an epistemological or consciousness-based kenotic mood in their work.

First, let us consider Thomasius's kenosis, as expressed in *Christ's Person and Work* (1857). Here, he focuses on the necessity of the limitation of God in the person of Christ; a "self-limitation" of the Logos that enables Christ's incarnation to be fully human and fully divine.[2] This limitation is exhibited in the psychology of Christ:

> The consciousness that the Son has of himself and of his universal governance does not come together as one with the consciousness of the historical Christ—it hovers, as it were, above him; the universal activity which the Son continuously exercises does not coincide with his divine-human action in the state of humiliation.[3]

When Thomasius writes of humiliation, this word is related to the state of intentionally limited consciousness. He goes on to point out that this limitation is necessary in order to fully participate in human life, but that it is "certainly not a divesting" of the divine, it is "manifestly a self-limitation."[4] Thomasius also addresses Philippians directly and concludes that the self-emptying in that passage is a reference to the necessity of self-limitation in

---

2. See Welche, *Incarnation*, 46.

3. Welche, *Incarnation*, 47.

4. Welche, *Incarnation*, 48.

order to be incarnated and not just an aspect of self-denial in the "temporo-historical life of Jesus Christ."[5]

The preoccupation with kenotic theology in the West continues Thomasius's attention to examinations of the character of Christ's consciousness. Charles Gore, Peter Taylor Forsyth and Hugh Ross Mackintosh, between 1880s and 1930s, wrote about "the person of Christ" in several differing publications, each of which wrestle with the practicalities of how "self-emptying" was experienced in Christ's mind.[6] Importantly, they each faced fundamental limits to their theorization of kenosis whereby it seemed prudent to "think no further." For example, Gore writes about whether self-emptying is to be conceived of as a continual refusal to exercise the free divine consciousness which Christ possessed, as something once and for all completed in the original act of entering into the self-limiting conditions of manhood and concludes: "if we are wise we shall not attempt to answer the question."[7] Forsyth also notes the limit of his thought when he acknowledges that we cannot fully understand how the kenosis could happen, and how a divine consciousness could reduce itself by volition. He writes: "If we knew and could follow that secret we should be God and not man."[8] Mackintosh also abandons reference to kenotic Christology in his later work. However, it is the very questions raised by modern psychology that have forced these Scottish thinkers to engage in a reinterpretation of kenosis and fostered a pronounced revival of this idea among them.

Now, let us consider Fedotov's definitions in *The Russian Religious Mind*. There, he draws attention to ancient and medieval examples of kenosis in the lives of the saints and holy fools.[9] He points in particular to the martyrdom of Boris and Gleb and the lives of St. Theodosius and St. Sergius of Radonezh. In his recounting of the various hagiographies he emphasises that these saints follow the example of Christ's humiliation, or kenotic humility.[10] The clear, unifying trends between these saint's lives are more readily identified as martyrdom and sacrifice, however, and not a peculiar form of "self-limitation." The curious case of the saintly brothers Boris and Gleb is certainly worthy of note as an exceptional Russian example of sainthood because the submission to martyrdom is unusually unselfconscious and related to political power, but it is also described by

5. Welche, *Incarnation*, 52.

6. See Giorgiov, "Kenotic Christology."

7. Giorgiov, "Kenotic Christology," 54.

8. Giorgiov, "Kenotic Christology," 59.

9. See Fedotov, *Russian Religious Mind*, 1:94–123; 2:195–230, 316–43.

10. See Fedotov, *Russian Religious Mind*, 2:212.

Fedotov as being a "partaker of Christ's passion" which is more akin to martyrdom than kenosis.[11] In the case of Theodosius, humiliation is emphasised as in the form of "self-impoverishment" form childhood, which is more alike to self-limitation but not alike to Thomasius's focus on the humiliation of consciousness.[12] He also identifies kenotic humility in Sergius of Radonezh's "repudiation of the metropolitan see."[13] Collectively, including descriptions of the uniqueness of holy fools, it seems that an incompatibility with power could be a unifying kenotic ideal, but this is still a very loose unity of disparate life narratives.[14]

With the aforementioned aspects of kenosis in the West and as identified by Fedotov as a crucial aspect of the Russian religious tradition in mind, the sacrificial aspects of *sobornost'* can clearly be seen to connect to both definitions. Kenosis is apparent in Khomiakov's work. With regards to *sobornost'*, the "kenotic mood" is articulated in relation to submission. In *The Church is One* (written in the 1840s) he opens with: "The unity of the Church follows necessarily from the unity of God, for the Church is not a multiplicity of persons in their personal separateness but the unity of God's grace living in the multitude of rational creatures who *submit* themselves to grace."[15]

The sobornal unity of the Church community is only possible through a submission of the individual to that community, and by placing this observation at the very introduction to his essay he establishes submission in the foundation of the meaning of the Church. He further extols this as a virtue of Orthodoxy in his letter to the Serbians (1860), writing: "It is no accident that the commune, the sanctity of the communal verdict and *the unquestioning submission of each individual to the unanimous decision of his brethren* are preserved only in the Orthodox countries."[16]

It is clear that in Khomiakov's descriptions, submission is laudable, and in this letter Khomiakov associates pride and individuality, having pejorative connotations, with Western Christianity. Therefore, in order for *sobornost'* to exist in the community, the community must be one of special, kenotic individuals. In this, Khomiakov is supported by other Slavophiles who, as group, discern between "the personhood as such and

---

11. See Fedotov, *Russian Religious Mind*, 1:103.

12. See Fedotov, *Russian Religious Mind*, 1:116.

13. Fedotov, *Russian Religious Mind*, 2:212.

14. See Fedotov, *Russian Religious Mind*, 2:217.

15. Khomiakov, "Church is One," 17.

16. Khomiakov, "To the Serbs," 94.

self-enclosed individuality."[17] Wood argues that "the Slavophiles advance a relational approach to personhood, grounding personhood in one's participation in a large corporate body" that was against individualism.[18] In this sense, communality is in the very definition of personhood, there is no choice to submit to a group, instead it is an ontological condition of personhood to be a part of another whole, the community. Wood describes Aksakov, Khomiakov's Slavophile contemporary, as defining personhood cast "in kenotic rather than possessive terms. Personhood finds its highest self-realization only in self-renunciation."[19] It is important to note, however, that the kenoticism central to Khomiakov's conception of the person included freedom and volition.

Another part of this ontological communality implied by *sobornost'* is the idea that individuals retain their personal freedom within it. This connotation clarifies understanding life in *sobornost'* as a distinctly personal life by emphasizing personal freedom. Khomiakov relies on the example of the free relationship of persons within the Trinity to reinforce a situation in which the members of society maintained their individuality. True Christians are also freely participating in *sobornost'*. In his third letter to the Oxford scholar William Palmer (1846), Khomiakov is explicit that free or voluntary submission is a quality of Orthodox Christianity:

> [Western theology] is no vice of the mind but an *involuntary submission* to the tendencies and direction of the past. When the unity of the Church was lawlessly and unlovingly rent by the Western clergy the more so in as much as at the same time the East was continuing is former friendly intercourse and submitting to the opinion of Western Synods the Canons of the second Council of Nicea.[20]

Here, the involuntary submission of Christians in the West contrasts unfavourably with the voluntary submission of the East.

The idealized sobornal community has unique and paradoxical attributes that transmute the personal will of its members to the group and in so doing remove the potential for political agency from the community (something of a mixed blessing for the Serbs, no doubt). Khomiakov treated *sobornost'* as non-political, as a quality which connects to Fedotov's kentoic ideal, and implied that it should maintain a counter-political element in

17. Wood, "State Authority," 186.

18. See Wood, "State Authority," 186.

19. Wood, "State Authority," 186.

20. Khomiakov, "Letters to William Palmer," 151.

every manifestation.[21] Shevzov writes, "In fact, *sobornyi*, as Khomiakov understood it, had nothing in common with secular democracies or any other form of purely human social organization since its underlying ordering principle was a metaphysical, divine, spiritual one."[22] *Sobornost'*, then, denotes an apolitical society and opposes hierarchies representing the state in favour of collaborative decision-making.[23] According to Shevzov,

> nowhere in [Khomiakov's] writings did he equate the idea of *sobornyi* with the 'will of the people,' juxtaposing the hierarchical principle [most meanly manifest in the hierarchies of the Catholic Church] and the communal as two diametrically opposed principles.[24]

If *sobornost'* supports ontological conceptions of community but not active volition within a community, it is possible to question the place of justice in such a community.

To use Khomiakov's own words, it is easy to "submit" to a unanimous decision of one's brethren when one shares in that unanimity, but what of the liberal individual and his "rights"? Without political agency, *sobornost'* is open to the same accusations of a "slave-mentality" that also dog kenosis. In Chaadaev's *First Philosophical Letter* he was critical of the Orthodox Church's sanctioning of the continued situation of slavery among the Russian people.[25] The self-renunciation that is an important component of kenotic personhood opens those people to abuse. Indeed, modern feminist theology

21. Stoekl points out that the anti-Western and anti-modern aspects of some Orthodox fundamentalism involve no critical revision of "Church subservience to the autocratic state" and use the concept of *sobornost'* to "justify the suppression of individual rights," something entirely contrary to Khomiakov's intention. See Stoeckl, "Lesson of the Revolution," 295.

22. Shevzov, *Eve of Revolution*, 3. In terms of this observation of Shevzov's, it must be considered that contemporaneous theories of democracy were far more coarse, crude and populist than our current understanding of democracy. It might be more useful to think of the development of democratic theory along with *sobornost's* own development in time. Thus, this special understanding of communal life is able to influence ideas of governance in Russia positively and negatively. For example, in Frank's *Spiritual Foundations of Society*, the underlying element of *sobornost'* facilitates a beneficent democratic governmental system. Alternatively, the assumed natural inclination of the Russian peasantry to Socialism strongly influenced Mikhailovsky's disregard for pursuit of democratic political reforms (Billington, "Intelligentsia," 807–21).

23. See Pain, "Sobornost," 93.

24. Shevzov, *Eve of Revolution*, 31. This observation is a counter to arguments that Khomiakov's attention to the whole Church was too focused on the role of the laity and therefore Protestant.

25. See Khomiakov, "To the Serbs."

criticises the valorisation of imitating Christ in circumstances that condone abuse, so this conflict is not isolated to the Orthodox Context.[26] Rancour-Laferriere describes this as a "masochist's idea of freedom."[27] Wood disagrees, even though it seems less with the content of Rancour-Laferrier's argument than with the terminology.[28] A masochist is one who takes pleasure in pain, but the voluntary submission to (presumably) a beneficent community does not involve pain. It is a false assumption embedded in liberal-individualism that such a community would have a need for dissent, or that the needs of the community's members would go unmet. As Wood writes: "Khomiakov's great insight was to recognize that kenotic personhood could only be a gift of grace made possible by the people's communion with God."[29] In this articulation, Wood echoes the German theologian Johann Möhler as much as he does Khomiakov.[30] Chaadaev sustained his disagreement with this point of view on Russian communality in correspondence with Schelling (1842), writing that this Slavophile tendency was an arrogant apotheosis of the Russian people, and not evidence of the "religious humility, modesty of spirit, which has always been the train of our national character."[31] Khomiakov and the Slavophiles wrote prolifically about the Russian national character, but sheer volume of material is not the only scale on which to judge testimony, so it is important to bear in mind that other contemporary ideas of "Russianness" were just as keenly observed.

The tension between individualism and community, exemplified by the difference of opinion between Wood and Rancour-Leferrier, is a product of standpoint, on whether *sobornost'* is considered to be a theological or philosophical idea. Understanding *sobornost'* as restricted to Church life, as Wood does, helps maintain the idealism that is necessary to preserve individual freedom. Outside of a Christian community, voluntary submission no longer seems benign. The view point of *sobornost'* as a part of Church life endures to varying degrees in religious philosophy after Khomiakov. For example, Florovsky's later discussion of *sobornost'* in *The Ways of Russian Theology* significantly uses the word to represent a spiritually united apolitical society.[32] Such a distinction can allow for simple co-existence, but

---

26. See Mercedes, *Power For*.

27. Rancour-Laferrier, *Moral Masochism*, 41.

28. See Wood, "State Authority," 187.

29. Wood, "State Authority," 187.

30. See Valliere, "Modernity of Khomiakov," 132.

31. Kline, "Russian Religious Thought," 182.

32. See Florovsky, *Ways of Russian Theology*.

spiritually-gathered-people can also be considered a force opposed to any political power that is able to oppose it.

Khomiakov's use of *sobornyi* with reference to Russian communities connotes a gathering across space and time that structures ideas about the ideal Russian community in émigré writings. Khomiakov describes an idealized "whole Church": "*Sobor* implies the idea of assembly, not necessarily gathered in some place or other, but existing virtually without a formal gathering"[33] that endures or perpetuates throughout time. "It is unity in plurality."[34]

By building on Khomiakov's *sobornost'* Russian émigré thinkers also joined the discussion about whether *sobornost'* applies more to Church life or the all-Russian experience. Notably, Bulgakov in The Orthodox Church (1935) and Berdyaev in Freedom and the Spirit (1927) both invoke *sobornost'* in their discussions of community in order to describe the émigré experience as a legitimate part of the overall Russian experience. Berdyaev further moves away from looking at how *sobornost'* affects Church hierarchies to consider its role as an agent organizing people. In *Dream and Reality* (1949) he also emphasizes this distinction between *sobornost'* and Church life:

> All the value of the thought of Khomiakov was in that he thought of *sobornost'*, which was his creative discovery, in an imperforated connection to freedom. But, he did not think this idea to its end. Not in any way can *sobornost'* be turned into an external authority. Absolute primacy belongs to freedom. In the case of conflict, of which Khomiakov little thought, conscience chooses freedom.[35]

Freedom, though, is most relevant when *sobornost'* is used in a wider discussion, outside of the Church. As I have mentioned, it is not easily compatible with liberal thinking on personal freedom. Rosenthal interprets the religious philosophy of Bulgakov and Berdyaev as antagonistic to personal freedom because of the very close distinctions that must be made in order to understand *sobornost'* as supportive of democracy. She writes that although fin de siècle Russian idealist thinkers:

> condemned authoritarianism, compulsion, and force, by 1917 they were as opposed to individual freedom as the Bolsheviks. . . . Unwittingly and unintentionally, their lofty ideal of

33. See Khomiakov, "Letter to the editor," 139.
34. Khomiakov, "Letter to the editor," 139.
35. Berdyaev, *Dream and Reality*, 53.

sobornost' degenerated into an ultra-communalist vision in which the individual virtually disappeared.[36]

A criticism like this is bold, and hard to square with the accepted understanding of the Christian humanism also apparent in religious philosophy. While Rosenthal's critique is justified, and some thinkers did indeed use Slavophil language to advocate for theocracy or dictatorship, it is helpful to consider these ideas within the context of the wildly idealist approach religious philosophy had to all practical problems and the stresses of self-governance exhibited in the Provisional Government after the February Revolution. Rosenthal identifies and condemns the strong anti-individualist aspects of traditional *sobornost'*, but she also acknowledges that the fracture in revolutionary society might have made the ideals of *sobornost'* appealing to religious philosophers.

Clearly the legacy of Khomiakov's *sobornost'*, and in turn its kenotic mood, was influential for later thinkers. The use of his terminology and ideas brought forward older questions of freedom and raised the Russian character in more modern debates. Fedotov, himself a contributor to those same conversations, put considerable emphasis on kenosis, and used the terminology as well as the concept of kenotic ideal much more aggressively than his Slavophile predecessors had done. This perpetuating circumstance is particularly interesting because Russian émigré thinkers, Fedotov among them were, like Khomiakov, engaging with the West. It is important to note that Khomiakov's dialogue with Western Protestantism took place directly, such as in the correspondence with William Palmer cited above, and indirectly through the influence of German thought on his overall world view. Later Russian emigres would also have direct and indirect dialogues with Western thinkers and ideas.

In terms of German influence, this is most visible in Khomiakov's *Exegetical Note on the letter to the Philippians* where he emphasises that "Christ humbled himself and united the Divine and the human in himself." In *The Modernity of Khomiakov*, Valliere uses this blatant connection to the kenotic tradition in Germany as evidence of German influence. Yet, it is important to highlight that the bulk of Khomiakov's writings are in the form of letters; and therefore in a dialogic mode. A dialogue that is, furthermore, between himself and the West, not in and among the Orthodox community. German thought also influenced the kenotic theories of Scottish protestant theology. At this point it is necessary to point out that the Slavophile thinkers offer a remedy to the Scottish problem mentioned above, namely that at a certain point kenotic inspections of Christ's person must cease. The ontological

36. Rosenthal, "Lofty Ideals," 181.

epistemology of "Integral knowledge" expanded on by Kireevsky offers an avenue to exit the limitations that has stopped these Western thinkers, and creates a whole new way to continue on with thought about kenosis and the human mind, and this was not available to the Scottish theologians. These confluences of influence help to show why it therefore seems less than co-incidental that ecumenical meetings between Russian émigré theologians and Western thinkers (especially British thinkers) should have attention to these problems and topics. In the first publication of *Sobornost'* the journal of the Fellowship of St. Alban and St. Sergius, it is no coincidence that Gore and Khomiakov are mentioned on the same page in two considered book reviews, and that Fedotov himself writes about sacrifice just a few pages later on in the same publication.

These two groups, Russian and Western thinkers, were brought to this one topic, kenosis, by different forces, but they nevertheless arrived at the same space. Joanna Hubbs, in *Mother Russia* suggests that the Russian intelligentsia abroad in the mid-twentieth century identified with the kenotic mood: "The meekness, self-abasement, voluntary poverty, humility, obedience, non-resistance, acceptance of suffering and death" identified by Nadia Gorodetsy in the *Humiliated Christ in Modern Russian Thought*.[37] I would venture to build on Hubbs's assertion, and suggest that the intelligentsia made a virtue out of necessity, drawing out the positive implications of suffering because they could not avoid it. The appearance of the term "kenosis" could be attributed to similar causes; Western academia were interested in Russian emigres and their thought, especially in ideas that had resonance to them. It may be that their own interest in resolving the questions of kenosis urged a retroactive appellation of the name "kenotic thought" to the trend of valorising submission in Slavophile thought, and Russian cultural work in general. This hypothesis can be tested further by looking more closely at the differences between Fedotov's and Florovsky's kenotic moods, which I do not have the space to do here. Florovsky's kenosis bore much more pressure from dialogue with continental audiences who were less interested in kenosis as a whole. Valliere argues that this dialogue has a bearing on the connection between Godmanhood and theosis in the Western scholar's mind; that this connection had been implanted, and cultivated by neo-patristic scholarship, and that in fact the idea of kenosis (emptiness) is equally connected to Godmanhood.[38] It may simply have been the case that the strongest proponents of neo-patristic thought were also furthest from

---

37. See Hubbs, *Mother Russia*, 230; Gorodetsky, *Humiliated Christ*, ix.

38. See Valliere, *Modern Russian Theology*, 14.

dialogue on a kenotic ideal, and less in need of connecting their work to the West through this theological tradition.

Another hypothesis, demonstrated by the search for kenosis in Khomiakov and in *sobornost'*, is that the kenotic theologies identified in Russian thought might not be best described as *theologies*, but instead fit better among thinkers who did not aim to theologise. Khomiakov and his contemporaries were primarily interested in explaining Russia. In Valliere's words, they were concerned to define Russia's place in an aggressively expanding Europe.[39] This is indeed also akin to the émigré project of defining Russia, albeit as a shrinking enclave or Russian emigres within Europe instead of as a nation poised against a rising Europe. Perhaps thinking about sacrifice and *sobornost'* both fit better in the context of national thought and extolling the virtues of Orthodoxy in that context than they do in the context of global academic Christian theology, which, as can be seen in the Protestant cases, can dispense with kenosis when the idea becomes theologically problematic.

Bibliography

Berdyaev, Nicholas. *Dream and Reality: An Essay in Autobiography.* Translated by Katherine Lampert. London: Bles, 1950.

Billington, James H. "The Intelligentsia and the Religion of Humanity." *American Historical Review* 65.4 (1960) 807–21.

Fedotov, George P. *The Russian Religious Mind.* 2 Vols. Cambridge, MA: Harvard University Press, 1946–66.

Frank, Semen. *The Spiritual Foundations of Society: An Introduction to Social Philosophy.* Translated by Boris Jakim. Athens, OH: Ohio University Press, 1987.

Giorgiov, Adrian. "The Kenotic Christology of Charles Gore, P. T. Frosyth, and H. R. Mackintosh." *Perichoresis: The Theological Journal of Emanuel University* 2.1 (2004) 47–66.

Gorodetsky, Nadezhda. *The Humiliated Christ in Modern Russian Thought.* New York: AMS, 1973.

Hubbs, Joanna. *Mother Russia: The Feminine Myth in Russian Culture.* Bloomington, IN: Indiana University Press, 1988.

Khomiakov, Alexei S. "The Church is One." In *On Spiritual Unity: A Slavophile Reader,* edited by Robert Bird and Boris Jakim, 29–53. Hudson, NY: Lindisfarne, 1998.

———. "Letter to the Editor of *l'Union Chrétienne* on the Occasion of a Discourse by Father Gagarin, Jesuit." In *On Spiritual Unity: A Slavophile Reader,* edited by Robert Bird and Boris Jakim, 135–39. Hudson, NY: Lindisfarne, 1998.

———. "Letters to William Palmer." In *On Spiritual Unity: A Slavophile Reader,* edited by Robert Bird and Boris Jakim, 141–59. Hudson, NY: Lindisfarne, 1998.

39. See Valliere, "Modernity of Khomiakov," 131.

Khomiakov, Alexei S. "To the Serbs. An Epistle from Moscow (Extract)." In *A Documentary History of Russian Thought from Enlightenment to Marxism*, edited by William J. Leatherbarrow and Derek C. Offord, 93–94. Ann Arbor: Ardis, 1987.

Kline, George L. "Russian Religious Thought." In *Nineteenth-Century Religious Thought in the West*, edited by Ninian Smart, et al., 179–230. Vol. 2. Cambridge: Cambridge University Press, 1988.

Mercedes, Anna. *Power For: Feminism and Christ's Self Giving*. London: T. & T. Clark, 2011.

Pain, J. H. "Sobornost: A Study in Modern Russian Orthodox Theology." Phd diss., University of Oxford, 1967.

Rancour-Laferriere, Daniel. *The Slave Soul of Russia: Moral Masochism and the Cult of Suffering*. New York: New York University Press, 1996.

Rosenthal, Beatrice. "Lofty Ideals and Worldly Consequences: Visions of Sobornost' in Early Twentieth-Century Russia." *Russian History* 20.1–4 (1993) 175–95.

Shevzov, Vera. *Russian Orthodoxy on the Eve of Revolution*. Oxford: Oxford University Press, 2004.

Stoeckl, Kristina. "The Lesson of the Revolution in Russian Émigré Theology and Contemporary Orthodox Thought." *Religion State and Society* 35.4 (2007) 285–300.

Valliere, Paul. *Modern Russian Theology: Bukharev, Soloviev, Bulgakov. Orthodox. Theology in a New Key*. Edinburgh: T. & T. Clark, 2000.

———. "The Modernity of Khomiakov." In *A. S. Khomiakov: Poet, Philosopher, Theologian*, edited by Vladimir Tsurikov, 129–44. Jordanville, NY: Holy Trinity Seminary Press, 2004.

Welch, Claude. *God and Incarnation in Mid-Nineteenth Century German Theology*. New York: Oxford University Press, 1965.

Wood, Nathaniel. "Sobornost', State Authority and Christian Society in Slavophile Political Theology." In *Religion Authority and the State from Constantine to the Contemporary World*, edited by Leo D. Lefebure, 17–98. New York: Palgrave, 2016.

5

Sobornost' as a Linguistic, and Therefore Religious, Trap

ELENA TVERDISLOVA

Andrzej Walicki, the Polish historian of ideas, once wrote, "Our perception of Khomiakov's thinking is not the same thing as the thinking of Khomiakov himself."[1] That scholar's words, which could have served as an epigraph for this article, have come to reflect the chief feature of Khomiakov's narrative key, the feature which determined the receptive mobility of his discourse with all the consequences which stemmed from it. Up to a point, Khomiakov is a typical curiosity in Russian history, and in its thinking and its faith, similar to Tsiolkovsky in space exploration and rocket science (an "exhibit in a museum" is what engineers used to call him). Taken together, these reflect the yearning, typical of the Russian outlook, toward a mythologizing of thought and idealization of reality, which played a ruinous role in the country's fate. No revolution ever takes place without that sort of yearning. It was not enough that the ones on the bottom wanted nothing that was old, and the ones on the top could not do anything the old way.[2] There was already fertilized soil. The Slavophiles worked to loosen it up, and everything started with them. What they planted grew to their glory.

Much has been written about Khomiakov, most of it panegyric, and his pronouncements in various forms and structures can be ascribed to a multi-variable model which is nevertheless complete in terms of its internal statement: Russia has a special path, and it requires consistent self-defense. Up till now, the most interesting and convincing work about Khomiakov as

1. Walicki, *Rosja, katolicyzm*, 76.
2. See Lenin, "Collapse."

a philosopher has been done by Khoruzhy,[3] who put in order, if not to say actually rethought, his teachings, thanks to which Khomiakov is no longer so contradictory, while also inserting under Khomiakov's ideas his own justifications—in which, incidentally, Khoruzhy is not alone. His interpretations included Slavophilism as a "symbol" of Russian theology,[4] as an "innovation" by Khomiakov in his "synthesis" of Russian thought and analysis of the notorious new development of *sobornost'*.

Most would agree that Khomiakov and the Slavophiles' ideas were in a leading position in Russia's philosophical, social, and religious palette in the second half of the nineteenth century. Slavophilism was laid down as a stable alliance of like-minded people, the first genuine focus in the philosophy which drew a dividing line between westernization and Slavophilism, which still persists today, and the distinguishing factor which, it seemed, would be brought to an end with a new generation, indifferent overall to its origins, forebears, and the Slavic ethnos (and not just in Russia); they would lose themselves in their gadgets, as people say, in order to tear themselves away from what binds them.

In the run-up to its own history, the Slavophilic pathos, *how we are different*, dictated theory. The concept was not long in coming, and it mixed philosophical terms and concepts which had been worked out in the West over the centuries (Thomas Aquinas, Descartes and others). It violated the rules of cognition and complementarity on the basis of which systems of law, religion, science and the interactions between them had been built, which allowed for the expression of the specifics of legal thinking, self-awareness, philosophical thinking, faith, and morality. The Slavophiles' system was living flesh, pulsing in time with the ecstasy of the heart (even the English could, if they wished, turn out to be of Slavic origin).[5]

The Slavophiles' ritualistic attitude toward the Slavs, and later the similar attitude of the "Rusichists" to the Slavophiles, gave rise to a new

3. Khoruzhiy, "Sovremennye problemy"; "Uchenie o sobornosti i Tserkvi." Both works have a wealth of scholarly observations, lack pathos, and contain profound analysis. But they all seem to have been written in a manner detached from the actual practice of the Russian Orthodox Church, and therefore, the scholar's remarks about *sobornost'* are shot through and replete with deep religious meaning, and are utopian, just as with its creator.

4. "As a symbol, Slavophilia is eternal, for it is the symbolic expression of Russian self-awareness," wrote Florensky, inventing a sort of typology for reading Slavophilic heritage as specifically a creative one (Florensky cited in Khoruzhiy, "Alexei Khomiakov i ego delo," 1).

5. "His love for the English even went so far, that he seriously considered the English to be Slavs" (Berdyaev, *Aleksei Stepanovich Khomiakov*, 41; cf. Khomiakov, "Letter to the 'Moskvitjanin,'" 73–75).

field of polemics in which the Slavophiles were more likely to turn to the West and least of all to domestic Westernizers; their passion was directed against Catholicism, while the Westernizers were continuing their debates with the Slavophiles. The concept of *semeistvennost'*, or "familyhood"—the patriarchal, Slavophilic Mafia family—helped strengthen the position of the latter, and almost all participants of the movement were connected with each other by birth, through their wives, husbands, brothers and sisters. Their position was unwavering. The clan was at war with the splintered minority of Westernizers, and was invincible: jaws grip more strongly when the struggle is based on blood. And, while the Westernizers held different opinions due to the wide spectrum of their views (Peter Chaadaev, Sergey Soloviev, Ivan Turgenev, Alexander Herzen), and their camp was, as a result, less than monolithic, the Slavophiles always struck as a single fist. The main narrative of this polemic was built to reveal the underlying sign: *svoy*, "our own." Everything that did not correspond with their orientations, views, and understandings, whether those pertained to religion and philosophy or merely to culture or way of life, was liable to being marked as *chuzhoy*, "foreign." This same scale by which worldviews are measured is still present in Russian today, and finds expression in all priorities of faith, knowledge and art. Aggression, in the form of an offended soul, is noticeable in the very refusal to accept a joint existence with other confessions. It is striking to note that in the final analysis, in Russia today, the only ethical system which has risen above all confessions, with orthodoxy in the lead, is found among the organized criminal underworld, the *vory v zakone*. They themselves admit that no such society exists in any country of the world.

To the Slavophiles, according to Khoruzhy, the situation in Russia

> has been seen as a confrontation, a standoff between opposites, a conflict; it has come across as existentially fraught, saturated with negative emotions, or even with neurotic elements: both interpretations of this situation, in Samarin, depict a harsh mismatch, in which by one account Russia is much lower, and in the other, much higher than, "advanced peoples." The profound inequality between Russia and those peoples served as the primary fact for thinking this through; and it was here that the task of self-reflection converted into the task of self-confirmation: to overcome the inequality, to prove that we are not lower, not worse. ... The primary fact has turned out to be the primary trauma, as well: inequality was interpreted as injustice; disregard, judgment, and passivity were read into both this fate and the situation of the orthodox Slavic world. ... Therefore, the Slavophile's construct is not a pure scientific-philosophical nor

theological discourse. Both philosophy and theology, and their
historical and sociocultural theories, always include specific
ancillary motives: polemical, ideological, emotional, and even
"psychoanalytical," expressing certain complexes.[6]

These complexes brought the Slavophiles along with them, not to
search for the truth, but to fight to defend the values which still needed to be
described and justified, for all of them were bonds of the past. Gradually the
passéist spirit, with its genuflectory attitude toward history and tradition,
was let out onto the surface. Future plans were examined and built based on
the matrices of the past, in the pluperfect, preserving the necessary mark-
ings for the future. This was the position that laid the well-beaten path for
revolution, a leap to a time brought to pass. When the future does not come
together naturally and harmoniously, but rather is assembled ideologically,
the call to remake the world has real meaning, for the potential readiness for
war is always vindicated.

Hence the temptation to discover the purely Russian, original foundations of theology, building it up not so much along the lines of a unified
Christian discourse that extends back for over a millennium as in contradiction to those "not with us." The problem is far from trivial, as is the question of who is more powerful and more convincing.

Khomiakov entered the history of Russian philosophy and, most of
all, ecclesiology, having awoken domestic Russian thinking as "a defender
of the roots of old Russia" (Florensky's words leave a sense of subtext).[7] He
won fame with his love for Russia and its people, personifying on its face
all the good of the world, and with his curt dismissal of the West, most
of all Catholicism. Everything bad, of course, came from there, from their
nihilistic attitude toward life, although why did "western nihilism" strike a
blow on Russia and give the West a pass? What's more, how did allegiance
to the people reconcile with serfdom? After all, in those years, Russia was
the only country in Europe still to boast the legal authority to exploit and
enslave human beings.

The usual model—everything vile is from the Catholics, while the
genuine and the future ripens in Orthodoxy—came to life in full color in
the works and artistic compositions of Khomiakov, the West's most rabid
detractor, who was not only a historian and theologian, but also a poet and
dramatist. And although openly and officially he managed to achieve almost
nothing, during his lifetime, of the ideas that were most widely voiced and
disseminated, he nevertheless attracted people who celebrated and would

6. Khoruzhiy, "Sovremennye problemy," 2.

7. Florensky, "Around Khomiakov," 322.

continue his work (Ivan Kireevsky, Yuri Samarin, Alexei Koshelev, and later Nikolai Berdyaev, Georges Florovsky, and others), and also laid the strongest possible (but, I would say, potentially explosive!) foundation for Russia's mythologization, of its past, its people, the Church, and science, tossing a sort of veil onto the actual situation and authentic history. Furthermore, as of today, the mythologem of Russian holiness is the most destructive and most popular "crown" of all political systems and structures, and indeed of Russian thinking in general. With it, you can eat up everything. The only strange thing is that these qualities of Khomiakov's—spiritual impressionability and fantasizing—found their expression not in his verses and plays, full of pathos and sermonizing, but rather in ecclesiology, which demands, precisely, a rhetorical approach. It seems as if his ability for creative work, on one hand, and for theology, on the other, switched places. There must have been a reason he said about himself, "without pretense of humility I know for myself, that my verses, when good, depend on the thought, i.s. the prosifier everywhere peeks out, and subsequently, one has to ultimately throttle the versifier."[8] Having successfully suffocated the poet in him, he directed the whole of his inexhaustible creativity in full to the study of orthodoxy. The town crier was ringing the bells at full volume, for only he knows what his Church needs. "It seems that three quarters of all questions regarding the Slavophiles or Slavophism boils down to the question of . . . 'Khomiakov and the others.'"[9]

In its own way, his nature was harmonious, and people saw in his type "a captivating and aesthetic completeness"[10] although he "was not an aesthete."[11] Along with rejecting "rights of ownership," "a special attitude towards the people, an unique trust for the collective life of the people,"[12] he was more inclined to a moderate and family-oriented life than the intellectual life; in that sphere, he was a dilettante. Khomiakov could not have been called an aristocrat of the spirit; he was a Russian lord of the manor through and through, one convinced that only the lord of the manor could save the majestic Rus'. As the bard of the "collective unconscious," his contribution to the development of patriotic ideas in Russia—which, it must be noted, rose to an apex due to the overthrowing of the ideas of its neighbors—is indisputable. In confirming the distinctiveness of the Russian faith, he planted the seeds of self-isolation, and planted an allergy to tolerance, painting a picture,

8. Berdyaev, *Aleksei Stepanovich Khomiakov*, 42.

9. Florensky, "Around Khomiakov," 319.

10. Berdyaev, *Aleksei Stepanovich Khomiakov*, 23.

11. Berdyaev, *Aleksei Stepanovich Khomiakov*, 53.

12. Berdyaev, *Aleksei Stepanovich Khomiakov*, 25.

within the framework of the serfdom that then existed, of the *organic* relationship between master and bondman.

At the end of the eighteenth century, following the partition of Poland (the third one, in 1795), the Russian people received Polish land as well as the Polish and Jewish people (some of them Ukrainians and Belarusians) who lived there. But the Russian people never recovered from that forced enrichment. The central reason for that was not the psychology of the Russians, who so keenly discerned what was foreign, but rather their wholesale illiteracy, which rendered them completely helpless in comparison with the Polish peasants (the churches ran schools) and even more so with the Jews who had finished *cheder*, where they more or less learned Hebrew from the Book of Life, the Torah. The Slavophiles, Ivan Aksakov most of all, shed more than one tear over the lot of the unlucky Russian people, but few of them acknowledged how unprepared that people was for a new life and what sort of yoke slavery had been for them. In the end, serfdom was ended not under the influence or at the demand of the Russian intelligentsia (there's no point mentioning, here, the Russian revolt as Alexander Pushkin described it, "senseless and merciless"), but instead as a result of the attempted rebellions by the Polish peasants, who were in no way satisfied by this unseemly dependency, since in their own homeland—which by then had been broken into pieces—they had once had the ability to buy themselves membership in the gentry, while now, under the law of the Russian Empire, they faced the prospect of being tied to the land and its owner.

But what was most curious was that it was very early on, in this patriarchal figure at the center focal point of Slavophilism who thirsted for love and family happiness, that the spirit of resistance was aroused. Berdyaev could not avoid noting it, and indeed nearly rejoiced in this peculiarity, using the "Letter to the Benedictines" as an example, which had been written by a young Khomiakov and was shot through with Derzhavin's anthem, "Let the thunder of victory sound": "And so the day of victory, glory, and revenge has come: / And so our imagined dreams have come to pass."[13] These lines by Khomiakov, by the way, are barely half a century removed from Derzhavin's verses. How powerful is the pathos of ratting weapons!

> The military nature of Aleksei Stepanovich found expression
> very early. At seventeen years of age he attempted to run away
> from home, in order to take part in the war for the liberation of
> Greece. He bought himself a bootleg knife, grabbed with him a

13. Khomiakov and Koshelev, *Stikhotvoreniya*, 61.

small sum of money and secretly left home. They caught up with him at Serpukhov gateway and returned him home.[14]

Then there is this: "Everything, which was romantic in the nature of Khomiakov, always assumed the form of a military stirring."[15] And after that:

> The military bearing—is a characteristic feature of Khomiakov. This feature was evidenced also, in that he often lapsed off onto a war motif, both in his martial manner of writing, and in his love for dialectical skirmishes. . . . He is always the dogmatist. A dogmatic tenacity runs through all his nature.[16]

His dogmatism was indeed invincible, for it was all too transparent— not "in favor of," but rather "in spite of." Here is the most instructive: "The bad warrior is the one who fights himself instead of the enemy. Khomiakov always fought the enemy," whom, we will note, he had no need to invent: the Catholics, the Pope, and the West were always conveniently at hand.

One of the biggest errors of not just Khomiakov, but also of Berdyaev who wrote about him, was in their idealization of the idealization to which Khomiakov periodically succumbed. "He sees the mission of Russia to be first of all in this, that it reveal to the Western world the mystery of freedom."[17] And until that "secret of freedom" was revealed, one stroke of the tsarist pen deprived converts to another faith of all their rights granted by birth and their property. One example was the prince Ivan Gagarin, punished "for willfully appearing and speaking before the monks of the Jesuit order."[18] And how could anyone speak of the "secret of freedom" when serfdom was so blatant?

> His own everyday rural landlordly freedom seemed to him to be the organic freedom of the Russian people as a whole, of the whole Russian way of life. Here there was a limitation connected with everyday culture, with the historical conditions of place and time, but Khomiakov's love for freedom, itself, was unlimited.

Berdyaev wrote this clearly in adoration of the lingering "rural landlordly freedom" in old Rus' (in the West, that had long been an anachronism), and

---

14. Berdyaev, *Aleksei Stepanovich Khomiakov*, 26.

15. Berdyaev, *Aleksei Stepanovich Khomiakov*, 27.

16. Berdyaev, *Aleksei Stepanovich Khomiakov*, 37.

17. Berdyaev, *Aleksei Stepanovich Khomiakov*, 37.

18. See Yudin, "Gagarin."

not remarking upon the sort of crisis that had long pained the Russian intelligentsia and about which he had written in a study vibrantly entitled "The
Spiritual Crisis of the Intelligentsia" back in 1910.

Such a clearly idealized "rural landlordly freedom" was the analogue
not to simplicity, but to the informality of everyday culture which had replaced spirituality. Khomiakov's prophecies fed a view to the past, and the
ancient history of Rus' showed the way. Passéism settled into the Russian
soul for a good long time, if not forever, and it defined an attitude and a type
of behavior. It is telling that in art passéism is inherent to decadence: this is
the biggest paradox in Khomiakov, the one he bestowed on his countrymen,
without handing them either the keys to the gates or the reins of government. His philosophy worked only like "memory" and as a guide for taking
action against the enemy. But it saved nobody in their moment of (ruinous!)
need. What help could it offer to people who immediately lost everything
after the revolution, or who were the former owners of cherry orchards, who
had lost courage in the face of what was flying so quickly around the garden,
with life changing so rapidly?

A conviction built on rejection, it turns out, can have a long life. Khomiakov's "Khomiakovstvo" remained within the bounds of the research
by his students and followers, who concentrated mainly on their teacher's
legacy. So Florensky is justified in writing that and therefore Khomiakov's
doctrine is regarded as a problem and asks "Who was Khomiakov?"[19] And
clarifies, "the subjective loftiness of his person and the elastic freshness of
his thought their due is not jet to go very far in objectively assessing his
inner life and the system of his thought" to any conviction.[20] In exactly
the same way, it remains a mystery what Khomiakov had to teach future
generations. To love a life from which only a charred framework remained?
To bow down to the Church, which had partially surrendered itself and
partially been defeated? "*Vse v proshlom* [Everything is in the past!]" is a
benign painting from Tretyakov, without a future. What people write about
Khomiakov today is a rethinking of his idea in the form of the very same
nostalgia or ascetic faith in the truth of the Orthodox Church's teachings,
which reject the concrete individual as a subject, while after all the true
sign of democracy is in *liberum veto*. Khomiakov's Church, excluding its
singling out of individuality, based its authority, in the end, on allegiance
to government authority.

Khomiakov was a discrete, closed-off individual, and what could soul-
less theory teach anyone? What's more, in his verse he "is the soldier, he

19. Florensky, "Around Khomiakov," 322.
20. Florensky, "Around Khomiakov," 321.

shoots precisely to the point," but at the same time he is "is aloof and re-served" (Berdyaev).[21] Khomiakov carefully hid from everyone all the work-ings of the soul, something that Kireevsky also wrote about; but it was that experience—rankling, personal, and deeply hidden—that was inevitable and vital. In life, as a rule, openness is a sign and guarantee of talent. Here there is not even a hint of creative freedom. What was hindering Khomia-kov? Perhaps it was writer's block. That happens: thoughts fly easily, but get hung up on the paper. And this was during the period when in Russian lit-erature, with the arrival of Lev Tolstoy, immanence was acquiring ever more power, and that immanence, as Florensky alertly observed, had spread to Khomiakov's "theologizing," especially in how he imagined the Church, but not to his poetic self-expression. He seemed to replace his closed-off soul not with God, nor faith, but with the Church, the only place where human fates were being played out, for here was the genuine assembly, or *sobiranie*, of the people. *Sobornost'* comes partially from here. He clearly exaggerated the power of the people, and this, half a century later, backfired powerfully on Russia during the years of bloody revolutionary score-settling. The Rus-sian people are a people who can be led. And they can be well organized. Even against their own benefactors, for which the ransacked, burned manor house at Yasnaya Polyana stands as an example. Yet these people's owners had treated their illnesses, educated them, helped them develop. To what did that lead? This is not an idle inquiry. Khomiakov speaks nowhere of this, but it emerges on its own: the Russian people are obedient and devoted, as long as they are enslaved. And they do not know what to do with their freedom. They have not been trained for that. Khomiakov replaced a sort of guilt complex over the uneducated and forgotten peasantry with an author-ity that the people in reality did not possess, but which, in his social teach-ings, was implied. He extended a private experience from his own practice to the whole Russian social order, opening the gates to a pseudo-populist mythologization. Instead of educating the people, at length and relentlessly, the Slavophiles invented the people, missing their chance to reform Russia in actuality rather than in words.

Through his modeling of the Church, Khomiakov built up religious relationships within the bounds of nearly the entire world, extending his program at least to all humankind. Judging by his historical, "intuitive" searching, his thinking covered not just spatial and geographical, but also temporal relationships: from facts not known to the chroniclers to the present day, and centuries beyond. And in all his pronouncements, the Orthodox Church was in first place. The ecclesiastical instructor of the

21. Berdyaev, *Aleksei Stepanovich Khomiakov*, 31.

Slavophiles considered the Christianity contemporary to him, with its multiple branches, as apostasy. And there is no avoiding the simplest failure of understanding: why did the Russians pounce on the West, blowing its whole system to bits with such abandon, and most of all with so much certainty that they had the right to do so? (And it was not just the religious system which, let's assume, was absolutely foreign to the Slavophiles, but also the political, ideological, and social order.) That was not their motherland and not their state, after all. And such an approach led to a habit, and it became, almost, the Russians' fundamental rhetorical trump card.

> What did the creatively virginal "East," the world of the Byzantines and Slavs, have to counterpose this cultural wealth [the West!]? The blank pages of its history, occasionally reddened with the blood spilled in wild orgies of fratricidal enmity or explosions of unbridled barbarism.[22]

Florovsky exclaims, as if echoing everything Chaadaev had said on the topic. And he finds an explanation: The Slavophiles counterposed their ideal of organic life in spirit and love, their "rural communism" against an enlightened Europe.[23] And what about Europe? Did it not have problems of its own? In providing an account of how the Slavophiles made their own errors, about which Florovsky speaks with great caution, he strives by every scholarly method to justify the triad they announced, or more precisely, assigned—"orthodoxy, autocracy and nationality"—as the "symbolic expression of their ideal of organic life."[24] This heady brew could not be reduced to its parts. Florovsky characterizes the Slavophiles as "historical old believers," assuming that they must be interpreted strictly within the framework of their own tradition, without crossing outside of that time, in order to avoid succumbing to the temptation of the "children" to create their own "legends of the fathers."

Florensky never tires of asking who Khomiakov actually was. His question is not ontological, nor is it essentially immanent; it cannot even be classified as strictly theological, since this is a question which lies in the realm of morality. The responsibility that obliges a scholar to restrain excessively zealous thinking:

> Did he desire to Strengthen and elevate the imperial throne or, on the contrary, should we see in Khomiakov the creator of the most popular and therefore the most dangerous form of

22. Florovsky, "Vechnoe i prekhodyashchee," 59–77.
23. Florovsky, "Vechnoe i prekhodyashchee," 35–36, 39.
24. Florovsky, "Vechnoe i prekhodyashchee," 41.

egalitarianism? . . . A defender of the roots of old Russia or an up rooter of her primordial foundations in the name of a dreamy vision of a projected Russia of the future? . . . For to prescribe, on the basis of one's own authority, even with the purest of intentions, what the Church should be, is not to recognize the Church, but only to recognize oneself.[25]

The conclusion is purely methodological. Florensky had no complexes in his approach to scholarship. What guided this thinking was a precisely structured and evidence-based idea, which always had a logic to it and a place in his systemic-structural approach ("Iconostasis" is the ideal model of structural analysis, and he was located at its source).

Certainly, his attitude toward Khomiakov could not be unambiguous. Florensky was one of Khomiakov's most forthright and unbiased critics, and he emphasized that this was "This question is not a formal one. Khomiakov makes himself vulnerable to a dualistic interpretation."[26] Then there is Walicki, who in characterizing Khomiakov's teachings as "utopian," called the author "two-faced,"[27] explaining: "Khomiakov earned his reputation as the great forebear of modernist trends in Christianity,"[28] and even played an important role in reconsidering Catholic dogmatics at the Second Vatican Council. Meanwhile, within Russian thinking's eternal debate with Catholic thinking, "a completely different side of Khomiakov is revealed: that of the Orthodox fundamentalist, who rigorously supported centuries-old principles and was hostile both to anything foreign and to the ecumenical tendencies of the general renewal of Christianity in the nineteenth century."[29] His ideas were targeted at "anti-Catholic fundamentalism, isolationism and a feeling of superiority over the other Christian world."[30] What is the origin, then, of the quite obvious enthusiasm for his images and ideas in the West? Khomiakov, who built up his ecclesiology exclusively in opposition to Europe and Catholicism, turned out to be much in demand among those very same Catholics. His understanding of unity, *sobornost'*, makes the rounds from the theologians to Pope Francis. Clearly, the Catholicism of the time, thirsting for change, laid its hopes on Khomiakov's writings without taking note that in his own country those

25. Florensky, "Around Khomiakov," 322–23.
26. Florensky, "Around Khomiakov," 323
27. Walicki, *Rosja, katolicyzm*, 75–80.
28. Walicki, *Rosja, katolicyzm*, 75.
29. Walicki, *Rosja, katolicyzm*, 76.
30. Walicki, *Rosja, katolicyzm*, 79.

had long since transformed into an idealistic construct of aggressive self-determination, essentially justifying religious intolerance.

But today, *sobornost'* is also associated with Islam, with its confidence in the rightness of the religion and its insistence on maintaining cohesion. If we closely examine the essence of *sobornost'*, taking into account all the originality of Khomiakov's systemic construct, it is difficult not to see how it manifests in the ISIS movement, in a perverted form, of course: "Only one task is possible for Russia: to make of itself the most Christian of all human societies."[31] Sometimes the seditious thought arises that Russia became orthodox accidentally; an Islam which at present has still not moved beyond paganism is a closer match to its mentality and ideological taste. The influence of *sobornost'* is only picking up speed with time—not as a religious term, but more as a nationalistic invocation, always metamorphosing and transforming.

Almost ten years ago, on October 22, 2008, not far from Magnano, within the walls of the Italian Catholic monastery in Bose, close to the village of Biella in northern Italy, between Turin and Milan, where the independent, mixed-type monastic community first emerged, a place which has become a center for creative, theological and artistic activities with an ecumenical focus, a conference was held with a curious name: "*Sobornost'*, *kontsiliarnost'* and communication: From Khomiakov to Zizioulas." John Zizioulas, the Greek metropolitan of Pergamon, is now one of the most prominent Orthodox theologians, an advocate for ecumenicism and closer ties with Catholicism, despite its passion for the *Filioque*. One participant in that conference, Archpriest Igor Tsvetkov, notes, in part:

> The philosophers of the so-called Slavophile movement—and they were all passionate adherents of Orthodoxy—were in fact trying to carry over what people now call the discourse of Orthodox theology into the realm of inclusive ecclesiology—with no success, unfortunately. The symbolic naturalism which Prot. Alexander Schmemann lamented both during the American diaspora and hundred years later remained impervious.[32]

The first and central question that arises in relation to all this is what *sobornost'* actually means, and why it became not just the very favorite treat of the Slavophiles and, later, of Orthodoxy (its official representatives first battled against this innovation), but also an alluring prize for practically all religions. Catholics and Anglicans openly admit this, *sobornost'* has a great deal in common with Islam, and *sobornost'* meets the main requirements of

---

31. Khomiakov, "O yuridicheskikh voprosakh," 335.

32. Tsvetkov, "Sobornost'."

Protestantism even if it doesn't admit it. Florensky exposes the underlying differences between Orthodoxy and Protestantism, governed again by the logic of comparing the "Iranian" and "Cushite" origins in the work of the Church's Slavophilic master:

> For Khomiakov, the essence of Protestantism consists *only* in protest against Romanism, but with the fundamental premises and characteristic modes of thought of the latter preserved. But is that really the case? The development of Protestantism and its derivatives *after* Khomiakov has undeniably shown that Protestantism, as the chief expression of the culture of recent times, is based on humanism, the elevation of humanity, the divinization of humanity. To us a term borrowed from philosophy, Protestantism is based on *immanentism*, meaning humanity's intention to create all reality out of itself, outside of and apart from God, that is, out of nothing, and, first and foremost, sacred reality; to create this reality in all senses, beginning with the formation of concepts and ending with spiritual reality.[33]

Given the flexibility of the discourse surrounding it, *sobornost'* applies to Protestant communities. But in Russia it still exists at the word level. How could that have occurred? Apparently, as a result of exchanging the hatred toward Catholics for what has become the customary "image" of the Church and its "inclusive unity." However, what turned out to be the closest fit with the Russian mentality was this aggression targeted at the battle against the "fallen churches." Berdyaev eloquently calls Khomiakov "a genuine Orthodox knight,"[34] again, in an analogy to Western knighthood, echoing Herzen's expressive portrait of him, about which he must have known: "He was like the medieval knights who guarded the Madonna and slept fully armed"[35] (chock-full of Catholic associations). It is unlikely that the Slavophiles ever made an accounting of how much they were able to predict the spirit of Russian self-identification. What could have made *sobornost'* so attractive beyond Russian borders? First and foremost, it arose in the environment of the Russian abroad as that very same nostalgia and demand for unity. It was not immediately that *sobornost'* took on the nature of a meme of Russian Orthodox ideology, with its mandatory components of multifunctionality, polysemanticism and inscrutability.

33. Florensky, "Around Khomiakov," 323.

34. Berdyaev, *Aleksei Stepanovich Khomiakov*, 45.

35. Herzen called Khomiakov "the Ilya of Murom, the *bogatyr* who, on the side of Orthodoxy and Slavophilism" (Herzen, *My Past and Thoughts*, 2:535).

In terms of persuasiveness and clarity of application of the concept of *sobornost'* so central to the system of Khomiakov's theological studies, Florovsky, who may well have been the biggest fan of his theory, having called it "a systematics of Slavophilic teaching" and "systematic expositor of Slavophile"[36] (while cautioning against a literal understanding of "system," given that in Khomiakov's work and thoughts what ruled supreme was "a born dialectician" but testimony and description[37]), makes reference again to the Catholic theologian Johann Adam Möhler (the Tübingen Catholic school), one of whose works happens to be entitled "Unity in the Church or the principle of Catholicism" (Möhler, *Die Einheit in der Kirche oder das Princip des Katholicismus*, 1825), which Florovsky interprets in translation in his own way: "Unity in the Church or the origin of *sobornost'*." With that, he replaces the previously accepted and long-recognized term "catholicism" with "*sobornost'*" as evidence of the rightness of Khomiakov's position, and the conditionality of the meaning of *sobornost'*, and the vagueness of what it entails, immediately becomes self-evident.

Incidentally, the word *sobornost'* which Khomiakov brought into fashion arose, in the Russian language, not out of the noun *sobor*, a council or assembly, as it would be easy to assume, but rather out of the adjective *sobornyy*,[38] which means, in translation from the Greek *katholike*, whole, all-encompassing, universal (or "catholic," spelled in Russian either *katolicheskiy* or *kafolicheskiy*)—these are all synonyms, which, put together side by side, suggest Khomiakov's thought about ideological subversion. He does not simply cause different translations of one word go head to head, as in *vselenskiy* and *sobornyy*, in attempting to "dethrone" the Catholic creed, but also makes the case for his own interpretation against the structure of "catholic universality" that had developed, conducting an overt argument with other Christian confessions to confirm the Orthodox rules, the only true ones. "Here, the significance of human agreement or disagreement is exaggerated and the dignity and value of the truth are diminished."[39] His striving for a metaphysical conceptualization of Church traditions returned as an ideological reckoning with European Christians, the Catholics and the Protestants, and a desire for revenge. Such a mutiny on the ship of Christianity, with one term being absorbed in order to cast off another, could hardly have facilitated mutual understanding. Today the last thing people

36. Florovsky, *Ways of Russian Theology*, 38.

37. Florovsky, *Ways of Russian Theology*, 39.

38. For the terminological component of this concept, see Khoruzhiy, "Uchenie o sobornosti i Tserkvi."

39. See Florensky, "Around Khomiakov," 325.

remember is the way in which Khomiakov introduced the concept which was intended to unite all the faithful under the canopy of the Spirit of God. The Creed of Constantinople (381) mentions faith in the *katholike ekklesia*, which, in Old Church Slavonic, is rendered *v sbornuiu tserkov*, and later became *sobornyy*. In this way, *sobor* was borrowed from Old Church Slavonic. According to Vasmer, the word *sbor*, which originally meant an "assembly of clergy," is a calque from the Greek word *synagoge*,[40] "to gather together," or *sobor* (meaning "assembly" or "synagogue").[41] Khomiakov, however, had in mind a completely different meaning of *sobornost'*, as "conciliarity" (from the Latin *concilio*, meaning "council," implying the form or the body of church management, thereby expansively interpreting *sbor* and giving it its own substantive packing. In the end, he mixed both concepts together. It is interesting to note that today, in order for the Orthodox *sobornost'* to fit into a working model, commentators have resorted to the Latin term "conciliarity," written in Russian as *kontsiliarnost'*, on the basis of which there have been built modern-day Catholic theological concepts appropriate to *sobornost'* in its modern meaning.

"Naturally, the question arises of whether a word existed in the Slavic language that completely corresponded with the concept of catholicity," writes Khomiakov, in reference to an issue pertaining to his dispute with the Jesuit Gagarin regarding the Creed.

> It is they who chose the word *sobornyy* that one can judge about the meaning they attributed to *katholikos*. Was there a word in the Slavonic language that could express the concept of universality. . . . The first of these words occurs in very old homilies. The second is indisputably ancient and is used to render the idea for the universal Church (*vselenskaya tserkov*) or in the ecumenical sense (*vselenskii dobor* = ecumenical council). Thus, the first translators could have used such expressions to render the universal sense. I am certainly not denying that *katholikos* (deriving from kath'-ola and implying *ethne*, *klimata*, or some other related expression) can have this sense of university. But I assert that the Apostles of the Slavs did not understand this term in this enter their heads. It appears that such a definition was not part of their theological system. The word they chose was *sobornyy*. *Sobor* implies the idea of an assembly, not necessarily gathered in some place or other, but existing virtually without a formal gathering. It is unity in plurality.[42]

40. Vasmer, *Etimologicheskiy slovar'*, 704.

41. D'iachenko, *Tserkovno-slavianskiy slovar'*, 627.

42. Khomiakov, "Letter to the Editor," 138–39.

Meanwhile, as Igor Tsvetkov notes, "The first Church Slavonic texts containing the Creed are quite distant in time from the equals-to-the-apostles Methodius and Cyril; we know that they translated this Creed, and it follows that we cannot prove that it was they who invented the adjective *sobornyy*."[43] Consequently, the word *sobornyy* has a historically more distant meaning: *sbornyy* as "gathered together," or catholic, while *sobornyy*, with the feminine ending in the phrase *Sobornaia Tserkov'*, has its own meaning: "it includes the believers in Christ of all places, times and peoples,"[44] which is also expressed by *vselenskii*, "universal," but this, at its root, contradicts Khomiakov's attitude towards other confessions due to his disagreement with their doctrines. To recognize *sobornyy* as the source of Khomiakov's *sobornost'* would be to introduce still more confusion.

Khomiakov built up his idea of *sobornost'* on the basis of words taken out of context (*sbor—sobor—sobornyy—sobornost'*), and there was a need to distinguish them from the European type, meaning the general Christian tendency, and to make a break from the Catholic notion of universality (as in *vselenkost'* or *vsemirnost'*); that idea, which had arisen to gloss the Greek term *katholike*, from a list of synonyms immediately made the leap into the category of antonyms. "He looked into himself more penetratingly and consistently than the others."[45] In Florensky's opinion, Khomiakov believed that the label *sobornyy* precisely conveyed the original Greek meaning of the word "catholic," considered a scientist, and so he refused to call the Western Church "catholic," and used instead terms like "Romanism" and "Latinism" Khomiakov signed himself up for open disavowal of the dogmas of Catholicism (the infallibility of the Pope, for instance, and the problem of the *Filioque*). That opened the way to justifying national individuality and laying out the principles of isolationism on that basis. The Russian Orthodox Church was proclaimed to be different, with its own special path, and, most importantly, it was faithful to tradition. Personal individuality was replaced by collective, *sobornyy* individuality. In dividing the institute of the Church and the Church as a unified spiritual whole, Khomiakov separated it along the same lines of infallibility he had protested when the idea was applied to the Pope according to Catholic dogmatic principles. Such a methodology quite strongly resembles the Marxist-Leninist one, which adapted the ideas and concepts of the German "classics" to show, for example, that revolution was possible in one individual country with a weak economy, and therefore the USSR was

43. Tsvetkov, "Sobornost'."
44. Svirelin, *Tserkovnoslavianskiy slovar'*, 206.
45. Florensky, "Around Khomiakov," 319.

declared the example for the whole world. The connection with the logic of suggestion which Khomiakov demonstrates is very clear.

Essentially, after obtaining its terminological freedom, *sobornost'* became an Orthodox hit, expressing everything and nothing, justifying the enmity toward people "not our own." This new development, this neologism which had arisen out of the already-accepted and standardized concept of *vselenskost'*, heaped together within its multivector system of associations both the catholicity/universality of the imperial Church and the Church's form of government, implying that it was managed through an assembly/council of its authorized representatives.

Khomiakov's main trick—the deconstruction of word and meaning, image and significance, thought and action—anticipates modernism in general, and not just in theology as Walicki has stated. It is strange that in the West, with its ongoing interest in Khomiakov, they have not picked up on this paradigm, practically the first portent of modernist art. Khomiakov boldly takes from the word his own understanding and fills it with his own content, violating the laws of translation. If only he had composed music, he might have been in the forefront of cacophony.

Multidimensional and multifaceted, *sobornost'* resembles a grenade that is just about to explode. Khomiakov believed that he was figuratively laying a path for the future Orthodox Russia, but in fact he was laying a snare that distorted Orthodoxy's palette of religious expression, a linguistic substitution of words, *vselenskost'* for *sobornost'*, and diverting theological discourse toward the ideological, destroying at the roots the processes of democratization whose champion he himself had once been and of which he had even seemed to be the initiator. He reduced the scale of all humankind down to the profoundly private community of the temple. Having mixed causes and effects, Khomiakov's configuration of terms inside his own theory introduced a cognitive dissonance to the spiritual world of the Russian man, for all the components of his ecclesiology had turned out to be in conflict with each other, causing damage to the very idea of its cunning verbal imprecision, which was characteristic generally for Khomiakov, when one thing is presumed and a different thing written, and the more dangerous expressions are the ones chosen; for example, the Church is *boryushchayasya* (fighting, grappling) but in fact it is *voinstvuiushchaya* (bellicose or up in arms); the Church is "visible" and "invisible"; the Church as a place that serves God and the Church as an *obraz* (image, pattern or symbol); the Church as a unified organ obtained a status almost higher than God's, while the unification of people different in status but adhering to the same faith excluded all rights for any one separate individual. This was now not just a linguistic trap, but a genuinely religious, moral one. The

conceptual proof of the victory of Orthodoxy as a unified whole degenerated into the oratory of expansionism which fed on the songs of the Russians' victories of yore, over the Tatars, the Swedes, the French, the Turks.
And just as the stimulus to develop industry, which was always prodded
awake with a warlike slant, the religious surge, in exactly the same way,
is accompanied by far-reaching sociopolitical and geographical intentions.
Bearing up the people, his believers, in that sort of surge was an important
part of Khomiakov's program and that of his successors.

The constitutive model of *sobornost'* with its pathos of interconnect-
edness, in the hands of an able player, could easily toss a chip onto the
necessary territory, gradually moving its pawn from national consciousness through religious and social consciousness to, soon, revolutionary
consciousness. In altering the lexical narratology, it was pursuing purely
ideological goals, relying on the innate propensity of the Russian people
for acting communally, "huddling together." And in sensing this specificity,
which, to Khomiakov's credit, was discovered and formulated by him, not
to mention philosophically grounded, the Slavophile teacher of the Church
placed his bet on the people as a coherent nation, without considering the
sources of such a unification, the reasons underlying that specificity, and
the circumstances which accompanied that coherence. One factor having
an impact on the formation of this monolith was the warlike culture of the
Tatar-Mongol hordes, who taught the Russians about the "gathering of the
hordes," the "collective subconscious" in search of a form: either social (for
the *obshchina*, community) or religious (*sobornost'*). The mythologems of
social or community development with their inherent whiff of a special path
led to within a hair's breadth of revolution. The "expansionist" analogy lay
on the surface, while everything else sunk into the darkness.

Religion infers life. Khomiakov chose the fight.

One can also look at Khomiakov's idea from the other side: in refusing separate individuals the right to freedom within the unified collective,
according to the *sobornost'* project, the Slavophiles also refused the Church
as such the right to its own position and personal views, not to mention the
individual selection by a parish of its internal regimens or development of
a liturgy within the system of the church hierarchy. Unanimity of spirit, in
effect, becomes the standard, a sort of sign of quality to which all are subject.
There was a reason that Khomiakov defined his vision of the Church as
Tserkov' odna (the "one Church" or the "single Church") rather than *Tserkov'
edinaya* (a "unified Church"). At first, it gives the impression that this is
an imprecise word, but later one understands the true meaning: There is
one Church, one faith, one people. It is a rallying cry. The *sobornost'* which
gained popularity in the West became, for Russia, somewhat of a prototype

for communism, along with an experiment in self-hypnosis: there can be no doubt about the hypnotic impact of Khomiakov on the subsequent development of the Russian mentality.

Subsequent generations straightened out Khomiakov's thinking and injected it with a certain dose of spiritual sadness, the kind practically all believers in Russia had experienced, dreaming that another person thought the same way, shared their worldview, or so to speak ontology and immanentism at the same time, in order so that everyone could sense everyone at once.

To a certain extent, *sobornost'* was a complaint against the legitimation of a special, as it were, neo-Protestantism in the Orthodox consciousness; there was a reason that Florensky saw a similarity with Protestantism in Khomiakov's teachings (something to which Florovsky took offense). Meanwhile, Khomiakov himself acted as a sort of Luther, turning spiritual humankind to a new interpretation, fighting with other churches, including his own, which ripped out by the roots the concept of *sobornost'* as a unifying factor rather than a dividing one. For Florensky, this was only "masked socialism," inspired by western ideas: "Of the idea of *sobornost'* (though it should be noted that the idea of *sobornost'* of consciousness is not completely foreign to Western philosophy, for instance, to Kant, not to mention Schelling of the final period, Feuerbach, Comte, and so on)."[46] He writes, while Khomiakov's contemporaries considered his dialectical pathos of churchhood as genuine wholeness to be a living voice from within. Without engaging in outright polemics with Khomiakov, but only bringing to light the clear alogism of his theological judgments that mixed dogma and law, religious feeling with socialism, and distorted the laws of historical development, here we can add, as well, Khomiakov's skillful combining of the poetic with the artistic in his teachings about the Church; sufficient examples are his declaration about the Church as *obraz*, and forthrightly the "Legend of the Invisible City of Kitezh," which Florensky—not directly, but only through his review for a book by Zavitnevich[47]—finds to be a deviation, a contradiction, underwater reefs which are difficult to circumvent.

Khomiakov builds his texts like modular histories which demand to be laid down in layers, but he switches the places of these components: their clear subjectivism obscures the picture, and when ontology disappears, it is not simply the individual symbolism (which somehow holds up to any description) that unravels, but also the semantic idea, without which there is neither writer nor reader. And it does not matter what sort of discourse

---

46. Florensky, "Around Khomiakov," 323–24.
47. Zavitnevich, *Alexei Stepanovich Khomiakov.*

we face: philosophical, theological, poetic or autobiographical. Slavophilic thinkers knew how to guess, leading their teacher's thoughts far from the intellectual path. Might this not be the source of the simplicity which revealed itself in the portability of his ideas? He can be interpreted any which way, which has been demonstrated by the subsequent number of those encouraging a "synthesis" of his thinking. Khomiakov built his own parallel, ethereal paths, and today efforts are being made to bring them down to earth, to find them their proper place. But just as that place did not exist then, it does not exist now—as long as you do not publish his texts with commentary, of course. The audience did not concern him; he seemed to prepare his performances for the members of his household, who in any case would be happy to listen. The subjective idea of two global elements, the "crooked mirror" of "Cushitism" and the "embellished" one of "Iranianism,"[48] as the *element of necessity* and the *element of freedom*, which made Khomiakov (in Berdyaev's opinion) almost congenial, essentially acted in contradiction with their author: in posing himself the task of "guessing" unknown facts of history, not recorded in the chronicles, he relied on historical intuition, at the same time rejecting mysticism, even though those two spheres were tangential. And he tossed out entirely previous work which he had studied thoroughly, assuming that, in the study of history, everything was ambiguous. His faith in his own rightness was unyielding. "Khomiakov is superior to the other Slavophiles in talent, intelligence, learning, and conviction."[49]

> The lofty founding principle of which he sang as a poet—writes Florensky—and in which he saw security for the fortress of the peasant community, as a master—this turns out, now, to be the loftiest founding principle in history. But—stresses the Russian theologian—against this founding principle in history, as it happened earlier in poetic images and then in everyday peasant life, another force is fighting. Against the "Iranian" principle, which is what Khomiakov called the higher spiritual principle of history, there is arrayed the materialistic, "Cushite" founding principle, which eats away at it. After that discovery, Khomiakov tries to seek out the living centers of these founding principles in their pure form. These centers turn out to be the historical Church and Romanism, that is, the root force which made the Roman Church into a community of heretics and, in its further development, gave rise to Protestantism.[50]

48. Florensky, "Okolo Khomiakova," 157.

49. Florensky, "Around Khomiakov," 319.

50. Florensky, "Okolo Khomiakova," 146.

Then Florensky performs a careful tracing of Khomiakov's thoughts, trying for an all-around analysis of his *whirling vortices*. It remains to be understood for whom or for what Khomiakov created his system of cultur-ological elements, which does not explain evolution; its logic of development is too conditional and it exerted no influence on subsequent scholarship. Evidence of the purity of Orthodoxy despite the apostasy of Catholicism is another matter.

Khomiakov's ability to keep his head above all the "axioms" served him well. As a great debater, he loved to argue and knew how to do so, practically all evening at some affair or other, as Herzen noted,[51] and Alexei I. Koshelev specifies in his famous "Notes" that this was "by the Socratic method,"[52] meaning that he knew how to occupy the other's point of view, which is also called "pretending," due to which people who did not know him well even presumed that he easily changed his own views to make people think he respected other people's opinions, although he was more likely fishing what he needed out of other people's opinions, as well as argu-ing for the sake of the argument.

But that was a view from the outside, from the salon; Florensky, as a theologian and priest, could not reconcile himself to such a subjective in-terpretation of the Eucharist.[53] And Florensky only accepted with major reservations the outwardly beautiful, full of seemingly deep thoughts, and nearly fantastical concepts which Khomiakov introduced and insisted upon, in heralding not so much the "visible and invisible Church" as its image. Kho-miakov's understanding of the unity of the whole Christian Church in the lap of Orthodoxy devolved into the temptation to conquer the whole world. This phantom exposes the "dialectics" and "metaphysics" of Khomiakov's

51. "Only Khomiakov argues for the sake of arguing; for him, vital questions are only a subject for conversation," wrote Herzen in a letter to Samarin (dated November 27, 1845). Herzen had a scathing attitude toward the "early" Slavophiles. He assessed them as "a mad movement becoming a hindrance in the course of formation. It takes the form of a gloomy, absurd fanaticism," records Teslya, quoting an entry in his di-ary from November 18, 1842. In general, Herzen's attitude toward Khomiakov did not change. "This mundane forty-year-old man, Khomiakov, who has been laughed at his whole life long and who has caught the awkward ghost of the Russian-Byzantine church, always making them universal, always repeating the same thing" (entry from September 1844). See Teslya, "Gertsen i slavyanofily," 66, 63, 68.

52. Koshelev, *Zapiski*, 99–116.

53. "Khomiakov fundamental idea, which he shared with all Slavophiles, was that the source of all theologizing and all philosophizing should be the integral life of the spirit, organic life, and that everything must be subordinated to the religious life, only in the life of the Church." And specifically, the emotional emphasis falls on the word *vera*, faith, in the sacrament, and not on the sacrament itself as a subject of faith. See Florensky, "Around Khomiakov," 333.

"supracustomary,"[54] a concentration not on debate (despite all his inclination toward it), but rather on the non-acceptance of belief-based positions where there was talk of the exclusive role of the Russian people not just in the context of Slavic Orthodoxy, but in religion worldwide: "This Church, if may be permitted to use the words of the apostle, is temptation in the of the judaistic Romans and holy folly for the hellenizing Protestants, but for us it is the revelation of God's infinite wisdom and grace in the world."[55]

This is how Khomiakov concludes his central work, the tract "*Tserkov' odna*," asserting the self-sufficiency of the Church outside of its "historical reality."[56]

Having set a course for Slavdom, which he imagined at the scale of all humankind (and here Khomiakov had his most conscientious "student"— Herzen—with all his categorical rejection of Khomiakov as an individual and scholar), Khomiakov on the one hand foretold the potential of such a strategy and the arising in the far future of such a unity, the "social camp" resting on Slavdom, but on the other hand,

> an unresolved dissonance was introduced into Slavophilic doctrine. The common human ideal was tied with the "people's spirit" of one ethnographic group, and the goal of human life was squeezed into a narrow, nation-oriented historical perspective. Slavdom acted in the role of the "highest" people. This, in and of itself, was fallacious,[57]

says Florovsky, not without some regret, trying to cleanse the interpretations of Slavophilic teachings of their expansionist seducements. History, alas, knows how such seducements end.

It is curious to note that *sobornost'* as a religious concept arose not out of a religious, social or philosophical movement, but out of society's demand for some sort of consolidational appeal, a slogan, a manifest, and out of the idea of the separate mind. There was no challenge of time here; instead, Khomiakov was issuing a challenge to his epoch, reanimating it. That challenge came with great delay and with a split away from Europe, in which the same problems—the interaction of the individual and the social, the subjective and the objective, the general as individualistic, the everyday occurrence of the immanent and the ontological, faith and the Church, the spiritual recognition of the divine gift and the overall concept of interaction

---

54. Florovsky, *Ways of Russian Theology*, 41.

55. Khomiakov, "On the Church," 91.

56. Florovsky, *Ways of Russian Theology*, 41.

57. Florovsky, "Vechnoe i prekhodyashchee," 44.

with God—had received completely different interpretations and meanings, and had been made to fit the demands of specific societal changes, and not at all as a consequence of a spiritual reincarnation.

However, while *sobornost'* as a vector of Russian Orthodoxy did not bear up, in practice, within the borders of Russian lands, it did prove to be competent abroad, within the Russian diaspora. It is enough to simply name the cities where Russian emigrants gathered, starting with the first wave, reviving, simplifying, and developing Russian theological thought around the temples: Berlin, London, Paris, Rome. This was reflected, in particular, in the words of Berdyaev, although one of his first monographs on Khomiakov dates to 1912, and to those of Bulgakov, who strove to connect together the concepts of *sobornost'* and *kafolichnost'*: "*Sobornost'* is only a *consequence* of *kafolichnost'*," he wrote, literally rescuing *sobornost'* by not using it to replace *kafolichnost'*, as Khomiakov does, pushing *kafolichnost'* from the stage, but rather by putting *sobornost'* in line with it, as its result. He goes on to warn, "It is very important to distinguish catholic conciliarity [*sobornost'*] from collectiveness or external society," deftly catching the practical meaning which stems from *sobornost'*, no matter where you put it.[58] Also indicative here are Semen Frank's assessment of *sobornost'*, recently brought into current scholarly use by Teresa Obolevitch, as fully relating to the émigré period, which I mention here to make it obvious how distant Frank's interpretation of *sobornost'* is from Khomiakov's:

> The concept of *sobornost'* and the difference between the Orthodox Church and the Catholic one is not at all that the Catholic Church is managed individually and the Orthodox Church collectively. If that were true, then of course the usual objections of the Catholics would be completely correct when they say that there is no difference in principle between the infallibility of one person and the infallibility of several people gathered together. In fact even the Pope must listen to the opinions of his cardinals in order to make a decision *ex cathedra*. No. *Sobornost'*, as a principle of the Orthodox Church, means that for the Catholics the head of the Church is the pope, Peter's regent, while in Orthodoxy it is Christ himself. And, consequently, there can be no other empirical head. But empirically, the one making the decisions in the Orthodox Church is the collective [*sobornoe*], meaning the unanimous opinion of the church, the opinion of the Church body as a whole. . . . From this it certainly does not follow that the Orthodox Church is a collective

58. Bulgakov, *Unfading Light*, 58.

Church, but it fundamentally and under every circumstance must be managed collectively.[59]

There is more:

> The principle of *sobornost'* simply says nothing about the management process. It is the principle on the strength of which there is no infallible power anywhere in the church, and infallibility belongs only to the voice of the holy Church itself, in its unity, not in any kind of individual or collective organ of the church. Of course, I am not at all denying that out of this principle of *sobornost'*, or church unanimity, it follows that in the general order of things and to the extent practically possible, it is preferable both that the hierarchy communicates amongst itself, and that each individual hierarch does not take too much on his own shoulders; and that everywhere, always, under all circumstances, it would be absolutely necessary and it would stem from the dogmatic principle of *sobornost'* that collective management is required.[60]

Lossky saw in Khomiakov's theological works "the germ of the metaphysical system," subsequently developed further by Russian philosophy.[61] It is worth taking into account that his work on the history of Russian philosophy, also written in emigration, was in fact the only work in which an overview of scholarly ideas is interspersed with a description of the biographies of philosophers and facts from concrete history. His laconic language, nevertheless, allowed him to feel out the most important original points in Russian religious thinking and in his calm, gentle manner provide his elucidation of extremely acute problems:

> In his criticism of the Roman Catholicism and Protestantism, Khomiakov takes for his starting point the principle of *sobornost'*, or *commonalty*, namely, the combination of unity and freedom based upon the love for God and his truth and the mutual love of all who love God. In Catholicism he finds unity without freedom, and in Protestantism freedom without unity.[62]

But even he did not pass by Khomiakov's leading thesis about Russia's priority of place on the world map. In his words, Russia is destined to stand at the center of the action in global civilization. "Russia's ideal vocation is

---

59. Frank, "Rech' professora," 150–51.

60. Frank, "Rech' professora," 149–51.

61. Lossky, *History of Russian Philosophy*, 33.

62. Lossky, *History of Russian Philosophy*, 37.

not to be the richest or most powerful country but to become 'the most Christian of all human societies.'[63] This idea is a favorite quotation from Khomiakov, and it began to destroy itself before the revolution with its massive explosion of atheism; the revolution itself finished the work, which could be interpreted as proof of the utopianism and even the error of Khomiakov's deductions, to which Russians abroad, who felt differently, yielded more easily than those still in their homeland. And yet, it was they who did all the work of justifying and rescuing that mission which, the Slavophiles thought, was foreordained for Russia. It was another matter that the most important such experiment in Russia, the Novgorod *veche*, which had become to a certain extent the precursor of one of the meanings of *sobornost'*, had completely fallen out of sight of everyone who in one form or another took upon themselves the role of caryatid of Russian philosophy.

The immanent history of Russia has not received from the Slavophiles the thought due to it. It was swallowed up by a passéist discourse that was far removed from the traditions of the Novgorod *veche* and from the *veche* itself as primarily an assembly or council, a *Sobor*. A concept seemingly close to Khomiakov, but without a religious inspiration, was realistically manifested only locally, within the borders of Novgorod, and also in fantasy worlds like the city of Kitezh, presented in its pure form as Khomiakov's *obraz* of the Church.

Two essentially different but similar-sounding phenomena exerted a noticeable influence on the advent of *sobornost'* as a concept that melded the nation with a category of faith, and on the very recognition of the fact that Russia had its own mission: messianism and missionarism, which differ only by a single vowel in Russian (there was a reason nineteenth-century Russian philosophers warned against confusing them[64]). Lossky unfolded it in different directions in his own way, dedicating a monograph to the philosophical difference between good and evil.[65] Florovsky lamented over how great the temptation of messianism was,[66] and he was certainly right. As Lossky reminds us,

> In Muscovite Rus', national messianism had already been vibrantly expressed in the early sixteenth century in the ideology of Philotheus of Pskov, which stated that "two Romes have

63. Lossky, *History of Russian Philosophy*, 40.

64. Tutlis, "Obshchechelovecheskiy smysl russkoy idei," 120–32.

65. Losskiy, "Russkiy messianizm i missionizm," 321–31.

66. Florovsky, "Vechnoe i prekhodyashchee," 43.

fallen, the third remains, and the fourth is never to be." The third
Rome is Moscow.[67]

By the period when the Slavophiles were writing their "Orthodox symphony," messianistic ideas had long transformed into a peripatetic topic, and
every people was ready to ascribe to itself a messianistic, prophetic spirit,
though they missed the most important component: the national forfeiture
of governmental independence. That was the soil in which messianistic pre-
sentiments grew. The very idea of messianism has its roots in the history
of the Jewish people, and a wave of hopes and expectations swept over the
Jews not due to their being "chosen" (although that also played a role), but
rather as a result of their exile from Israel, from their ancestral lands, after
which began the extended period of the Jewish diaspora. This is also the
origin of the Polish messianist experiment (Sarmatism, and the later vibrant
"romantic" promulgators Adam Mickiewicz and Andrzej Towiański), supported on the Jewish one, which was close to them even in geographical
terms: Jews had lived on Polish territory for almost five hundred years, and
their hardships and hopes were a good fit for the Poles during their loss of
governmental independence and the partition of their country.

The problem of Russia's mission had the beginnings of its development
in Vladimir Soloviev, and many of his ideas were harshly rejected by the
Slavophiles, although in the end, decades later, his theory "the true unity of
nations does not mean a single nationality, but an all-embracing nationality,
that is, interaction and solidarity of all nations for the sake of each having
an independent and full life of its own," the true unity of the peoples is
not uniformity, but universality (*ne odnorodnost', a vsenarodnost'*) came to
dominate as the cornerstone of the problem, according to Lossky.[68]

The unity of the Russians in Russia, alas, found complete fruition in
how, with a revolutionary passion reflecting, in all likelihood, the "Cushite
element," they together razed churches and destroyed cemeteries, burned
icons and books, and annihilated other relics of religion along with its instruments, which were later found in trash heaps, basements, and the most
unexpected places. No other country has ever had the distinction of such a
massive destruction of its holy things.

In the final analysis, Khomiakov, one of the instigators of the awaken-
ing of religious life in Russia and a champion of the renewal of the church,
put into law the most troublesome shortcomings characteristic of Orthodoxy
even today: the isolationism against which Vladimir Soloviev argued, and
against which Chaadaev had earlier led his battalions. With all its similarity

67. Losskiy, "Russkiy messianizm i missionizm," 321.

68. See Solovyof, *Justification*, 426; Losskiy, "Russkii messianizm i missionizm," 323.

to Protestantism (about which many theologians write with barely concealed hatred), Khomiakov's Church seems to manifest itself as a gathering bulwark, but with its own disciplinary measures, and even splits the Christian community as a whole. And the spiritual unity of the Russian people and the Church turn out to be simultaneously in different, sometimes mutually exclusive, registers: hordes, fabulousness, missionary service, messianic calling, a special religious path, rejecting, in the end, other confessions. But again, just as with the word *sobornost'*, the salvation of Russian philosophical thinking in Russia comes from the West, from the scholars who were mercilessly banished from Russia on a ship of wise men. They preserved and multiplied its culture and traditions, and prevented its value from being denigrated: the Russian Orthodox Church abroad and the Catholics.

Is this not a victory of *vselenskost'* over *sobornost'*?

I would like to thank Dina Gusejnova (Sheffield), Ruslan Loshakov (Uppsala) and Innokenty Pavlov (Vyborg) for their consultations and support.

Bibliography

Berdyaev, Nicolas. *Aleksei Stepanovich Khomiakov.* Translated by Fr. Stephen Janos. Mohrsville, PA: Fr. Stephen J. Janos, 2017.

Bulgakov, Sergius. *Unfading Light. Contemplations and Speculations.* Translated by Thomas Allan Smith. Grand Rapids: Eerdmans, 2012.

D'iachenko, Grigoriy, ed. *Polnyy tserkovno-slavianskiy slovar' v 2 t.* Vol. 2. Moscow: Izdatel'skiy otdel Moskovskogo Patriarkhata, 1993.

Fasmer, Max. *Etimologicheskiy slovar' russkogo yazyka v 4 t.* Vol. 3. Moscow: Progress, 1987.

Florensky, Pavel. "Around Khomiakov." In *On Spiritual Unity: A Slavophile Reader,* edited and translated by Boris Jakim and Robert Bird, 319–25. Hudson: Lindisfarne, 1998.

———. "Okolo Khomiakova." *Simvol* 16 (1986) 140–226.

Florovsky, Georges. "Vechnoe i prekhodyashchee v uchenii russkikh slavianofilov." In *Georgij Florovsky. Iz proshlogo russkoi mysli,* 59–77. Moscow: Agraf, 1998.

———. *Ways of Russian Theology.* Vol. 2. Translated by Robert L. Nichols. Vaduz: Büchervertriebsanstalt, 1987.

Frank, Semen. "Rech' professora S. L. Franka, proiznesennaya na otkrytom zasedanii Russkogo Akademicheskogo Soyuza v Berline, 24 sentyabrya 1926 goda." In *Semen Frank. Shtrikhi k portretu filosofa,* by Tereza Obolevich, 145–54. Moscow: Izdatel'stvo BBI, 2017.

Herzen, Alexander. *My Past and Thoughts.* Translated by Constance Garnett. 4 vols. London: Chatto and Windus, 1968.

Khomiakov, Alexei S. "Letter to the Editor of *l'Union Chrétienne* on the Occasion of a Discourse by Father Gagarin, Jesuit." In *On Spiritual Unity: A Slavophile Reader,* edited by Robert Bird and Boris Jakim, 135–39. Hudson, NY: Lindisfarne, 1998.

———. "Letter to the 'Moskvitjanin' about England." In *Letter about England, in Russia and English Church*, by Alexei Khomiakov, 73–76. London: Rivington, Percival, 1895.

———. "O yuridicheskikh voprosakh." In *Polnoe sobranie sochineniy Alekseya Stepanovicha Khomiakova*, by Alexei S. Khomiakov, 323–37. Vol. 3. Moscow: Universitetskaya tipografiya, 1900.

———. "On the Church." In *A Documentary History of Russian Thought from Enlightenment to Marxism*, edited by William J. Leatherbarrow and Derek C. Offord, 91–92. Ann Arbor: Ardis, 1987.

Khomiakov, Alexei S., and Vyacheslav Koshelev. *Stikhotvoreniya*. Moscow: Progress-Pleiada, 2005.

Khoruzhiy, Sergey. "Alexei Khomiakov i ego delo." *Institute of Synergetic Anthropology.* http://synergia-isa.ru/?page_id=6158.

———. "Alexei Khomiakov: uchenie o sobornosti i Tserkvi." *Bogoslovskie trudy* 37 (2002) 153–79.

———. "Sovremennye problemy pravoslavnogo mirosozertsaniya." http://predanie.ru/horuzhiy-sergey-sergeevich/book/72497-sovremennye-problemy-pravoslavnogo-mirosozercaniya.

Koshelev, Aleksandr. *Zapiski (1812–1883)*. Moscow: Izdatel'stvo MGU, 1991.

Lenin, Vladimir. "The Collapse of the Second International." In *Collected Works*, edited by Julius Katzer, 205–59. Vol. 21. Moscow: Progress, 1964. http://www.marx2mao.com/Lenin/CSI15.html#p207.

Lossky, Nikolai. *History of Russian Philosophy*. New York: International Universities Press, 1951.

———. "Russkiy messianizm i missionizm." In *Usloviya absoliutnogo dobra*, by Nikolai Lossky, 321–31. Moscow: Izdatel'stvo politicheskoy literatury, 1991.

Solovyof, Vladimir. *The Justification of the Good: An Essay in Moral Philosophy*. Translated by Natalie A. Duddington. London: Constable, 1918.

Svirelin, Alexandr. *Tserkovnoslovianskiy slovar'*. Moscow: Izdatel'stvo "Khristianskaya biblioteka," 2011.

Teslya, Andrey. "Gertsen i slavyanofily." *Sotsiologicheskoye obozreniye* 12.1 (2013) 62–85.

Tsvetkov, Igor. "Sobornost' v interpretatsii sovremennykh bogoslovov." http://www.kds.eparhia.ru/www/script/ps18_3_68497800926.html.

Tutlis, Vadim. "Obshchechelovecheskiy smysl russkoy idei." In *Obshchechelovecheskoe i natsional'noe v filosofii. Kantovskie chteniya v KRSU*, edited by Irina I. Ivanova, 120–32. Bishkek: KRSU, 2004,

Walicki, Andrzej. *Rosja, katolicyzm i sprawa polska*. Warsaw: Prószyński, 2003.

Yudin, Aleksei. "Gagarin." In *Katolicheskaia entsiklopediia v 5 tomakh*, edited by Grigoriy Tserokh, et al., 1166–70. Vol. 1. Moscow: Izdatel'stvo frantsiskantsev, 2002.

Zavitnevich, Vladimir Z. *Alexei Stepanovich Khomiakov*. Kiev: Tipografiya I. I. Gorbunova, 1902.

6

Khomiakov's Idea of *Sobornost'* as a Regulatory Ideal of Intercultural Communication

LADA SHIPOVALOVA AND YULIA SHAPOSHNIKOVA

The idea of *Sobornost'*, like many other philosophical concepts, presupposes many different contexts in its interpretation. Of those, three relevant contexts will be discussed here. The first context is of Russian philosophy, which regards the emergence and the development of the ideas of Slavophilism, as opposed to Westernism in its various interpretations, as fundamentals of practice. These include a fidelity to abstract principles as well as pragmatism and particularism. In this context, the idea of *Sobornost'* can be interpreted as one of the key concepts of Slavophilism. As Robert Bird puts it, "The Slavophiles' thought it is all about *sobornost'* and integral knowledge; these concepts stand both at the beginning and at the end of their writings."[1]

The second context is religious, ecclesiastical and even confessional. Within it, Khomiakov contradistinguishes between the words "*sobornyi*" and "catholic" in his famous *Letter on the Occasion of a Discourse by Father Gagarin*. Whereas in the second context the tenets of Church are discussed and the word *Sobornost'* has a very specific meaning, the third context, which we may call the "philosophical," allows for a broader interpretation of this term. *Sobornost'* can be viewed as a construct which determines human interaction, a sort of normativity of intercultural communication. The three contexts do not oppose but rather complement one another. However, the fact that they can be discerned with greater or lesser accuracy creates curious

---

1. Bird, "General Introduction," 8.

collisions within both theoretical investigation and the possible applications of its results. One such collision will be discussed in the paper.

Despite the well-recognized significance of the first two contexts and the relevant literature (religious studies and studies in Russian philosophy), this article will mainly focus on the third context. This may be considered something of a provocation, which indeed it is. In the philosophical literature, critical arguments against such a broad understanding of *Sobornost'* are quite common. For example, Sergey Khoruzhy describes the transformation of this concept in Russian philosophy and condemns those scholars who attribute epistemological or social meaning to it and thus obliterate its primarily religious origin.[2] Alternatively, the objective of this article is to prove not only the possibility, but in fact the necessity of such an expansion of meaning. Moreover, this paper argues that if one only uses the restricted confessional meaning of the concept of *Sobornost'*, he or she will most likely face theoretical problems in terms of interpretation and practical problems in the application of this idea. Grounds for this expansion, as well as the proof of its necessity, will be presented by means of the analysis of Khomiakov's writings.[3]

This paper focuses primarily on the third context also for the reason of its universal, and concrete applicability of the idea *Sobornost'*, which allows it to fully manifest its essence and potential. Why does applicability matter? In fact, this term plays an important role in the context of hermeneutics as a sort of methodology of the social sciences and humanities. Hans-Georg Gadamer, one of the key figures in modern hermeneutics, emphasizes the fact that a theory in humanities is not complete until it receives an application in any particular activity. Religious exegesis accomplishes in preaching and sharing the understanding of the Holy Scripture with parishioners; understanding the law unfolds itself when applied to judicial practice; philosophical hermeneutics provides rules and patterns for various interactions with the Other.[4] If we consider the idea of *Sobornost'* in a philosophical (and, therefore, humanitarian) context, the description of a possible application (if not *the* application) must precede or at least accompany its investigation.

In the first part of the article, two possible aspects of the current applicability of the idea of *Sobornost'* will be discussed. In the second part, the basis for the interpretation of this idea in the broadest sense of the word will be offered. Finally, in the third part, dangers of the distortion of this idea

2. Khoruzhiy, *Posle pereryva*, 25–31.

3. On the expansion of meaning realized in Khomiakov's texts and the possibility of discovering the principle of *Sobornost'* in gnoseology, as well as in moral and creative activity see Zenkovsky, *History of Russian Philosophy*, 1:171–205.

4. Gadamer, *Wahrheit und Methode*, 312–17.

caused by the restriction of its meaning will be demonstrated, and ways of interpretating its expanded meaning will be shown.

I

In the modern world, two extremes define the norms of social and inter-cultural communication. On the one hand, there is totalitarianism, which deploys terror against those who do not agree with what it views as the only normative approach to organizing society and culture. It can raise the pos-sibility (and ultimately declares the necessity) of destroying entire nations. The term "terror" is treated here in the sense introduced by Jean-François Lyotard, when he emphasizes the obligatory suspicion towards consensus tools in postmodern conditions.[5] This extreme is obvious for those who retain memories of the Second World War in any way, or who are conscious of certain features of colonialism. It is important to understand that such an extreme is associated with activity on the behalf of unity—no matter what is at stake: the unity of a state, a certain ideology, any value declared as the highest, or a scientific approach.

On the other hand, one may find liberalism, which is expressed in terms of pluralism, individualism, and disunity, of the abstract recogni-tion of the diversity of cultural, ideological, and social ways of being, or of cognitive practices, often manifesting itself in a lack of attention to some particular Other in all the specifics of his or her cultural preferences and beliefs. This state of affairs is described in the area of cultural studies as rela-tivism, the principles of which include the recognition of the difficulty, or even the impossibility, of translation between different cultural meanings. The reason for this untranslatability is the self-sufficiency of homogeneous cultures, each obtaining very diverse and at times incompatible features. Such relativism can lead to the same terror as totalitarianism when the interaction with the Other (now Alien) is unavoidable and the incompat-ibility is irreconcilable. In one extreme example of this interconnection be-tween pluralism and terror Carlo Ginzburg, a noted Italian historian, cites a speech by Adolf Hitler on cultural problems and the incommensurability of national cultures:

> Each clearly formed race has its own handwriting in the book of
> art, as far as it is not, like Jewry, devoid of any creative artistic

5. Lyotard, *Postmodern Condition*, 63–67.

ability. The fact that a people can imitate which is formally alien to it does not prove that art is an international phenomenon.[6]

And concludes:

> If each civilization is a homogeneous phenomenon, both stylistically and racially, Jews and foreigners could not play any intrinsic role in the development of the German nation because by birth they were excluded from it. The implications of these ideas—from Auschwitz to the former Yugoslavia, from racial purity to ethnic cleansing—are well-known.[7]

Isolation, homogeneity of cultures and, consequently, a fundamental lack of unity between them, leads to the fact that one culture claiming to be the best and strongest, begins to speak on behalf of unity, claiming the right to judge on behalf of this unity. In this way, individualism and pluralism lead to totalitarianism.

These two extremes, these two types of rules for social interactions—the regulative of the totality and the regulative of plurality—converge in a general concept: the power of one. In the first case, someone having a position empowered by the whole (world, state, ideology, value, class interest, etc.) does not notice or admit the otherwise-minded, does not take into account the interests of all. In the second case, some retain a particular or "provincial" (Khomiakovian term) mode of thinking. They may also declare themselves as the power holders of the whole and, as a result, destroy those who are different. The situation described in these two cases, when the power of one (person, culture, world) is related to the rejection of another, Khomiakov regards as unique to Protestantism.[8] It seems that rules of social and cultural relations should determine the conditions of the moving away from these extremes to the golden mean of Aristotle. Developing the rules of factual communication provides the first possible application of the idea of *Sobornost'*.[9]

The important role in the establishment of such rules belongs to the study of the interaction of cultural traditions. This course of interaction has two aspects. The first concerns the *influence* of one culture upon another, when the specific characteristics of the first are recognized and accepted by the second. If this aspect comes to the fore, it establishes a hierarchy of the first (active) and the second (passive) cultures. Such an aspect of interaction

6. Ginsburg, "Style as Inclusion," 45.

7. Ginsburg, "Style as Inclusion," 45.

8. Khomiakov, *Quelques mots*.

9. On the conditions of such practices see Shipovalova, "Praktiki poiska soglasiya."

is interpreted either from the position of an active agent, who is convinced of the justification of one's own power, or from the point of view of a passive object of influence, who sinks in the depth of resentment. The second aspect deals with the *reception* which assumes not only the submission to influence or its imitation but the active rethinking of ideas of another culture, an organic combination of these ideas with "the original life of people" (Khomiakov). The study of the reception of Russian thought abroad, as well as the reception of Western thought in Russia, is currently a topical direction of scholarly interest.[10] Furthermore, the results of this study are not confined to the theoretical domain alone but can serve as the basis for practical actions, that is, contribute to the development of norms of intercultural communication. This study can be interpreted as the second possible application of the idea of *Sobornost'*.

Accordingly, two possible applications of Khomiakov's idea of *Sobornost'* were introduced: a methodological basis for theoretical cultural studies, and a way to explain and justify existing norms of interactions between cultural traditions.

II

It is time to pose a particularly relevant question: how does the idea of *Sobornost'* fulfill both the aforementioned tasks—emphasizing constructive reception and not solely influence, as well as providing the possibility for the avoidance of the extremes of totalitarianism and individualism?

In the above-mentioned Letter,[11] Khomiakov emphasizes the difference between two terms: "catholic" and its Russian translation "*sobornyi*" which was suggested by St. Cyril and Methodius in ninth century. He warns against ascribing meanings of "geographical universality" to the latter, as well as numerical or imperious superiority, which historically became characteristic of the former in the West. What does this warning indicate? Although both terms signify the unity of Church, unity can easily be mistaken for oneness and singularity if the criterion of the unification is limited to spatial, ethnographic, quantitative, or any other one-sided characteristic. It is this unambiguousness that makes it too narrow for universal application. Consequently, Khomiakov highlights the meaning of "the unity in plurality" and free consentience as a possible regulatory ideal of social and cultural practices.

---

10. See Obolevitch et al., *Russian Thought*; Nazarova, "Recepciya russkoy religioznoy filosofii."

11. Khomiakov, "Letter to the Editor."

The question of the meaning of *Sobornost'* is not a question of num-
bers, extent, or geographical universality, but "something much loftier."[12]
"*Sobor* implies the idea of assembly, not necessarily gathered in some place
or other, but existing virtually, without a formal gathering."[13] We should
take note of this tricky word "virtually" and explain its meaning in the following way. Khomiakov tells us about the assembly without any compulsion
from the outside, from the leader of any sort—top or bottom, the assembly
of co-thinkers, which is real even if not occurring in a fixed place and time.
This interpretation of the meaning of the word "virtually" approximates
it with the word "potentially," revealing an overtone of "ever-existing possibility for gathering."[14] This meaningful element of the definition suggests
that no factual assembly ever fulfills the idea of *Sobor* as such; the unity of
the Church. The final gathering as one remains only a virtual yet awaited
event in human life.

Khomiakov speaks about the "possible church" in his writing "On the
Old and the New" (*O starom i novom*).[15] In the work *The Church is One*
he divides the Church into two parts—visible and invisible—and asserts
that this division is relevant only to humanity. However, all of us, including
Khomiakov, are human and as humans we define the rules of our cultural
interaction. What can we humans possibly say about the invisible Church
and the unity of Church, which—Khomiakov repeats it over and over
again—has never existed?[16]

> Since the earthly or visible Church is not yet the fullness and per-
> fection of entire Church, which the Lord appointed to be made
> manifest at the Last Judgment of the entire creation, she creates
> and has knowledge only within her bounds without judging the
> rest of humankind (according to the words of Apostle Paul to the
> Corinthians [1 Cor 5:12–13]). For the Church only those who
> have removed himself from her are seen as being excluded—i.e.,
> not belonging to her. The rest of humankind, whether alien to

12. Khomiakov, "Letter to the Editor," 138.

13. Khomiakov, "Letter to the Editor," 139.

14. This expression is taken from the Russian translation of the Letter originally
written in French. It is far beyond the scope of interest of this paper to explicate the
historical and logical interconnections between these words in different languages and
the ancient Greek "*on dynamei*." It is noteworthy that in other works written by Khomiakov in Russian, the same aspect of potentiality is present when he discusses the
unity of the Church.

15. Khomiakov, "O starom i novom," 49.

16. On this division of the entire Church and the impossibility of understanding this
Church rationally, see Khomiakov, "Remarks on the Occasion of a Brochure," 58–59.

the Church or tied to her with bonds that God has not desired to reveal to her, she leaves for the judgment of the great day. The earthly Church judges only herself by the grace of the Spirit and by the freedom granted to her through Christ, summoning the rest of humankind to unity and to adoption by God in Christ, but she does not pronounce sentence over those who does not heed her call, knowing the command of her Savior and Head "not to judge another's servant" (Rom 14:4).[17]

This passage also has a potential modality. Thanks to Khomiakov's explanation, the unity of the Church symbolizes openness; an invitation for those who have not yet agreed to the unity. This unity presupposes work and care of oneself. This modality makes *Sobornost'* the essence of unity of the Church, a dynamic idea, characterizing action and movement rather than describing an existing state. It defines unity as a sought-for relation, as a link not specifically confessional but universal and meaningfully uncertain; open to the future (or eternity) in its uncertainty. This broadening of the pure confessional context can be endorsed by a statement of Pavel Florensky that at times Khomiakov makes judgments about the Church which should seem quite suspicious to an Orthodox Christian. He further writes:

Khomiakov is made indignant not by the falsity of decrees of Western councils but by the fact that they represent violations of *unity.* And the fault of the Catholics appears to consist not in the fact that they profess false dogma, but in the fact that they are not *together* with the East. Here, the significance of agreement and disagreement is exaggerated, and the dignity and the value of the Truth are diminished.[18]

By contrast, an unambiguously defined actual unity leads to a dictate of one in relations with other cultures and emphasizes the discourse of the influence of cultures and their hierarchy in cultural studies. From the standpoint of such an interrelation, one culture represents originality and "colonialism of knowledge," and the second—only imitation and "servile reverence." Khomiakov writes about it in the works "Foreigners' Opinions of Russia" (*Mnenie russkih ob inostrancah*)[19] and "The Opinion of the Russian about Foreigners" (*Mnenie inostrancev o Rossii*)[20] stressing the importance of identity and development of "one's own creative principles" as opposed to the power of one.

17. Khomiakov, "Church is One," 31–32.
18. Florensky, "From 'Around Khomiakov,'" 324–25.
19. Khomiakov, " Mnenie russkih ob inostrancah."
20. Khomiakov, "Mnenie inostrantsev o Rossii."

Thus, the possibility of expanding (and not distorting) the meaning of the idea of *Sobornost'* beyond the limits of the visible or any historical church is due to the fact that, in its interpretation, Khomiakov intentionally includes characteristics of potentiality and makes the definition of unity (gathering) uncertain. Thanks to his definition, one can comprehend the expression "unity in plurality" as a possible assembly of all as it is expected in eternity, to view human life as an opportunity to fulfill this idea, to make it a norm of cultural interconnection, and use it as a methodological tool for the study of cultural interaction.

III

However, it is necessary to raise some disturbing doubts related to the above-mentioned applications of the idea of *Sobornost'*, and also to point out a possibility of its distortion and the reasons for it. Reading some of Khomiakov's works, and the above-mentioned "Opinions" in particular, one may get an impression that the struggle against "imitation" for "originality," as well as against "servile reverence" for the development of "one's own creative principles" has as its result not an acceptance but rather the rejection of one by another. Sometimes in his criticism Khomiakov seems to forget that "the earthly Church judges only herself" and "does not pronounce sentence over those who does not heed her call"; for instance, he condemns and thus rejects Protestantism. As a result, the defense of one's own right to identity is surrogated by the non-recognition of the rights to identity of Others. In fact, Khomiakov speaks on behalf of the actual idea of Orthodoxy and not in defense of the unity of Church. We could say that the concept of the unity of the Church and *Sobornost'* in Khomiakov's writings sometimes look similar to an instrument of ideology.

We can find one of the reasons for such a transformation in the Introduction to *On Spiritual Unity*. And this relates to the above-mentioned division of the Church. Robert Bird writes:

> Khomiakov's Concept of Church involves a complex dialectic between her transcendent and immanent aspects. Transcendently the Church is one untouched by human conflict and discord; the historical Church, however, does not fully manifest this transcendent unity. ... Khomiakov affirms that the community of believers as long as it remains truly *sobornyi*, is essentially identical to the transcendent Church. ... Stressing the

immanent aspect of Church can lend Khomiakov's expressions the appearance of national and cultural exclusivity.[21]

These doubts are confirmed by reading the work by Khoruzhy on Khomiakov's idea of *Sobornost'*. He not only describes the features of this idea (freedom, organicity, accordance, grace and love)[22] but also gives us examples of the transformation of the concept.[23] Khoruzhy cites Khomiakov's expressions: "The Christianity of the West has committed suicide because it stopped being Christianity"[24]; "In Romanism ... [there is] not a word, not act that bears the stamp of spiritual life which is the life of the Church"[25]; "Two protestantisms, Germanic and Roman ... bear death within their bosoms. Unbelief has only to remove the corpses and sweep the arena."[26] It is noteworthy that, in different works by Khomiakov, one can find expressions of impartiality and disinterestedness. He writes:

> An external unity which rejects freedom and therefore is not a real unity—that is Romanism. An external freedom which does not bestow unity and therefore is not a real freedom—that is Protestantism.[27]

And again: "The West has rejected the fundamental doctrine of mutual love that alone constitutes the life of the Church"[28]; "I will say that in the Western confessions there is at the bottom of every soul a profound hostility against the Eastern Church."[29]

> Why has the West lost this divine tradition? The answer is quite clear. Germanic Protestantism could nor reconstruct this tradition because it could never and can never build anything, because it could only reject and destroy, because it consists entirely of critique in thought and isolation in spiritual life.[30]

And:

---

21. Bird, "General Introduction," 15–16.

22. Khoruzhiy, *Posle pereryva*, 20–22.

23. Khoruzhiy, *Posle pereryva*, 24.

24. Khomiakov, "Remarks on the Occasion of the Letter," 102.

25. Khomiakov, "Remarks on the Occasion of the Letter," 111.

26. Khomiakov, "Remarks on the Occasion of the Letter," 113.

27. Khomiakov, "Some More Remarks," 127.

28. Khomiakov, "Some More Remarks," 134.

29. Khomiakov, "Remarks on the Occasion of the Letter," 67.

30. Khomiakov, "Remarks on the Occasion of the Letter," 86.

Human beings were isolated within the narrow bounds of individuality; they turned out to be separated from their sisters
and brothers. Furthermore they turned out to be separated from
God himself.[31]

These and many other cases make one think that Khomiakov has forgotten
his own words about the possible Church, about universal assembly, and has
pronounced judgment on Protestants, placing plurality outside unity.

However, we are not going to condemn Khomiakov or to share the
spirit and the letter of his statements. We will try to understand the reasons
for such a transformation. The text of Khoruzhy could help us in this en-
terprise. He writes: "The heterodoxy for Khomiakov is an external subject,
and in judgments about it, his thought obviously loses the character of the
'witness's testimony,' which is its main value."[32] We try to link this attitude
to heterodoxy as to external subject with particularism, which Khomiakov
demonstrates in relation to the Western confessions. But how does this attitude echo in Khomiakov's texts? The answer to this question reveals another
important feature of the idea of *Sobornost'*.

Khomiakov associates particularism with rationalism.[33] He does not
contrast rationalism with irrationality of faith, life and love, but with rationality which presupposes a synthetic unity of knowledge and tradition, of
law and life, of reason and faith. Rationalism abstracts reason, knowledge
and law from life, tradition and faith. That is, Khomiakov speaking from the
standpoint of rationality against rationalism admits the necessary mediation
of "living reality" (material or intellectual) by law and knowledge.[34] Notably,
he discusses the law in his work "On the Old and the New" as a way of overcoming an unjust tradition.[35] The law and judgments of reason should be
derived from the understanding of leaving the reality of the people, which
is provided by one's own participation and "witness's testimony" already
mentioned. In respect to the Russian reality, Khomiakov is an eyewitness
and testifies to both the positive and negative in the custom. His rationality
in this case presupposes a switching of focus from life to norms, and shows
the contradiction between life itself and the conditioning of the norm by
this inconsistency.

31. Khomiakov, "Remarks on the Occasion of the Letter," 86.

32. Khoruzhiy, *Posle pereryva*, 24.

33. See, for example, Khomiakov's Second Letter to Mr. Palmer.

34. See about this features of rationality Khomiakov, "O starom i novom"; "Some
More Remarks," 128–29.

35. Khomiakov, "O starom i novom," 46–47.

When Khomiakov makes judgments about Western confessions from outside the living reality of western people he is unaware of it. Florensky contends that Khomiakov "wishes to expel the law and compulsion, the element of the Roman nations and replace them by social relation and kinship, the element of the Slavonic nations."[36] We see that in the case of making judgments about westerners, Khomiakov does not follow the route of rationality but proceeds from the law (dogmas opposing the dogmas of Orthodoxy) to his external vision of Western life and sometimes in his accusations falls into rationalism. It is a lack of a broad philosophical context to his thought that makes him emphasize how much dogmas differ and proves to be an obstacle for him to think himself in place of the Other. His rationality turns into rationalism and the idea of *Sobornost'* becomes an instrument of ideology.

Conclusions

We believe that Khomiakov's writings not only clarify the meaning and highlight the importance of the idea of *Sobornost'* but also demonstrate the dangers of its distortion. They teach us to distinguish between the power of one and the interests of many gathering together as the prerequisites of unity. The idea of *Sobornost'* acts as a regulative basis for cultural interaction if two conditions are met. First, thinking about unity from the position of the already existing state of affairs should be supplemented by the potential modality. Second, rationalism of judgment should be replaced by rationality, grounded in the living reality with all of its contradictions but not in dogmatic principles. As a result, the use of the idea of *Sobornost'* in its confessional sense alone and the exhaustive efforts to find an adequate definition of this concept will leave open the opportunity of its use in a broader context: as a living dialogue based on the possibility of gathering together different cultures and people of different beliefs and confessions.

Bibliography

Bird, Robert. "General Introduction." In *On Spiritual Unity: A Slavophile Reader*, edited and translated by Boris Jakim and Robert Bird, 7–28. New York: Lindisfarne, 1998.

Florensky, Pavel. "From 'Around Khomiakov.'" In *On Spiritual Unity: A Slavophile Reader*, edited and translated by Boris Jakim and Robert Bird, 319–25. New York: Lindisfarne, 1998.

36. Florensky, "From 'Around Khomiakov,'" 325.

Gadamer, Hans-Georg. *Wahrheit und Methode*. Vol. 1. of *Hans-Georg Gadamer: Gezammelte Werke*. Tübingen: Mohr Siebeck, 1990.

Ginsburg, Carlo. "Style as Inclusion, Style as Exclusion." In *Picturing Science, Producing Art*, edited by Caroline A. Jones and Peter Galison, 27–54. New York, London: Routledge, 1998.

Khomiakov, Alexei S. "The Church is One." In *On Spiritual Unity: A Slavophile Reader*, edited and translated by Boris Jakim and Robert Bird, 31–54. New York: Lindisfarne, 1998.

————. "Letter to the Editor of *l'Union Chrétienne* on the Occasion of a Discourse by Father Gagarin, Jesuit." In *On Spiritual Unity: A Slavophile Reader*, edited and translated by Boris Jakim and Robert Bird, 135–39. New York: Lindisfarne, 1998.

————. "Mnenie inostrancev o Rossii." In Alexei Khomiakov. *O starom i novom. Stat'i i ocherki*, edited by Georgiy M. Fridlender, 82–102. Moscow: Sovremennik, 1988.

————. "Mnenie russkih ob inostrancah." In Alexei Khomiakov. *O starom i novom. Stat'i i ocherki*, edited by Georgiy M. Fridlender, 103–34. Moscow: Sovremennik, 1988.

————. "O starom i novom." In Alexei Khomiakov. *O starom i novom. Stat'i i ocherki*, edited by Georgiy M. Fridlender, 82–102. Moscow: Sovremennik, 1988.

————. *Quelques mots par un chretien orthodoxe sur les communions occidentales à l'occasion d'une brochure de M. Laurentie*. Leipzig: F. A. Brockhaus, 1855.

————. "Second Letter to Mr. Palmer." In *Russia and the English Church during the Last Fifty Years*, edited by William Birkbeck, 27–40. London: Rivington, Percival, 1895.

————. "Some More Remarks by the Orthodox Christian Concerning the Western Communions, on the Occasion of Several Latin and Protestant Publication (excerpts)." In *On Spiritual Unity: A Slavophile Reader*, edited and translated by Boris Jakim and Robert Bird, 117–34. New York: Lindisfarne, 1998.

————. "Some Remarks by an Orthodox Christian Concerning the Western Communions, on the Occasion of a Brochure by Mr. Laurentie (Excerpts)." In *On Spiritual Unity: A Slavophile Reader*, edited and translated by Boris Jakim and Robert Bird, 57–62. New York: Lindisfarne, 1998.

————. "Some Remarks by an Orthodox Christian Concerning the Western Communions, on the Occasion of the Letter Published by the Archbishop of Paris." In *On Spiritual Unity of Slavophile Reader*, edited and translated by Boris Jakim and Robert Bird, 63–116. New York: Lindisfarne, 1998.

Khoruzhiy, Sergey. *Posle pereryva. Puti russkoy filosofii*. St. Petersburg: Aleteyya, 1994.

Lyotard, Jean-François. *The Postmodern Condition: A Report of Knowledge*. Translated by Geoff Bennington and Brian Massumi. Manchester: Manchester University Press, 1984.

Nazarova, Oxana. "Recepciya russkoy religioznoy filosofii v sovremennoy zapadnoevropeyskoy khristianskoy filosofii." *Solov'evskie issledovaniya* 4.48 (2015) 148–57.

Obolevitch, Teresa, et al. *Russian Thought in Europe. Reception, Polemics, Development*. Krakow: Akademia Ignatianum, 2013.

Shipovalova, Lada. "Praktiki poiska soglasiya: mezhdu terrorom i rasprey." *Politika i obshchestvo* 11 (2015) 1495–503.

Zenkovsky, Vasiliy. *A History of Russian Philosophy*. Vols. 1–2. Translated by George L. Kline. New York: Routledge, 2014.

PART II

Contexts

7

Alexei Khomiakov and Blaise Pascal

BORIS TARASOV

I

Pascal found himself in the middle of the downfall of the medieval image of reality, when faith in God was replaced by faith in man, when theocentrism gave way to an anthropocentrism which declared man to be the measure of the whole reality which is fully submittable to man's actions, when religious dogmas were replaced by truths based on experimental data and rational analysis—those which our philosopher had applied so brilliantly to the realms of Mathematics and Physics. During the Renaissance, such a substitution gradually spread throughout every aspect of human activity but did not include its psycho-emotional and spiritual-moral limits. The endlessly rich, diverse, ever-changing and pulsating nature of these processes, which paradoxically combine in themselves, the "royal" (to use Gavrila Derzhavin's words)—that is absolute truth, goodness, beauty, justice, freedom, love, mercy, conscience, honor, nobility, self-sacrifice, etc., and the "slavish" (pride, vanity, envy, greed, love for power, money and fame, anger, vengefulness, etc.) aspects of self resist being restricted to a quantitative-experimental scientific approach. A good deal of man's motivation, his notions of emotion and will, his liberal and engaged relation to life, are a living denial of reductive rationalism, of the unifying patterns produced by it; which led Pascal to review his own scientific activity and the seemingly boundless might of "pure" and "autonomic" mind.

> I have spent much time in the study of abstract sciences, but the little intercourse to be had concerning them has disgusted me with them. When I began the study of man, I saw that these

105

abstract sciences are not proper to him, and that I should be going further out of my sphere in penetrating them than others in
ignoring them, and I pardoned others their little knowledge of
them. But I at least thought to find some companions in the study
of man, because this is the study which is truly proper to him. I
was deceived: those who study man are even fewer than those
who study geometry. It is only for lack of knowing how to study
him, that people seek other things; but is it not also because this is
not the knowledge that man ought to have, and because it is better
for him to be ignorant of himself, in order to be happy?[1]

A close examination of the world of man showed Pascal that the grandness of the emancipated man separated from the misery of insignificance,
as declared by the revivalists, is a kind of an exaggeration, a dangerous tilt
which may lead to his mad self-deification, the oblivion of the core contradictions of his nature and of the fundamental paradoxes of his existence.

The Renaissance conception of reality implies that man, liberated
from the divine grace, can find the rational explanations of all the facts
of his existence in the inexhaustible abundance of Nature herself which
is taken to be uniform, healthy and without any need for transformation;
that man can define, by his own syllogisms, his mission and then accomplish it; that he can provide the complete and balanced development of his
abilities and powers and in the end of all conquer and defeat, Prometheus-
like, this very Nature.

Pascal found it necessary to discuss such programs of mind and to
demonstrate the limitations of these ideals of "living by nature," "God-less-
ly," relying on one's self-constituted will and the autonomic mind by using
the anthropological method discovered during the Renaissance, the specific
observations upon the complex content of the actual inner life of people and
the fathomless contradictions in any given area of the mundane reality. Pascal provides a critical analysis of the ontological and cosmological abilities of
mind limited in its understanding of the beginning and end of all things, of
the relation between the whole and the parts, of the mysterious twinning of
the spiritual and the bodily principles in man, his existence between "the two
infinities" as he momentarily materializes from nothingness before slipping
unto eternity. The true sagacity should be concentrated on the realization of
man's destiny and on the consequences of that: "Imagine a number of men in
chains, and all condemned to death, of whom every day some are butchered
in sight of the others, those remaining seeing their own fate in that of their

---

1. Pascal, *Pensées*, 120–21.

fellows, regarding each other with grief and despair while awaiting their turn; this is a picture of the condition of man."[2]

According to Pascal, the deep awareness of the fleeting nature of man's life must change the will and actions of the person in correlation with their hopes regarding eternity. Exploring the anthropocentric idea and phenomenon of turning eternity into nothing and making nothing eternal, he unfolds before us the struggle between reason and feelings, imagination and other "deceiving powers" which govern and penetrate the mind—power, career, fame, honors, wealth, pleasures—anything but the meaning of life before the face of death. In Pascal's interpretation, imagination is seen as social-evaluating and irrational-persuasive force connected with feelings, subverting and controlling most people's minds, creating various, far from being strictly logical, views on hierarchy, values, authorities, reputations, appearances, fame, achievements, beauty, justice, goodness, etc.

Self-esteem, pride, vanity, ambition, lust, greed and other "slavish" aspects of human nature are the "deceiving powers" which interfere, in a way, with the "autonomic" decisions of the mind, leading it away from the "royal" realization of truth, the supreme good, true justice; induce *nothing* and *eternity* to change their places. All of that creates the ever-doubling images of the world where good and evil fuse through the various entanglements of actions and events into a solid unbreakable knot, and man, flying up to the great spiritual heights, just as regularly ends up in the mud. And the more mysterious the truth, justice and good are for the anthropocentric "king" in earthly history, the more fiercely he presses toward the new searches and understanding of these, finding—not without the assistance of the "slavish" deceiving forces—nothing but poverty and death.

> What chimera, then, is man? What an oddity, what a monster, what a chaos, what a subject of contradiction, what a prodigy! Judge of everything, senseless earthworm; depositary of truth, cloaca of uncertainty and error; the glory and the refuse of the universe. Who shall unravel this tangle? . . . Know then, proud creature, what a paradox you are to yourself. Humble yourself, impotent reason. Be silent, imbecile nature. Know that man infinitely surpasses man, and learn from your master your true state, of which you are ignorant: hear God.[3]

Left to himself, man cannot find his way out from the deep contradictions of a split, shattered world. Yet the bottomless soul and principal irremovability of these contradictions by neither social changes nor

2. Pascal, *Pensées*, 135.

3. Pascal, *Pensées*, 99.

philosophical doctrines indicate, in Pascal's thought, the mystery which lies behind them and holds the explanation. Thus the very limitations of anthropology, of the "God-less" life, take him to theology, to the "God-full" life. The initial image of God was deformed by pride and original sin, leaving its mark on all of man's "royal" manifestations. "Self-interest became the foundation and the material of the most splendid rules of social life, morality, justice; but it remained the foul core of man, the application didn't prevent it from being the foul foundation of human nature, the same *figmentum malum*—the clot of evil; it's covered up but not destroyed." This "slavish" clot of evil which delivers its poisonous juices to every layer of *isness* is not covered but destroyed when—and only when—in the cleansing heart of man there springs faith in Jesus Christ who embraced, in his sacrificial Love, man's sins and created by his death on the cross the springs, the sources of forgiveness and grace. This source interacts with the supersensory grace in people's souls and the sinful nature, with "black" and " . . ."—as Pascal explains the paradoxical . . . *ism*, the glory and the misery of man's existence. The human heart as the center of one's inner life, the root of the man's active abilities, the source of good and evil will, loves *figmentum malum* which it bears inside and hardens against God no more and no less than it loves God and hates its *figmentum malum*. "You have rejected the one and held to the other: is it by reason that you love yourself?"[4]

Yet it is exactly from such deep feelings-intuitions, as from invisible underground seeds, that the understanding of life and its activities springs forth on the social surface.

Having no faith in God, which is the source of the highest enlightened awareness, Pascal concludes that it is impossible to reach true goodness. Only in the pure heart will the true and perfect Love awake—this absolute foundation of our *isness* which in the personal experience acquires the highest reliability as compared with the arguments of reason; the mighty force, the force beyond the control of any human power, the super-natural force which affects the transmutation of the inherited Adamic nature and joins the kaleidoscopic dots of life together. So the infinite abyss between the body and the spirit, both under the influence of *figmentum malum*, serves but a pale reflection of a much greater abyss between Spirit and Love—and only the latter alone can overcome this influence and bring the "New Adam" forth to the transformed reality.

Kings, rich men, generals don't see the grandeur of the men of wit— who, in their turn, don't notice the external appearance of these "great men of the whip"; for some people can only marvel at the earthly splendor, as if

4. Pascal, *Pensées*, 13.

there had never been anything spiritual under the sun; and others marvel at the spiritual grandness alone, as if there isn't the infinitely greater presence of Wisdom.

All bodies, the sky, the stars, the earth with all her kingdoms, all are worth less than the weakest mind, for it knows them all and itself, and the bodies know nothing.

> From all bodies together we cannot succeed in getting one single little thought: it is impossible, thought belongs to another order. From all bodies and all minds together, we cannot draw one movement of true love: it is impossible, for love is of another order, and above nature.[5]

II

Pascal's logic as presented here is in harmony with the very framework of Russian religious thought, creating a deep connection between the philosophers on the level of the spiritual *pneuma*.

Achieving God's Revelation which was given to Christ's disciples, developing one's personality and knowledge in all wholeness is naturally linked with the belief in the common action of mind, will and heart—the fundamental alternative for the man who either relies on his dark and passionate nature spoiled by the original sin, on the limited mind and the "deceiving powers" and, as a result, "progressively" degrades amidst the illusions of his flat empirical experience and his stumbling rationalism; or speeds forth in his free and focused spiritual doings—in order to transmute this nature, to reach God's grace and to unite with the Church as with the body of Christ; the question of the flow of history as it either "descends" or "rises" depending on this alternative—such questions can be found at the root of the works of the most profound Russian philosophers and writers, making them Pascal's kinsmen.

Georges V. Florovsky points out in his article "The Metaphysical Premises of Utopianism" that the Renaissance-Antiquity school of thought could not possibly leave the boundaries of this world and overcome the naturalistic concept of God being an immanent cosmic force and Providence, a law-like consistency of the Universe. He believes that such a manner of thinking suffers not so much from monism as, on the contrary, from the unifying objectivism which he sees as the lunatic obscuring and distorting the goals of creative activity.

5. Pascal, *Pensées*, 28.

The fact that man is "possessed" by the world obliges him to seek out and concretize the image of unconditional perfection that is inherent to his soul. This is the enigma of the paradoxical combination of the slave consciousness and arrogant self-assurance. Precisely because man is conscious of his own metaphysical insignificance, he feels that he is but a "dream of nature," "the medium of the external objectivity," he is incline to ascribe objective significance to his own dreams. Hence the Luciferian confidence in the complete cognizability of the mysteries of the world and in the realizability of the "striving" vainly exerted by nature.[6]

According to Florovsky, any monism emanates nihilism—for "*isness* is dualistic." And the main obstacles on the way from the potential nihilism and onto the true understanding of duality are the habitual cosmological settings of the naturalistic mind which is powerless to "embrace God's Revelation which transcends the mortal mind." The exit from this essentially natural dead-end or, as Khomiakov would have said, "the egotistic coffin" lies solely through the "*transformation of experience*" when one begins to see, by the virtue of the renewed religious consciousness, the "metaphysical schismatism of existence," "a harrowing abyss. And only in the experience of faith, the experience of freedom, is the noble path of true speculation revealed."[7]

On this path

the heavens descend to earth in answer to the celestial flight of the human soul. And the withdrawal of "nature" into itself, into its own "this-wordliness," is the root of the downfall and error. He who does not rise in cognition, does not remain immobile—he falls.[8]

So within the boundaries of the anthropocentric, naturalistic self-seclusion, immanence and despair we find the pre-programmed "wasteful," "descending," "falling," "shattering," and "deluded" development of the world and man, as well as the insensibility of the "natural" awareness to both the "abysses" and "chasms" of sinful human nature and the impossibility of overcoming these without "leaping" into the transcendental and acquiring God's grace in order to remove the fundamental damage done to human will. The man creature is imperfect, as Lev Karsavin brings to our attention, as during the Renaissance it prefers and obtains imperfection, when "the created unity hides the divine unity from the view, sometimes even seeming

6. Florovsky, "Metaphysical Premises," 91–92.

7. Florovsky, "Metaphysical Premises," 93.

8. Florovsky, "Metaphysical Premises," 78.

to part from it"—which inevitably leads to degradation and decay. Vladimir Soloviev, too, comes to the following "Pascalian" conclusion:

> As long as the dark core of our nature, evil in its exclusive ego-tism and mad in its desire to exercise this egotism, to connect all that is with itself and to measure all that is by itself—as long as this dark core is evidently present in us—not changed—and this original sin stays undefeated—we cannot perform any mean-ingful deed, and the question, *What to do?*, has no real meaning. Imagine a crowd of people who are blind, deaf, deformed, pos-sessed, and suddenly there's a voice coming from that crowd: "What do we do?"
>
> The only sensible answer is: seek healing; unless you are healed there is no business for you, and unless you stop pretend-ing being whole there is no remedy for you. . . . The true deed is possible only when both man and Nature hold the powers of light and goodness, free and positive; but neither man nor Nature can obtain such powers without God.[9]

Russian religious philosophy and literature preserve the anti-Renais-sance "Pascalian" understanding that man's blissful liberation from the hold of bad infinity is impossible without the radical "transmutation of self" in Spirit and Truth, that the empirical realm does not exceed the *allness* of *isness*, that the world can't be perfected by itself but requires supernatural support.

This fundamental alternative between the nihilism of naturalistic mo-nism and self-sufficient anthropocentrism (on one hand) and the blissful reliance on the values and relics of the "other world," on the ability of the transformed self to find, by the act of faith, the truth of God's Revelation (on another hand) is an integral part of the "mystery of man" which is rooted far beyond the known world and explains the original split and the dual nature of our existence here—on which Pascal was so keen (man is not an angel or a beast but their coexistence in one being) in his analysis of the substantial consequences of the original sin. Man, by his original nature which relates to God's own image and likeness, was created for love, freedom, truth, good-ness and beauty like a bird was created to fly or a fish was to swim. Yet after the Fall this spiritual nature was distorted, the "righteous source" of living ("But seek ye first the kingdom of God, and his righteousness; and all these things shall be added unto you"—Matt 6:33) was weakened; and in the wake of Adam the "dark core of our nature" sprung to being, together with its "deceiving forces" and, to use Khomiakov's words, "the random

---

9. Solov'ev, "Tri rechi v pamyat' Dostoevskogo," 311, 315.

centers upon leaving which the human soul, having lost the ontological connection with God's will and longing for its original nature, for the lost Absolute, started chasing their imitations in the search of various ghosts of 'happiness' in 'every thing' else"—in Promethean aspirations, in the ever coming-and-going creative projects, earthly ideologies, political interests, scientific and technological progress. As Aleksandr Gradovsky in his article "Two Enemies" wrote:

> One has to ask oneself this question—Khomiakov insists—or else you might discover that the whole history of the Roman Empire, to its last day, was "progressive"; sciences might be perfected while virtues degenerate and countries die. Where is the progress in that? Progress is a word which needs a subject. Unless you have the subject, progress remains an abstraction—or, to be more precise, sheer absurdity.[10]

Russian religious philosophy agrees with St. Paul's idea of the man being a lie, that is, being hardly human or even inhuman in himself. No man is worthy of praise, Vasilii V. Rosanov states, every man needs to be pitied. The paradox of man's existence is that man, to become human, has to surpass himself (as Pascal says, "man infinitely surpasses man"[11]) and to revive, in himself, the image and likeness of God by the virtue of "transformation of experience," "new birth," "act of faith," and example of which is Pascal himself. The word "act," as in "act of faith" which in Russian is related to heroic deeds, is close to Khomiakov's paradigm and can often be seen in the works of the Russian philosophers and writers, indicating the extreme difficulty of the task to find, as Vladimir F. Ern says, such a curvature of perception that upon following it all that appeared to be standing firmly would suddenly stand on its head, idols would fall, ideal images overthrown and "all creative and essential aspects of self would begin to unfold and to establish themselves." In their Pascalian logic, however, that is what man can't do, God can; as his graceful help is attracted to the man's free desire to overcome his sin and to transform his natural state—to the "theocentrical movement of the soul." An ontological predicament, in this case, is Christ's Incarnation, birth, coming, earthly life, death on the cross and revival; as Christ unites in himself and in his Church this life and the "other world." Thus, obtaining grace, enlightening "the dark core of our nature" and having the communion with Christ are specified in the works of the Russian religious philosophers and writers as the chief creative goal in the search for love for God and our neighbors; this love, in their works as well as in

10. Gradovskiy quoted in Chaadaev, *Tsena vekov*, 26.

11. Pascal, *Pensées*, 99.

Pascal's ones, is the main sign that marks the enlightened "new creature" which overcomes the dark heritage of the "Old Adam" in itself. Another obviously expressed or underlying keynote of their works is St. Paul's words—that if I have not love, I am nothing (1 Cor 13:2). Hegel said once that if you have no idea then your eyes can't see the facts. Elaborating upon this concept, we can add that if man's heart has no love then the mind can't notice the innermost essence in the man himself and in what he observer around him. "Without love, you are aware of nothing; and with love you are aware of many things," Dostoevsky concludes.

"There is no truth without love," as Pushkin already expressed. Love as a cognitive category is closely connected, in Russian philosophy and literature as well as in Pascal's works, with Love as the highest spiritual state lacking which the man turns into "clanking copper" or "clanking cymbals"; until this state is present all good intentions and social changes were, are and will be locked in the small circle of "the dark core of our nature" and of "the meaningless fantasies."

III

This deep inner logic of Russian religious philosophy, as it reveals the fundamental consequences of man's (and the world's) development "with God" and "without God," brings Pascal close to Khomiakov who considered the former to have been his teacher. When the founder of Slavophilism refers to the "tomb of egotism" and the limitations of the rational empirical experience; when he is talking about the holistic individuality or about the holistic knowledge; or about the "conciliar gnoseology"; about faith being a fruit of revelation (and not of mere logical reliance) and it embracing spiritual depths; about "the subject of progress" and the necessity of admitting man's own ontological infirmity; about Christianity as the graceful identity of unity and freedom under the law of mutual love; about the toxicity of substituting the Church of Christ with government and authority; about the distorted version of Christianity which preaches lack of faith; and about many other issues; then his reasoning identifies typologically and partly genetically with the speculations of the great French scientist and philosopher upon the poverty and magnificence of man's existence; upon the ranking of the spiritual and psychological forces (mind, heart, will) in man; upon the limitations of scientific cognition of reality; upon the "deceiving forces"; upon the three orders of existence (the order of body, the order of mind, the order of love and mercy); upon the disagreement on the matter principles in the debates between the

Jansenists and the Jesuits, the Augustinian Hermits and the Pelasgians; and upon a number of other important questions.

Khomiakov's religious, philosophical, historical, social and artistic beliefs and preferences were based on his world knowledge in next to all fields of human activity and sciences—which also connects him with Pascal, this time in appearance. As was the case with many other Slavophiles he had an excellent education, knew a number of languages, understood world religions, linguistics and wrote theological studies in French. Khomiakov had a good understanding of economics, worked on projects to liberate the peasants and to improve rural industries, invented a long-range gun and a new steam engine which was patented in Britain, practiced winery, sugar-making and homeopathy, sought with great success mineral deposits in the Tula Governorate, made plans to improve the life of the Aleutians Islanders and worked on intricate artillery ammunition during the Crimean War.

A talented artist—portraitist and icon painter; a famous poet and playwright are some more of his faces. Aleksandr Koshelev, his fellow, wrote this about Khomiakov:

> He wasn't an expert in any field; yet he was interested in all things; he was working on everything; everything, more or less, was familiar to him; and everything met his sincere sympathy. . . . It was very helpful for him, apart from having an exceptionally lively mind, to be able to read extremely quickly and to keep in mind—forever—what he had read to extend his knowledge.[12]

There are many testaments by Khomiakov's contemporaries to his ability to assimilate new information on the spot and to use it conveniently in discussions; here, again, he resembles Pascal—in an intellectual, psychological way. For instance, the well-known attorney and Westernizer Boris N. Chicherin remembers that Khomiakov, who swallowed books "like pills," needed no more than a single night to study the most abstruse work and then, by the morning, he could summarize briefly and accurately its main conceptions—or, as Anna F. Tutchev remarks, its comic sides. His passion for his ideas and talent of eloquence made this tireless disputer, like Pascal, remain alert at all times, ready to interfere in any controversy of his time. Alexander Herzen called him "the swashbuckler of dialectics" as Khomiakov, in the image of the medieval knights guarding Our Lady's Temple, "slept in full armor."

Here we have to highlight another opposing and important aspect of Khomiakov's natural spirit and mental disposition: that he never becomes vague or veers off in various fields of knowledge and in intellectual wit.

12. Koshelev, *Zapiski*, 88.

This seeming "vagueness" of his vivid, brilliant mind conceals—the same as Pascal's—the real ongoing deep spiritual and moral concentration, the holistic unity of ideas, feelings and will, the unmudded clarity of the most serious questions.

In order to understand not only the personality but the whole spirit and meaning of Khomiakov and his works, it is appropriate now to refer to Ivan A. Goncharov's novel, *The Precipice*, where we come across the following speculation upon a harmonious relationship between the mental and the spiritual development, mind's might and the ability to "have a heart and to value its might, placing it if not above mind then, at least, treating them equally." And "as long as people are ashamed of this power, valuing the 'wisdom of serpents,' and are made to blush over the 'simplicity of doves,' equating this simplicity with naiveté, as long as intellectual excellence is preferred to moral excellence—the attainment of moral excellence is inconceivable, just as true stable human progress remains is inconceivable."[13]

Within such a context it's hard to underestimate Khomiakov's personal and creative experience; Pavel Florensky calls him "the purest and the most noble of all great men of the new Russian history." Khomiakov's contemporaries mark the initial wholeness of his paradigm, saying that even in his early youth he had never had any doubts nor did he waver. Yuri F. Samarin, having experienced Khomiakov's radical influence in *his* youth, writes this: "He was an emancipator of sorts for those who preserved the acuteness of the undamaged religious sense but were lost in contradictions, for those whole soul was split in two; he took them back to freedom, to God's light of the day, he gave them back the wholeness of religious consciousness."[14]

Samarin saw the chief cause of such a special state of his elder friend's self, of his influence upon the others, in Khomiakov being "in Church" since his early childhood and to his last breath, being a living particle of it.

Khomiakov's great education and vast tradition showed themselves in many different areas. He left a motley heritage of literary pieces, such as poems, plays, articles ("On Humboldt," "On the Social Upbringing of Man"), voluminous *Notes on World History*, theological works under the common title *Some More Remarks by an Orthodox Christian Concerning the Western Communions*, and other works.

Their diversity did not cancel one another out but, on the contrary, each time displayed, in one way or another, the firm and monolithic spiritual core of Khomiakov's mind and personality which Aleksandr Koshelev describes specifically in his *Notes*:

13. Goncharov, *Precipice*, 403.
14. Samarin, "Predislovie," xvii.

All Khomiakov's friends were passing through the age of doubt, little faith, even denial of God and got fascinated now by the French philosophy, now by the British one, now by the German; all of them had at some point been, to some extent, what was later called "the Westernizers." Khomiakov, who had studied attentively the works of the greatest *lubomudry*[15] of the world, read most books by the apostolic fathers, without neglecting the apologetic works of any significance written by the Catholic and the Protestant authors, had never drifted towards the denial of God, had always followed, according to his faith, our Orthodox Church and was obeying strictly the duties it implies.[16]

Khomiakov was called "the Knight of the Orthodox Church"; and this description tells a lot about his theological and philosophical logic. We are talking here about finding the Christian truth through the inner experience of the Church and by the voluntary communion with the love it holds, by the graceful, living faith akin to the Pascalian. According to Yuri Samarin, Khomiakov believes that "the Church is not a doctrine, nor a system or an institution. The Church is a living body, the body of truth and love, or, more precisely: truth and love embodied."[17]

To name this specific unity which man finds in the Church without losing his own identity and freedom but, on the contrary, obtaining these, the philosopher uses the word *conciliarity* which marks one of the greatest qualities of the Orthodox religion and spiritual life. As he defines it, *conciliarity* means "unity by God's grace, not by man's mind," "by the divine grace of mutual love." So the liberation from the slavery of natural necessity, personal or collective interests; and the movement within the ecclesiastic interaction towards "the Spirit of faith, love and hope" is the highest manifestation of human will and of the basics of self-realization, and, in Pascal's words, of "the right consciousness."

Khomiakov repeatedly stresses out that "above all is love and unity . . . union of holiness and love"—and the man, truly being in these, brings a super-natural quality to his existence. It is true—Khomiakov writes

that a grain of sand not receive a new existence from the pile into which chance has blown it. . . . But a material particle that has been assimilated by a living body receives an integral a new meaning and a new life from the organism of which it has

15. "Philosophers." The Slavophiles' own word based on Slavic roots: *lubo* is "lover of" (*philo*) and *mudr* is "wisdom" (*sophia*).

16. Koshelev, *Zapiski*, 87.

17. Samarin, "Predislovie," XXI.

become an integral part. Such is a person in the Church that is the body of Christ, whose organic principle is love.[18]

Being a part of such a Church, men find their selves but

no longer in in the frailty of spiritual isolation but in the power of intimate, spiritual union with their brothers and sisters and their Savior. People find themselves there in their perfection, or rather they find what is perfect in them—divine inspiration, which is constantly lost in the gross impurity of each individual existence. This purification operates by the invincible power of mutual love of Christians in Jesus Christ, for this love is the spirit of God.[19]

In Khomiakov's theology and philosophy, much the same as in Pascal's works, the blissful equality of oneness and freedom in the spirit of true love, connecting the "visible" and the "invisible" Church with its head—Christ—and with the divine energies—does not merely induce the expansion of the spiritual and moral qualities in the man who joined it but gives him a kind of a new sight which overcomes the limitations of the individual mind and the rational-empirical experience, allowing them to see other dimensions of being: "mutual love, spirit of grace that is the Eye through which a Christian beholds the divine matters."[20] To put it more scientifically, what we have here is a queer conciliar gnoseology and, so to say, an ecclesiastic methodology of apprehending reality; Khomiakov, in fact, demonstrates its advantages in providing the holistic truth amidst the numerous "half-truths":

Truth, inaccessible to any individual method of thought, is accessible only to the sum of methods of thoughts tied of love. This trait sharply distinguished Orthodox teaching from all other.[21]

Nikolai A. Berdyaev distinguishes a revolutionary new, fruitful theory of cognition, springing from the rich soil of the Orthodox paradigm and involving the "faith-full mind," in Khomiakov's works:

There is to be noted a very original gnoseology which might be called a corporate Church gnoseology. Love is recognized as the principle of apprehension; it guarantees the apprehension of truth; love is a source and guarantee of religious truth. Corporate experience of love, *sobornost'*, is the criterion of apprehension.

---

18. Khomiakov, "Some Remarks," 78.

19. Khomiakov, "Some Remarks," 78.

20. Khomiakov, "Eshche neskol'ko slov," 137.

21. Khomiakov, "On the Fragments," 313.

Here we have a principle which is opposed to authority; it is also a method of apprehension which is opposed to the Cartesian *cogito ergo sum*. It is not I think, but we think, that is to say, the corporate experience of love thinks, and it is not thought which proves my existence but will and love.[22]

According to Khomiakov's (or Pascal's) logic, the disruption of the union between grace, freedom and love, the impoverishment of its parts means the weakening of the conciliar link between man (in the Church and in everyday life) and Christ and the Holy Spirit. Then the "will-full mind" begins to follow the "human, all too human" settings of the contaminated *figmentum malum* of the dark egotistic nature and to consider the celestial in earthly terms which leads to various nihilistic consequences. So "in the matters of faith, the forced unity is a lie, and the forced obedience is death." Such forced unity which dominates freedom and substitutes the conciliar agreement in love by the authority of the ecclesiastic hierarchy is found, by Khomiakov, in Catholicism. In Protestantism, on the contrary, apparent freedom overcomes oneness and floods this harmony with the subjective opinions of the dominating mind. From Pascal's—or Khomiakov's—point of view, the Universal Church of love, freedom and truth is founded by Jesus Christ and in its relation to man divides into the visible Church and the invisible one—while as a part of the historical process it undergoes schisms, secessions and declines, deformation of unity and holiness.

Hence we shouldn't talk here about creating some "new" Universal Church based on the abstract speculative foundations of the Protestant reformations which led the way to the sovereignization of the limited mind, domination of the external knowledge and an atheistic civilization; but about the particular re-creation of the indivisible unity within the "visible" plane of the "old" Church in order to be reunited with its invisible Head—the same as that which happens on the spiritual path of an individual being.

Pascal's intellectual and spiritual efforts expressed in his *Lettres Provinciales* and approved by Khomiakov were, in fact, the guidelines leading to the renewal of this kind; which was struggling with the fires of the Inquisition, the Crusades, the selling of indulgences and so on.

In every quarrel between the Jansenists and the Roman Court—Khomiakov points out—both the spirit and the letter of all previous testaments spoke in the Jansenists's favor. Always ready to obey the decision of the Church, the only right they were asking for themselves was to preserve the freedom of their conscience until the expected decision would be taken. There is little doubt

22. Berdyaev, *Russian Idea*, 160–61.

that they had every testament of the first centuries speaking in their favor—the very spirit of Christianity.[23]

They were eager to correlate "life" and "thought," to raise the mind to faith with it and to purify every thought and every deed by the Christian truth. But when the divine order by which grace itself comes, through love, in the conciliar oneness and transforms the natural and the historical existence—when this divine order is corrupted it leads the "subject of progress" (as Khomiakov believes) towards either collectivism—which consumes the identity—or individualism—which annihilates human solidarity.

Unless the "will-full mind" is working towards grace, enlightenment and deification it will inevitably—as Pascal notes as well—feed on the energies and passions of the "hardened heart." When the heart contains no love which would direct the mind to the knowledge—the "living knowledge"—of the principles beyond reason and of their connection with the given reality; and which would liberate man for self-realization, for being in truth ("know the truth, and the truth will liberate you," St. John says)—when there is no love then the "hardened heart" locks itself in the naturalistic order of life, provokes the anthropocentric pride, whispers various rational theories and ideologies unto the mind distracted from the *allness* of being; which theories, being one-sided and ignorant of the divine dimensions of *isness*, of the fundamental split and the contradictory wholeness of man's spirit and soul, of the invisible poison of passions, etc., replace one another incessantly and each time prove to be more or less invalid and utopian.

According to Khomiakov's idea, it is necessary to be aware, at every turn of the historical progress, that the "scientific," "capitalistic," "socialistic," "communistic" and "civilizational" values based on the sinful, egotistic principles of the human nature, enthralled by the "deceiving forces" are one-sided, narrow and, basically, lead nowhere—a dead-end.

Khomiakov finds an alternative which could save us by rooting culture and social relations in Orthodox Christianity where the Eastern Church doesn't mix with the heritage of the Ancient Rome, preserves the purity of the teachings of the holy fathers and, as he keeps telling us, reflects "the wholeness, that is, the equality of oneness and liberty as revealed in the law of spiritual love."

Note that he didn't mean to revert to grey antiquity, as many of his "progressive" contemporaries understood him. He was talking about choosing the tactically preferential pointer from the perspective of the "highest awareness." Khomiakov calls in one of his letters to

23. Khomiakov, "Pis'mo k Utrekhtskomu," 311–12.

cast away any idea that somehow returning to the days of old
became our dream. . . . But the path already walked is bound to
define the future direction as well. Upon losing your path you
must first of all get back to it.[24]

The deep flow of his thought is defined not by the self-sufficient adoration of the past which contains its own manifestations of *figmentum malum* in its historical development; and surely not by wanting to borrow something "new."

The "old," or rather the eternal, is vital for keeping the proper harmony of the soul and of the best spiritual traditions—that high road which defines the moral state of an individual and of the whole society. For being indifferent to truth and to moral goodness can "poison the whole generation and to ruin many more that would follow," can corrupt the life of the state and of the society.

Thus the moral nobility has to be able to solve any civil questions before they even rise.

Khomiakov counters the Machiavellian politics with moral historicism which provides the spiritual fullness of human existence.

> One cannot mix the social goals with the political ones and stay
> unpunished. . . . A ridiculous teaching sprang to being since the
> revolution (although, of course, it had been around for a very long
> time); it mixes the life of the society under the government with
> its formal image. This teaching had plunged its roots so deep that
> it became the foundation of the political Protestantism (communism or socialism) which solves the social questions by merely
> assuming a new form, hostile to the preceding forms but on the
> whole indistinguishable from them. . . . To re-educate the society,
> to cut it completely from the political issues, to make it face itself,
> understand its own emptiness, its own selfishness and its own
> weakness—that is what the true enlightenment must be doing.[25]

When it comes to solving the daily issues of this kind of enlightenment, Khomiakov places the highest value on true religion, wise conservatism, unswaying traditions, everlasting national values—only through the lens of which can new achievements and progressive changes be successfully obtained. In his *Notes on the World History* he divides all religion into the Cushite (based on the principles of necessity and mechanical obedience to the authority) and the Iranian (relying on freedom and the conscious

24. Khomiakov, "O sel'skoy obshchine," 462.

25. Letter of Khomiakov to Popov from March 17, 1848 (see Khomiakov, *Pis'ma*, 177–78).

choice between good and evil)—with Christianity being the highest and the fullest manifestation of both.

Comparing the invigorating traditionalism of the "skillful ones" (to use Pascal's expression) and the nihilistic novelty of the "half-skillful ones" he was using his own, considerably extended interpretation of the activity of the British Tories and Whigs, perceiving them as two forces affecting the society, each in its own way. The Whigs represent here the "one-sided development of the individual mind neglecting the legends and the historical life of society"—neglecting the reliance on the ancient traditions, family upbringing, classical education—all of which are typical for the Tories—and activating the egotistic impulses of behavior, financial reward, and purely external, technological progress.

Meanwhile, without combining harmoniously the "old" and the "new," without their natural fusion, it is impossible to achieve any spiritual growth or the true moralistic prosperity of the people:

> Any state or civil society consists of two principles: of the living historical principle which contains all vigor of the society; and of the speculative principle governed by reason—it cannot create anything new by itself but it gradually brings the chief—the living—principle to order, sometimes suppressing it and sometimes supporting and developing. The English called it, albeit without realizing, the Whiggism and the Torism. Too bad if the soil . . . throws away all roots and all sprouts of the historical tree.[26]

Khomiakov believed that the Russian "Whigs," represented by Peter the Great and his followers, were unwise to throw away the radical values of Russian "Torism"—"the Kremlin, Kiev, the Sarov hermitage, folk life with its songs and rituals, and most of the rural communities." Reviving these traditions is important—not in itself but because the life-bringing trinity of grace, liberty and love is still alive in them—alpha and omega of the true enlightenment. Such enlightenment "is not just a code of social agreements or scientific achievements" but

> it's the sagacious enlightenment of the whole spiritual disposition of man or nation. It can be linked with science; for science is one of its aspects; but it will remain strong even without the "scientific" knowledge; science, in its turn, being only one of its aspects, is powerless and miserable without it. . . . As for the sagacious enlightenment of the human spirit, it's that living root

26. Khomiakov, "O sel'skoy obshchine," 461.

which produces the sprouts of both the scientific knowledge and the so-called civilization, or scholarship.[27]

Freedom enlightened by grace and spirit helps the individual man to collect his powers and to direct his will and his mind to the divine simplicity of the holistic knowledge which plants the immediate, living harmony with the truths of faith and Revelation within the soul.

Such knowledge and harmony, which can be achieved, as in Pascal's works, not by the mind alone but also by the heart, he opposes to the "poverty of rationalism." And, like Pascal criticizing the abstract rationalism of Descartes, Khomiakov speaks against "en-spiriting the abstract existence" within the framework of Hegelian "honest fanatic" and "the last Titan"— the mind. Khomiakov is sure that the German idealism, upon reaching the Hegelian heights of the rational knowledge, "bumped into its boundary" and "passed the ultimate sentence on rationalism itself."

The holistic, living knowledge, on the contrary, supports, in its turn, faith and love which is

> an acquisition; and the broader its sphere and the fuller it carries us beyond our limits, the richer we will become within ourselves. In sacrifice, or self-oblivion, we find a surplus of expanding life, and in this surplus we become radiant, triumphant and jubilant. Whenever we halt in our striving, whenever we lose what we have acquired (despite the law inherent within us), we are impoverished, squeezed more and within our narrow bounds, as if into a coffin that we find repellent and hateful, but that we are unable to leave, because we do not want to.[28]

Without the transformation of man's inner world by the act of faith and by means of sacrificial self-neglect (an example of which is Pascal's life) there is no true love, and without true love there is neither true knowledge nor the true ennoblement of human relations.

According to Khomiakov, upon leaving the egotistic "coffin" and liberating himself from the power of the slavish "deceiving forces" man ceases to perceive the world around him solely as an object of rational knowledge, a source of some benefits to be extracted; and by the "moral power of hearty love" becomes transgressed by the immediate fullness of his reality; the living knowledge of which is as different from the rational one as the actual perception of light by someone who can see is different from the speculative understanding of the physics of light by someone who was born blind. *Then*

27. Khomiakov, "Mnenie Russkikh," 26.
28. Khomiakov, "On the Fragments," 302–03.

man can see the "highest truth of the willful intention" and the "super-logical mysteries of the matters celestial and human," although the final, specific answer they give is beyond human comprehension.

Bibliography

Berdyaev, Nicolas. *The Russian Idea*. New York: Macmillan, 1948.

Chaadaev, Petr Ya. *Tsena vekov*. Moscow: Molodaya gvardiya, 1991.

Goncharov, Ivan. *The Precipice*. Translated by Laury Magnus and Boris Jakim. Ann Arbor, Michigan: Ardis, 1994.

Florovsky, Georgy, "The Metaphysical Premises of Utopianism." In *Collected Works*, by George Florovsky, 75–93. Vol. 12. Translated by Catherine Boyle. Belmont, MA: Büchervertriebsanstalt, 1989.

Khomiakov, Alexei S. "Eshche neskol'ko slov Pravoslavnogo Khristianina o zapadnykh veroispovedaniyakh po povodu raznykh sochineniy Latinskikh i Protestantskikh o predmetakh very." In *Polnoe sobranie sochineniy Alekseya Stepanovicha Khomiakova*, by Alexei S. Khomiakov, 169–258. Vol. 2. Moscow: Universitetskaya tipografiya, 1900.

———. "Mnenie Russkikh ob inostrantsakh." In *Polnoe sobranie sochineniy Alekseya Stepanovicha Khomiakova*, by Alexei S. Khomiakov, 31–69. Vol. 1. Moscow: Universitetskaya tipografiya, 1900.

———. "O sel'skoy obshchine." In *Polnoe sobranie sochineniy Alekseya Stepanovicha Khomiakova*, by Alexei S. Khomiakov, 459–68. Vol. 3. Moscow: Universitetskaya tipografiya, 1900.

———. "On the 'Fragments' Discovered among I. V. Kireevsky's Papers." In *On Spiritual Unity: A Slavophile Reader*, edited by Robert Bird and Boris Jakim, 295–313. Translated by Robert Bird. Hudson, NY: Lindisfarne, 1998.

———. *Pis'ma*. Vol. 8 of *Polnoe sobranie sochineniy Alekseya Stepanovicha Khomiakova*, by Alexei S. Khomiakov. Moscow: Universitetskaya tipografiya, 1900.

———. "Pis'mo k Utrekhtskomu episkopu (Zhansenistu) Loosu." In *Polnoe sobranie sochineniy Alekseya Stepanovicha Khomiakova*, by Alexei S. Khomiakov, 303–17. Vol. 2. Moscow: Universitetskaya tipografiya, 1900.

———. "Some Remarks by an Orthodox Christian Concerning the Western Communions, on the Occasion of Several Latin and Protestant Religious Publications (Excerpts)." Translated by Boris Jakim. In *On Spiritual Unity: A Slavophile Reader*, edited by Robert Bird and Boris Jakim, 63–116. Hudson, NY: Lindisfarne, 1998.

Koshelev, Aleksandr. *Zapiski (1812–1883)*. Moscow: Izdatel'stvo MGU, 1991.

Pascal, Blaise. *Pensées or Thoughts on Religion*. Translated by Gertrude Burford Rawlings. New York: Peter Pauper, 1946.

Samarin, Yuriy F. "Predislovie." In *Polnoe sobranie sochineniy Alekseya Stepanovicha Khomiakova*, by Alexei S. Khomiakov, i–xxxvii. Vol. 2. Moscow: Universitetskaya tipografiya, 1900.

Solov'ev, Vladimir. "Tri rechi v pamyat' Dostoevskogo." In *Sochineniya v dvukh tomakh*, by Vladimir Solov'ev, 290–323. Vol. 2. Moscow: Mysl', 1988.

8

Khomiakov's *Sobornost'* and *Naturphilosophie*

A Revolutionary Narrative of History

JENNIE D. WOJTUSIK

Unarguably, Imperial Russians felt an immense amount of anxiety regarding the influence of Western philosophy on their indigenous culture, the most persistent problem likely being the applicability of German philosophical ideas as a model for social and public life.[1] The migration of post-Enlightenment values eastward out of Western Europe saw most liberal Russian intellectuals pursuing the Enlightenment's models of individual moral responsibility, but conservatives at the time also believed that Russian life, religious life in particular, needed renovation, albeit along different lines. These shared concerns created an intellectual schism between those who sought faithfulness in a "Russian way of life," with an explicit recognition that Orthodox religion and the church were necessary components, and the many who espoused a view that Christianity was not suitable for the task of conquering this new intractable external world.

Accounts of how "foreign" imports factor into such debates are all too often presented in binary terms, as a dualistic history of East versus West, or Russian Religious Philosophy versus German Idealism, and thus as a kind of intellectual colonialism or dependency that must be overcome when recovering "Russian" thought. The present discussion will combat these commonplace assumptions by addressing the work of Alexei Khomiakov (1804–1860), and casting him as a legitimate heir to German intellectual debates associated

1. See Terras, *Russian Literature*, 171.

with the era of German Idealism and especially Romanticism. Scholars have long understood that Khomiakov's *sobornost'* is a call for a communal spiritual existence—gleaned from Russian Orthodoxy.[2]

My own reading of Khomiakov suggests a contrary reading of this particular moment of cultural *contact*, one, which produces an original and sophisticated Russian adaptation of European thought. As we shall see, in working out his epistemological views, Khomiakov strongly relied on and extended German Idealism's own internal critique of Western European rationalism, especially its attempts to counter the fragmenting rationalistic effects logocentric thought had on European individualism—a relatively common critique leveled by German Romantics against Enlightenment thought, as well.[3]

Khomiakov's work makes the case that Imperial era Russian intellectuals need to be addressed as active participants in contemporaneous debates about cultural traditions, national patrimony, and the roles of education and myth in national politics, aesthetics, philosophy, and history—he and many others in his era were anything but dependent on or colonized by Western ideas, but instead he uniquely and actively adapted European models to the cultural concerns of his time in order to derive a model for Russian social and public life, a model that he uniquely situates in the Orthodox church, faith, and patriarchy. Thus, Khomiakov's idea of *sobonost'* responds to principles from the *Naturphilosophie* of Friedrich W. J. Schelling (1775–1854). The tension between these two philosophical models, however, allows Khomiakov to open up a complex, multilateral space redefining knowledge acquisition and new knowledge production that answer to cultural anxieties and imperatives in Imperial Russia that could not have appeared in Germany. In consequence, Khomiakov's work documents how "German" traditions were not only extended, but also refuted and naturalized to Imperial Russian contexts—original contributions to debates about the nature of culture, nation, and history that took forms answering to Russia's distinct national challenges in emerging as both a nation and a state in forms undreamt-of in the West.

The Search for Russian Continuity and Unity

By the mid 1790s, German Romantics were disillusioned by the both the Enlightenment's scientific method and reductionism and the French

---

2. Engelstein, *Slavophile Empire*, 111.

3. For a state of the art overview to the background of this debate, see Beiser, *Romantic Imperative*.

Revolution, and while they would not abandon the principles of liberty, freedom, equality and reason that they felt defined human beings, they also could not approve of the growing alienation of civil society from the ruling elites, especially from culture produced in the courts and imperial bureaucracies.[4] Such discontent was also being expressed by Russian intellectuals like Khomiakov, who claims: "the revolution was not nothing but a bare denial, giving a negative freedom, but without making any new content."[5] Indeed, Romantics had been quick to recognize this negative freedom (the freedom to resist absolutist claims for cultural authority) as the social vacuum that resulted from the destruction of traditional social institutions in the various wars of the eighteenth and early nineteenth centuries, coupled with the materialism and atheism growing out of dissatisfaction about Church and State responses to new classes and historical forces.

By acknowledging this new modern fragmentation between self and others that arises when traditional understandings of society erode and are not replaced by new ones, intellectuals in the West and Russia alike were forced to reevaluate the overwhelming needs of the masses, searching for some "new content," a model that could help both the state and its national stakeholders to overcome the various social, cultural, and political divides arising. Slavophiles like Khomiakov were aware of a new, post-French-Revolution generation of German thought which was at least addressing national cultural concerns in these contexts. Nonetheless, the German solution seemed to Russian readers like Khomiakov to be a purely philosophical assessment of the French Revolution's principles—"Germany being too backward, politically, and economically, for these principles to have application in the real world."[6] That is, German thought from the Storm and Stress Era into Romanticism had little or no address to practical politics and economics, in no small part because these intellectuals were scattered through essentially provincial German-speaking states, un-unified and without claims to national development, let alone empire.[7]

Regardless of the limited political field for these German Romantics, the era's politics engaged them to contemplate the preconditions for fundamental social and political change and for the high moral ideals of a Republic.[8] In doing so, they struggled to find a model of the state that ensured

---

4. Beiser, *Political Writings*, 16.

5. Khomiakov, "Mnenie Russkikh ob inostrantsakh," 51.

6. Walicki, *Slavophile Controversy*, 33.

7. The Holy Roman Empire united some of these states into a dense alliance, but not as a European Imperial or national state.

8. Beiser, *Political Writings*, 15.

revolutionary principles but within a framework of community, continuity and tradition—to preserve a *nation* as an identity. It is this set of values, already explicit in the Romantic critique of Western European rationalism and the Western absolutist state, that informs Khomiakov's *sobornost'* and the Slavophile conception of history. Of course, in some ways, Imperial Russia was younger, even less advanced than Germany as a nation, since it had little claim to being an inheritor of Greco-Roman culture. Thus, the dominant role of historicism's "real world" applicability in Khomiakov's context emerged primarily in one aspect of national consciousness highlighted in German Idealism and Romanticism: the role of historical and literary narratives as a debate about the continuity of Russian national life and a vision of their future almost entirely dependent on their past, a model for history that insisted on identifying continuity between old and new Russia, even across profound political changes.

Russia had internal forms of this debate. With the rise in literary production and distribution in the nineteenth century, for example, Russian intellectuals intuited the social and political potential in material production as a means of securing a new Russian nature, thus ideologizing the question along known political divides: either Russia's unique continuous history independent of Western Europe, or the cultural necessity for Western ideas. The former; the search for community and tradition, is readily evident in Russia's dominant historical reference texts, especially in the comprehensive treatment of whether Russia depicts continuity from "ancient" Kievan Rus to the "modern" post-Petrine era.[9]

For instance, Russia's disparate political legacies impelled prominent historians to evaluate whether Peter I increased Russia's strength and transformed her into an important European power, or if the price of progress was demoralization in the Russian "family, marriage, friendship and society."[10] While both historians conclude that despotism was by no means a traditional form of government in Russia, both repudiated the Petrine reforms due to their secular corruption of morals, which they claim broke a way of life that had not been disturbed during the reign of Ivan IV. Thus they recognized the importance of "way of life" and national consciousness in tandem with politics and economic modernization. Eventually, the Slavophiles (Ivan Kireevsky, Alexei Khomiakov, Mikhail Pogodin, Ivan Aksakov and Konstantin Aksakov

9. Andrzej Walicki's *Slavophile Controversy* stages a thorough examination of Mikhail Shcherbatov's seven-volume *History of Russia*, demonstrating that as early as the Enlightenment, Russian historians were concerned with the importance of uninterrupted historical continuity.

10. Walicki, *Slavophile Controversy*, 25.

in particular) interpret and evaluate both Peter and Ivan's reigns based on similar premises and draw likeminded conclusions.

Khomiakov's own writing espouses a narrative that reflects this over-arching set of what were clearly Romantic-national identity aims and values as critical forces within the context of Russian historical continuity. This affirmation also has a distinct political slant to it. Given the restriction on political action in early to mid-nineteenth-century Russia, the "thick" (*tol-stye*) journals from literary societies like "Lovers of the Russian Word" and "Society of Wisdom Lovers"[11] served as the principal means by which impe-rial Russia discovered, defined, and shaped itself culturally and nationally in contexts *outside* official government action. This discovery of a different venue for political discussion as cultural debate often took the form of active polemics concerning Russia's role in the development of a modern society *vis-à-vis* its literary contributions.

As in German Romanticism, but with much more precise political objectives, seemingly formal aesthetic concerns about the status and role of the writer, the proper subjects and languages of texts (to name a few) be-came, in fact, contentious debates regarding the nation's historical continuity and just what precisely from the past was useful for a burgeoning national identity. For example, one highly political issue became whether Russian literature should incorporate Church Slavonic and folk traditions[12] or wage war against the prejudices, vices and absurdities of "backwards" Russia—an awareness illuminated most concretely by German Romantics (and by Ideal-ists in general since the work of Johann Gottfried Herder[13]). Their strategy did echo the German logic for embracing national heritage culture when they determined that education and enlightenment of the people was the precondition for political change, and that art was the "content" that could show humanity the principles of reason and the highest moral ideas of lib-erty and equality—a sentiment reflected in the "Lovers of the Russian Word," "Society of Wisdom Lovers" and later in Khomiakov.

11. This society consisted of Odoevsky, Dmitri Venevitinov, Nikolai Rozhalin, Ivan Kireevsky, and Aleksandr Koshelev, all young Russian intellectuals employed in the Moscow Archives of the Ministry of Foreign Affairs. Their 1824 almanac, *Mnemosyne*, depicts their search for wisdom in Germany philosophy.

12. This was an aesthetic demand for the creation of a truly national philosophy and literature.

13. The cultural science notions of Johann Gottfried Herder were already firmly established as the general conception and interpretive methodology of the Russian Academy of Sciences (1725). Herder's *Volk* sees peoples, in the *ethnic* sense and *nation*, as each having their own cultural movement or continuous history, which offers a na-tionalistic, or pluralistic, notion of history, rather than an Eastern Russian vs. Western Europe dichotomy.

These early Russian aesthetics, combined with the narrativization of history, constituted a sociopolitical program intuited from the ideals of Romanticism, many of which emerged in the wake of the Enlightenment and the French Revolution, as they well knew. Overcoming the modern fragmentation between self and others eventually posits art as the ideal mode of cultural and national ideologizing and of depicting continuity, first for the Romantics, and then for the Slavophiles. In regards to the concerns about historical continuity (which would espouse evolutionary change rather than open revolution), Khomiakov claims that, "Restoring our private mental strength depends entirely on the living connection with the ancient,"[14] i.e., looking to their indigenous culture rather than to the cultural legacies of the Greco-Roman world.

While Romantic politics questioned the liberal tradition, especially individualism, its concept of community and its ethics was also a means to counter the atomism and anomie they found in Immanuel Kant's philosophy (or in other seemingly logocentric philosophies of the Enlightenment era that left aside embodiment, affect, and the "natural people" of a culture in favor of formal education alone).

Among the German sources for this thought, it was Schelling, more than any other thinker, who exhibited the limitation and disillusionment that Kant's systemic metaphysics of the subject generates. Schelling combined theology with the new philosophy of Idealism in insisting that philosophy, religion, and art are the three coeval frameworks through which the world is understood (his evolution on "the true, the good, and the beautiful"). Thus it is his ideas that the Slavophiles felt most aligned with, because he reclaimed both affect and belief as critical to knowledge of the world.

As it is impossible to examine here the full depth of Kant's three critiques, this paper will discuss but one foundational aspect of Kantian dualism and Schelling's response, and only as it pertains to Khomiakov's religious thought. Kant's dualism is that of an epistemological dichotomy—a fragmentation of self from nature in his insistence that direct revelation is impossible, because the mind always mediates the data we experience though its understanding. Put more experientially, and in the context of Khomiakov's spiritual beliefs: human senses and instincts bear which might well be false witness, and therefore man can never apprehend eternal, unchanging truths that a direct apprehension of things *an sich* (in themselves) would guarantee.

To begin, in the *Critique of Pure Reason* (1781–1787), Kant sees nature as that which is understood only as subject to necessary laws—laws accessible

14. Khomiakov, "O vozmozhnosti," 97.

to us because human cognition brings forms of thought (categories) to bear on what it perceives. Man's capability of knowing these laws is dependent upon a self-caused ability to judge in terms of categories, making knowledge of nature determined by human cognition. "Nature's laws" are products of human cognition; nature itself is a *Ding an sich*, a thing inaccessible directly by humans. Knowledge of nature, then, is also subject to the link between sense perception and cognition (aesthetic judgment) and to ethical judgment (and thus also is available as an object of faith).

While Kant's epistemology should not be read as a demolition of reason's cognitive role, he does eliminate reason's pretensions to offer knowledge of a "transcendent" world beyond the senses. Essentially, for Kant, man can have no objective knowledge claims to cosmological ideas. It is Schelling's critique that offers Khomiakov a productive means of rejecting Kantian dualism and recouping transcendent values to which he aspires:

> Schelling gives a most reasonable justification of nature, recognizing it as the reflection of the spirit. He passes from rationalism to idealism, and later . . . on to mystical spiritualism.[15]

Kant's account is disturbing to Schelling, since, in his reading, it creates a distinction between nature as itself and nature as an appearance, begging the question of how nature "in itself" gives rise to appearances for man.[16] Schelling insists that Kant's philosophy created a false distinction between epistemology, ethics, and belief.[17] In order to resolve Kant's dualism in a way that does *not* restrict nature's scope and impact, Schelling's *Naturphilosophie* offers a more integrated model, creating and positioning humanity within nature, as part of an interrelated whole, which is structured in an ascending series of "potentials" that contain polar oppositions within them.[18] Khomiakov agrees with Schelling that Kant proved faith, for example, is a higher, unconditional knowledge that has a different status than logical epistemologies do, but concludes with the Romantics that unity is essential when he claims, "The phenomena of spiritual and intellectual life are infinite in variety, and (like the organs of sense perception in the physical world), in order to correctly and fully perform their functions, they must be congenial with the general laws of nature, not only in form and geometric outline, but also

15. Khomiakov, "Recent Developments," 225–26.

16. Schelling, "Vorlesungen," 277.

17. This is a charge which Kant would deny because all three kinds of knowledge are for him based on the same unity of apperception.

18. Schelling's model is a magnet, whose opposing poles are inseparable from each other, even though they are opposites.

in their entire chemical composition and dynamic structure."[19] Thus emerging as a religious thinker, Khomiakov posits a model of knowledge based on the existence of creation (an ontological base) rather than on mediation (an epistemological one), stating that knowledge from the senses must agree with nature and not just exist in relation to dialectical reason but to all living and moral forces of the spirit.

This was the model for an image of humankind within nature, the model that would ground a nation in its people. Moreover, Kant had also insisted that knowledge came as the result of human labor: he lived, he said, not in an enlightened era, but in one in the process of becoming enlightened.[20] Pragmatically speaking, the French Revolution had proved to the Romantics and Khomiakov that humanity was not ready for the political realization of a moral state with freedom and individual rights, so building a moral state must require moral individuals first. Hence, Schelling's model, with its Kantian underpinnings, reintegrates an epistemological model for human knowledge with ethics and beliefs.

Khomiakov also saw in Schelling's model a way to surmount the fragmentation of self from nature, replacing opposing, inseparable poles of nature and knowledge into a whole which offer him the assumption that humanity will also be characterized by unity and ethics. Ultimately, Khomiakov sought to overcome the modern fragmentation of self and others via the Romantic tradition of historical continuity and nation building though aesthetic means that appeal to both mind and material experience.

Faith as Lost Tradition and Aesthetic Education

At this point in *Naturphilosophie*, Schelling begins to discuss the implications of his own model in very religious terms, hewing the Protestant line that can analogize history and salvation history. He suggests that what had once been a union of state, church, and community, had given away to individuals—rational and free but rootless and attached to nothing, and existing without faith or allegiance. Post-Enlightenment society, he claims, did not reflect community or a feeling for nature because many integral traditions had been lost when the Enlightenment assumed reason as the highest authority—an account that many scholars have accused (or assumed in error) Kant of providing: a narrative attributing full autonomy and absoluteness to the intellect. Schelling's Kantian critique, however, provides an account of mind and world that insists on the need not to limit our conception of

19. Khomiakov, "On the Fragments," 310.
20. See Kant, *Was Ist Aufklärung?*

nature to what can be objectified by scientific methods, thus clearly opposing such a fragmentation between reason and sensibility. Schelling's concerns and conclusions remain evident in Khomiakov's writing as he argues that the mind should conform not only to its logical structure, but also to all laws of the spiritual world and the totality of its vital inner forces.

Khomiakov's reception of German Idealism is evidence that he knows his source materials well. The charges of a limiting logocentrism that he responds to describe the work of Hegel more than they do Schelling, since Hegel's work was often referred to as a rationalistic metaphysics than as a commitment to individuals within the nation. Khomiakov's writings demonstrate that he explicitly understood the differences between Hegel and Schelling, which derive from their respective approaches to understanding the absolute. For Hegel, the absolute is the result of the self-cancellation of everything finite, whose mode of being is to change into something different (rational knowledge becomes consciousness of the world spirit).

Like Hegel, Schelling argues that it is not a particular experientially based act of knowledge which tells us the truth about the world, but rather the aggregate of knowledge with reference to a whole, necessitating connections between one piece of knowledge to the next. However, for Schelling, a logical reconstruction of the process of knowledge can only be a reflection of thought by itself—the real process of acquiring knowledge of the work cannot be described in philosophy, because the cognitive ground for knowledge and the real ground of that knowledge in the world, although they are inseparable from each other, cannot be shown to *reflect* each other.

Likewise, Khomiakov argues that Hegel's philosophy ends at the mind (spirit, *Geist*), because rational knowledge does not embrace the reality of the knowable: knowledge of the abstract is only available as rational law and not as a reality to be experienced. What is most problematic for Khomiakov is that Hegel's rational knowledge cannot contain faith, which is a culture's tradition, and the spiritual bind that holds together the community of *sobornost'*. It is religious faith that is the final conclusion, not the mind. While Hegel tried to create a story that meets the requirements of the human mind as the driver of history, his rational historiography only "created a systematic ghost" according to Khomiakov, rather than a source of living spirit.

Like Schelling, he believed that, for Hegel, "strict logic sequence or perceived need is only a mask behind which hides an unlimited arbitrariness of scientific systematics."[21] For both Schelling and Khomiakov, then, Hegel's *Geist* is not a complete mind, for the mind in its entirety embraces beyond the whole realm of reason into the realm of experience and that of belief.

21. Khomiakov, "Mnenie Russkikh ob inostrantsakh," 49.

Khomiakov claims, in addition, that the realm of belief is what in German philosophy is sometimes "under the extremely indeterminate expression of 'unmediated knowledge,'" what can be called internal knowledge, but what due to "the preeminent character of its entire realm should be called faith."[22] Therefore, Khomiakov defines mind as living perception of the phenomenon in faith; mind in its fullness reflects the life of the known in the life of faith, and only the logic of its laws is in the dialectic of reason.

Schelling suggests in *Naturphilosophie* that art is the route to an understanding of what cannot appear as an object of knowledge, since art conveys something beyond its objective nature and logic, as well as requiring the subject to engage in free acts of judgment. Thus, for Schelling, art restores the qualities of continuity, unity, and tradition to nature, society, and the human sense of belonging to them. Like the vast majority of German Romantics, then, he believed in human nature as engaged in the social. As a consequence, Schelling affirms that the education and enlightenment of the people are the precondition for political change, with art as the "content" that inspires human minds and spirit and could show humanity the principles of reason and the highest moral ideas of liberty, equality, and community.

For Khomiakov, a coherent nation, the source of unity, and faith as a key to community are also reflected in the work of art. And while all of the Slavophiles openly discussed which Romantic writers most reflected these ideas (for example, Vasily Zhukovsky, Alexander Pushkin), and what they deemed essential for a truly national literature, the framework that Khomiakov most often employs for *sobornost'* is his sense that art is a social conception, not just a historical or material one. Furthermore, for Khomiakov, the subject's ability to judge freely and the art object's conveying of something beyond its objective nature will eventually lead back to belief in a nation, and thus also to the Orthodox church: it is forms of religion and faith that transcends the empirical truth of the nation and is experience, and the church, above all else, is its social organization in his Russia.

According to Schelling, then, philosophy cannot represent nature in itself because it cannot represent the experiential and the unconscious. Philosophy, like particular sciences, appeals to consciousness and theoretical knowledge; it can only address objects of experience within a chain of logical conditions, especially sufficient reason rather than explaining an object's necessary end and purpose as part of nature. Art is, then, "the only true and

22. Khomiakov, "On the Fragments," 310.

eternal organ and document of philosophy, which always and continuously documents what philosophy cannot represent externally."[23]

This statement also follows what German Idealism and Romanticism posited as the essential nature of the artwork: the artist does not simply capture reality by representing the object through the lens of his subjectivity. Instead, art conveying the highest insight to its viewers unites conscious, logical explanation, with unconscious experience, the bounded with the unbounded. In *Naturphilosophie* specifically, philosophy cannot be defined as representing the absolute because conscious thinking operates from a position where the identity of the subjective and the objective has always already been lost in the emergence of consciousness. Simply put, art shows what cannot be said, reaching beyond knowledge attained through logic.

In Schelling's system, nature begins unconsciously and ends in conscious philosophical and scientific knowledge, but also necessarily in the artwork: "the I is conscious according to the production, unconscious with regard to the product."[24] Khomiakov concurs with Schelling that only "artistic creation" depicts the ultimate harmony of opposites in the absolute and the eternal ideas behind the particular forms of physical nature. Frederick Beiser states this most aptly when he claims about the Romantics, "through aesthetic experience, they believed, we perceive the infinite in the finite, the supersensible in the sensible"[25] and the absolute in its appearances. Art, however, is also the heart of Romantic sociopolitical thought and the instrument that binds the community through common experience. Such experience, in turn, is the ground for the existence and identity of the individual, who automatically is situated within the community, as well.

Schelling's definition of the threefold origin for knowledge of the world also points toward a theory of the state in total defiance of the Enlightenment and its more instrumental approach to the citizen and the state. Khomiakov started from this Romantic premise, which had been derived from Plato and Aristotle. He shared with them the fundamental aim of educating the public through the development of its moral, intellectual, and aesthetic powers—its whole mind as part of nature. Thus the state as a community was also anchored in its unity by art, which educated human nature into its wholeness:

> Not from the mind of one art arises. It is not the work of single individuals and their egoistic rationality. It focuses and express-
> es the fullness of human life, with its education, will and belief.

23. Schelling, "Philosophie der Kunst," 627.
24. Schelling, "Philosophie der Kunst," 613.
25. Beiser, *Romantic Imperative*, 73.

> The artist does not create by his own power: the spiritual power
> of the people is to create the artist.[26]

For Schelling and the Romantics, the spirit of a nation is not just an assemblage of customs, habits, traditions, and local color, nor an abstraction. Instead, that spirit is an ideal quality embodied in its people who must bring forth a process of creative self-expression and self-cognition (Herder's *Volk*).

Khomiakov extends this pattern by making it progressive—that spirit must be continuously brought into focus with an engagement with the here and now. Thus he sees "the inner spiritual life of the Russian people as a unique and fruitful beginning for the future of education"[27] and promotes an indigenous form of education as necessary for national self-cognition, claiming that the vast majority of intelligent Russians also attested to a "Russian way of life." However, in no way does Khomiakov consider art to be the exclusive domain of the intelligentsia, because the people will find knowledge of itself only in a group, and principally thought the art which brings forth its expressions of self:

> Why is the school of Arts that which should be the people's?
> Everywhere is perfect. One must look for art, rather than a nation in the arts.[28]

Here, Khomiakov echoes the Romantic belief that the artist is the creator of the nation around him by giving people a world to see and leading them to that world, but people can only discover their individual powers through interaction with others.

So, for Khomiakov like Schelling, not just logical knowledge, but art restores the national community's critical qualities of continuity, unity, and tradition, establishing the humans' sense of belonging to nature and society alike. In *Naturphilosophie*, Schelling claims that "beauty unites logic and belief, and that the highest act of reason is the aesthetic act embracing all ideas and truth and goodness are made kindred only in beauty."[29] In other words, if the art object manifests what cannot be understood of its knowable conditions, it can express the spiritual and the moral in forms rendering them palpable and available to group experience.

While German aesthetics may have begun, in the Enlightenment and in Hegel's model, with concerns of good taste and great literature, it quickly

---

26. Khomiakov, "O vozmozhnosti," 74.

27. Khomiakov, "O vozmozhnosti," 99.

28. Khomiakov, "O vozmozhnosti," 74.

29. Schelling, "Abhandlungen, Recenzionen," 116.

became the hallmark of the nation with an extended role as providing "absolute knowledge, the unity of the personality, a mediator between man and nature and the source of social harmony,"[30] all concerns inherited by Imperial Russians like Khomiakov.

A Mythical Patriarchy For The Modern Age

What the German Romanics assumed was the fount of knowledge of the world and the nation; Khomiakov would make the core of a new national politics, as well. For Schelling, art was to create on a sophisticated, self-conscious level that unity between nature and society that had once been given on a naïve subconscious level to primitive man. Khomiakov's *sobornost'* affirms this Romantic ideal of unity, which attempted to reaffirm this wholeness in the divisive tendencies of nineteenth-century modern society. Schelling claims in *Naturphilosophie* that poetry is the all-embracing sense of human creativity that is the teacher of mankind. Art, then, is linked to the demands for a "new mythology," which would be in the service of ideas, a mythology that makes palpable the nation's reason (as a rational order of expression, not as rationalism).

Ideas must become aesthetic (i.e., mythological) in order to be accepted by the people to be effective in the civilizing mission of art. Schelling argued both for art's freedom and the subordination of art to the interests of humanity, as beauty serves as a symbol of the good. When Khomiakov claims, "German critics were right in proclaiming the freedom of art,"[31] that claim is rooted in the tradition of Romantic aesthetics he inherits—that which derives its meaning and purpose from its philosophical context and its underlying ethical and political values, and that which can form and re-form the national community as tradition and as a tool for its formation—its *Bildung* (education, culture, development, formation).

Bildung is at the heart of this aesthetic education, as it was a mainstay of the German tradition.[32] *Bildung* implies transformation and evolution, something potentially inchoate, something implicit coming to fruition, becoming something actual, organized and explicit. The Romantic—and consequently the Russian—search for continuity, unity, and tradition that

---

30. Beiser, *Political Writings*, 12.

31. Khomiakov, "Mnenie Russkikh ob inostrantsakh," 42.

32. For example, the value of *Bildung* was part of the accounts of human development common to the Storm and Stress, the Enlightenment and Classicism, and although they differ, they all affirm an ethics of on-going improvement toward perfection and self-realization.

we have examined so far were aspects of *Bildung*, so its full definition should be fully graspable and resonate as key to a practical scheme for making a self-conscious nation out of a community's tradition.

That education to nationhood begins in *Bildung* as an ethics of self-realization rooted in freedom—a freedom, the Romantics argued, that lies at the root of all moral obligations, whose impetus is *love*, the desire to unite in harmony. While freedom is the characteristic mark of subjectivity, the self cannot be realized through inculcation of general cultural norms and traditions and cannot simply be the result of education or conditioning of state or culture. Religion, then, is the key and the source for a unifying artistic inspiration for *Bildung*: art creates the people as a new religion with its own mythology by going back to the roots of all religion. Religion here is not morality or metaphysics, but rather its aim was to cultivate a spiritual sense, to "foster experiences of the infinite" and nurture man's "feelings of dependence"[33] and interdependence.

This is the framework within which Khomiakov makes claim to the roots of Russia's "spiritual" and "national beginning" as an "identity of freedom" saying that there is "spirit (they) could take and keep due to its internal unity."[34] When Khomiakov concluded his evaluation of the contradictory historical evidence that he deemed essential in determining a course for the Russia of the present and the direction of her development, his notions of history became hostile to the intellectual, social, and political developments which had taken place in Russia since Peter the Great. An art rooted in the nation (not in the rationalistic norms of elite aesthetic categories cultivated by an international upper class) could engage the minds and hearts of Russia and refund the nation. This was not the program of his era, since many Russian intellectuals in the early nineteenth century were convinced Westernizers. In contrast, Khomiakov always insisted on the necessity of an indigenous development for Russian people, on the meaning of Orthodox faith in man's spiritual and moral existence, and the superiority of the Russian Church in these teachings.[35] Eventually, he mythologized the patriarchal world of the Old Russian gentry, which had become inimical to the state, to the bureaucracy and urbanity of St. Petersburg, and to rational philosophy in general.

This was the site at which Khomiakov saw the origin of a new Russian nation. He insisted that pre-Petrine Russia "had the power of a government in harmony with the people, and (the) freedom of the Church pure and

---

33. Beiser, *Political Writings*, 19.
34. Khomiakov, "O vozmozhnosti," 83.
35. See Edie, "Alexis Khomiakov," 216–17.

lightened."[36] In fact, he would conclude it was precisely because Russia was not of the Greco-Roman world that she had retained unity and freedom as key to its spirit, arguing that the paganism of the classical world affected the Roman Catholic Church, bringing about the rational disintegration, which led ultimately to the Reformation. In contrast, Russian had never lost "the purity of its inward life."[37] In presenting the Orthodox legacy as a model for social and public life, then, Khomiakov sought to return the educated classes to the native tradition—to bring it to engage in *Bildung* rather than simple learning and to become a national community.

Overall, then, Khomiakov sought to chart an original course for the development of a new Russian nation, formed to realize its own soul. In so doing, he moved beyond the dominant and most limited understanding of Idealism's influence on Russian thought, and beyond an Idealism associated with Hegel to embrace Schelling's idea of knowledge as implicating both nature and mind, united by mythology. He embraces the Romantic's condemnation of the French Revolution and the Enlightenment's sole focus on reason, reductionism and individualism.

Khomiakov also recognized how Schelling's examination of Kantian dualism demand that students and philosophers of German Idealism reassess the notion of Idealism itself, which he himself exercises as internal critique. As he saw it, the Romantics believed in a pluralistic notion of history, where individual and national self-realization was attained only through societal interaction. For Russia, he would have to take up an art mobilizing mythology as the source of inspiration for projecting the political ideal as part of a new national community. For Schelling, this process of aesthetic education, grounded in freedom, reconciled human nature with the larger creation of nature, thereby unifying logic, belief and ethics as conjoint accesses to a deeper, more resilient form of national knowledge and identity. Most importantly, this move toward a new freedom of knowledge through aesthetic education was inherently political, which for Romantics implicated peoples in the *ethnic* sense as a national community, rather than as a state (machine). Consequently, each nation has its own spirit, its own cultural movement and importance—a continuous history that must be taken up as such if it is to grow.

When Russian historians, philologists, and theologians like Khomiakov began to examine their own region of highly distinct, pre-industrial, often non-literate peoples, cultural perspectives, and new nationalism naturally emerged—an image of the Russian people as a nation requiring a new

36. Gleason, *European and Muscovite*, 159.

37. Engelstein, *Slavophile Empire*, 112.

state form. Suffice it to say in summary: the "real world" applicability of these Romantic concepts to Russian culture was of utmost importance for Khomiakov. The result was his idea of a new quasi-religious national community, characterized as *sobornost'*, a communal spiritual existence gleaned from Russian Orthodoxy—the faith-based community that once historically surrounded the church—updated using tools drawn from Schelling.

Today's scholars generally agree that Khomiakov offers *sobornost'* as a guide to counter the fragmentation of European individualism that Imperial Russia had absorbed. Yet they overlook how he is drawing a new national paradigm for Russia, encompassing tradition, unity, education, and myth— the key factors in Schelling's own internal critique of the Idealism that in the West culminated with Hegel. It is thus critical that we understand how Schelling's *Naturphilosophie* reverberates in Khomiakov's *sobornost'* to demand a state of wholeness for society, combined with the personal independence and the individual diversity of the citizens. A state, which is possible only on the condition of a free subordination of separate persons to absolute values and in their free creativeness, founded on love of the whole, love of the Church, love of their nation and state. In his way, Khomiakov also sketches the new Russian nation by adapting, rethinking, and reworking Schelling's *Naturphilosophie* through the lens of Russian cultural debates around history narratives, literary theory, Orthodox theology, and national politics. He posits the knowledge of a new Russia to rest in stories of faith, ethics, and the exercise of reason rather than in the divine rights of great leaders—a new, revolutionary narrative of Russian history from below.

Bibliography

Beiser, Frederick C. *The Early Political Writings of the German Romantics.* Cambridge, MA: Cambridge University Press, 1996.

———. *The Romantic Imperative: The Concept of Early German Romanticism.* Cambridge, MA: Harvard University Press, 2003.

Edie, James M. "Alexis Khomiakov." In *The Beginnings of Russian Philosophy. The Slavophiles. The Westernizers*, edited by James M. Edie, et al., 216–17. Vol. 1 of *Russian Philosophy.* Chicago: Quadrangle, 1965.

Engelstein, Laura. *Slavophile Empire: Imperial Russia's iberal Path.* Ithaca: Cornell University Press, 2009.

Gleason, Abbott. *European and Muscovite.* Cambridge, Massachusetts: Harvard University Press, 1972.

Kant, Immanuel. *Was Ist Aufklärung?* Göttingen: Hubert, 1975.

Khomiakov, Alexei S. "On the 'Fragments' Discovered among I. V. Kireevsky's Papers." In *On Spiritual Unity: A Slavophile Reader*, edited by Robert Bird and Boris Jakim, 295–313. Translated by Robert Bird. Hudson, NY: Lindisfarne, 1998.

Khomiakov, Alexei S. "Mnenie Russkikh ob inostrantsakh." In *Polnoe sobranie sochineniy Alekseya Stepanovicha Khomiakova*, by Alexei S. Khomiakov, 31–69. Vol. 1. Moscow: Universitetskaya tipografiya, 1900.

———. "O vozmozhnosti russkoy khudozhestvennoy shkoly." In *Polnoe sobranie sochineniy Alekseya Stepanovicha Khomiakova*, by Alexei S. Khomiakov, 73–101. Vol. 1. Moscow: Universitetskaya tipografiya, 1900.

———. "On Recent Developments in Philosophy: Letter to Y. F. Samarin." In *The Beginnings of Russian Philosophy. The Slavophiles. The Westernizers*, edited by James M. Edie, et al., 221–69. Vol. 1 of *Russian Philosophy*. Translated by Vladimir D. Pastuhov and Mary-Barbara Zeldin. Chicago: Quadrangle, 1965.

Schelling, Friedrich Wilhelm Joseph. "Abhandlungen, Recenzionen aus bem Kritisches Journal der Philosophie." In *Sämmtliche Werke*, by Friedrich Wilhelm Joseph Schelling, 1–343. Stuttgart: Cotta, 1859.

———. "Philosophie der Kunst." In *Sämmtliche Werke*, by Friedrich Wilhelm Joseph Schelling, 353–736. Stuttgart: Cotta, 1859.

———. "Vorlesungen über die Methode des akademischen Studiums." In *Sämmtliche Werke*, by Friedrich Wilhelm Joseph Schelling, 207–343. Stuttgart: Cotta, 1859.

Terras, Victor. *A History of Russian Literature*. New Haven: Yale University Press, 1991.

Walicki, Andrzej. *The Slavophile Controversy: History of a Conservative Utopia in Nineteenth-Century Russian Thought*. Translated by Hilda Andrews-Rusiecka. Oxford: Clarendon, 1975.

9

Alexei Khomiakov and Sergey Uvarov

"Official Nationality" or Nationality?[1]

DMITRII BADALIAN

It would no exaggeration to say that the entire epoch of the Slavophiles passed in disputes over nationality (*narodnost'*). To some extent drawing it to its conclusion in 1873, Ivan Aksakov said about nationality that "around this term, as around a center, all struggle was grouped and swords were fiercely crossed for nearly twenty years."[2]

The debate over the nationality of literature initially broke out in the mid-1820s, i.e., literally before the eyes of a very young Alexei Khomiakov. As early as in 1834, Vissarion Belinsky asserted: "*nationality* is the alpha and omega of the new period . . . now every literary clown claims the title of a *national* writer."[3] Yet, the real time of the disputes over nationality was the 1840s and 1850s, when the Slavophiles entered into the debate. Their merit, and specifically Khomiakov's, is that they saw in nationality not only an object of cognition, and not even a complex of imagery, but a form of consciousness and perception of the world. Hence the expression the "Russian outlook."

---

1. The publication was prepared with the assistance of the Russian Federal Property Fund, Project No. 17-04-00170a.

2. Aksakov, "Pis'mo," 582.

3. Belinskiy, "Literaturnye mechtaniya," 91. For the evolution of this notion, see Badalyan, "Ponyatiye 'narodnost'," 108–22.

I

The notion of "nationality" initially appeared, as Mark Azadovsky[4] has noted, thanks to Prince Peter Vyazemsky. Before that, at the very beginning of the nineteenth century, this word often meant the popularity of a literary work.[5] But in 1819, in his letter to Alexander Turgenev, Vyazemsky, through the example of his poem, in which he saw "a Russian color," began to talk "about an imprint . . . about an accent . . . about a nationality of certain indigenous manners" and exclaimed at once:

> Why cannot we translate *nationalité* as *narodnost*? After all, the Poles did say *narodowość*.[6]

Five years later, this word appeared in Vyazemsky's public speech. And it was just in "The Manifest of Russian Romanticism," as he termed his article-dialogue "Instead of the Preface" in the first edition of "The Fountain of Bakhchisaray" by Alexander Pushkin. Here, Vyazemsky put into the mouth of the perplexed Classic these words:

> What is nationality in literature? There is no such figure in Aristotle's poetics or in Horace's poetics.[7]

To this, the Editor, the author's *alter ego*, answered that "it is not in the rules, but in the feelings." And at once, he emphasized "the imprint of nationality, locality"[8] as an unquestionable criteria of a piece of art. In the same year, Vyazemsky explained on the pages of *Damskiy Zhurnal*: "Every literate person knows that the word *natsionalny* does not exist in our language: that the word *narodny* corresponds to the two French words: *populaire* and *national*; that we say *pesni narodnye* (folk songs) and *dukh narodny* (national spirit) where the French would say: *chanson populaire* and *esprit national*."[9]

It is still unclear how and under what circumstances in the following years the notion of "nationality" appeared and formed in the usage of the young Khomiakov. It is perhaps unsurprising as the whole genesis of his outlook is very hard to analyze. It is notable that the archpriest George Florovsky wrote: "One gets the impression that Khomiakov did not 'become,'

---

4. Azadovskiy, *Istoriya russkoy fol'kloristiki*, 1:191–92.

5. Bogdanov, *O krokodilakh v Rossii*, 130–32.

6. Vyazemsky to Alexander Turgenev, November 22, 1819 (Saitov, *Ostaf'evskiy*, 357).

7. Vyazemskiy, "Vmesto predisloviya," 49.

8. Vyazemskiy, "Vmesto predisloviya," 49.

9. Vyazemskiy, "Razbor 'Vtorogo razgovora,'" 76–77.

but was 'born.'[10] Nonetheless, we will try to note some traits in the biography of the young Khomiakov which demonstrate his adoption of the notion of "nationality."

When talking about the education of Khomiakov, we should take into account the alignment of the forces in the literary and social struggle of the time. The traditional opposition between Moscow and St. Petersburg had a parallel rivalry in terms of two literary circles. After the Patriotic War of 1812, advocates of original culture, the *shishkovisty*, were concentrated in the Northern capital, while those oriented towards European cultural priorities, the *karamzinisty*, had their center in Moscow. Just at that time, in 1815, Khomiakov and his brother were brought from Moscow to St. Petersburg and met their literature teacher Andrey Zhandr, then a novice writer from the circle of Aleksandr Shakhovskoy, Pavel Katenin, and Aleksandr Griboyedov, who, to varying extents, were close to the literary society "Colloquy of Lovers of the Russian Word" (*Beseda Lyubiteley Russkogo Slova*).

When the family returned to Moscow, the university professor Aleksey Merzlyakov became their home tutor. As far back as about fifteen years before that, he showed an enduring interest in the issues of national identity and nationality.[11] Merzlyakov, starting with the activities in the Friendly Literary Society (*Druzheskoe literaturnoe obshchestvo*, 1801–1803), dealt actively with the problem of nationality. Among the aspects that were developed by him, we can mention the following: the question of depicting a nation in literature, which was solved, in particular, in translations from ancient authors through the image of an idealized nation; the study of folklore, rites, and customs as the sources of aesthetic and ethic basics; the aspiration to create an original national culture on the basis of national literature; and the attempt to express national character in literature.

Though Merzlyakov still had somewhat primitive, elementary ideas of nationality, they formed the soil from which, in twenty to thirty years, other, more clear and accurate ideas would shoot.

It is important to emphasize that it was in the *Works of Society of Lovers of the Russian Literature* edited by Merzlyakov (in only the nineteen volume, with its "The Letter from Siberia" of 1821, where the theme of nationality was clearly heard), that the young Khomiakov's first publication appeared. It is a fragment from the translation of *Germania* by Tacitus made by him at the age of fifteen and with an introductory note to it. The published fragment is saturated with ethnographic observations, and, in the note,

10. Florovsky, *Ways of Russian Theology*, 39.
11. See Kosyakova, *A. F. Merzlyakov*.

Khomiakov emphasized that the speech of Tacitus's characters corresponds to the national types which they represent.

The aspects of nationality typical of Merzlyakov were developed in Khomiakov's further works. His first known works where if not the notion of "nationality" itself is found, then certain aspects of the theme of nationality are defined, is a short article of 1838—"About Collecting Folk Songs and Poems" and the well-known article "About the Old and New" written in 1838–1839, and then the problem of nationality constantly develops, starting from the article of 1842—"About Rural Conditions."

What came before, in the first half of the 1830s? If not the answer to this question then at least a hint is contained in an article which came out in 1832—"The Moscow Scene," in Nikolai Nadezhdin's newspaper *Molva*. In 2002, the author of this article, based on a number of arguments, offered to attribute its authorship to Khomiakov.[12] This article is a dialogue about the production of Aleksey Verstovsky's opera "Vadim." In the center of its attention is a debate about the "nationality" of this opera (and exactly the same way, fifteen years later, a similar debate would be the main theme in another dialogue, "A Conversation in Podmoskovnaya"). Although we should note that the term "nationality" is not found here (and the author does not so much as praise "Vadim" for the nationality manifested in it, as refute the arguments of its weak critics and laugh at their inconsistency). Let us emphasize once again: the main character of "The Moscow Scene" is possibly an *alter ego* of the author (as well as the character of "A Conversation in Podmoskovnaya").

II

The first half of the 1830s became the time of the formation of the well-known formula "Orthodoxy. Autocracy. Nationality." It was originally presented publicly in 1834 in the first issue of the *Magazine of the Ministry of National Education*, published at the initiative of Sergey Uvarov (1786–1855).[13] The earliest mentions occur only in Uvarov's documents dated to 1832 and addressed personally to Emperor Nicholas I.[14] However, forty years later, this formula of Uvarov's was presented as the quintessence of "The Theory of Official Nationality."

12. Badalyan, "Dva neizvestnykh proizvedeniya," 346–48.

13. "Ministerskiye rasporyazheniya," L. In the same issue, Peter Pletnev's speech "O narodnosti v literature" was published.

14. Zorin, *Kormya dvuglavogo orla*, 343.

As it is well known, the expression "The Theory of Official Nationality" was originally introduced for scientific use in 1872 by Aleksandr Pypin, who for the sake of discrediting "Official Nationality" began to connect it not only with Mikhail Pogodin's and Stepan Shevyrev's activities, but also with Fadey Bulgarin, Nikolay Gretsch and Osip Senkovsky, who were almost universally disliked.[15] Although Pypin did not dare to equate Khomiakov's environment with the "official" ideology, some Soviet historians took the plunge on the way to it. Thus, in 1951, Aleksandr Dementyev stated: "Differences between Slavophilism and official nationality are not essential."[16]

However, since 1989, starting from Nikolai Kazakov's article "About one ideological formula of the epoch of Nicholas I," and thanks to the efforts of several researchers,[17] it was shown that "The Theory of Official Nationality" is a myth which was disseminated by liberal scientists and journalists in their struggle against figures of the traditionalist movement.

In fact, "Official Nationality" not only was not publicly presented by its "creator," the Minister of National Education, Uvarov, as an integrated extended concept (when exposing it Pypin did not quote any of its points), but became a subject of hidden struggle between state departments. This struggle went on in education,[18] literature and journalism. Uvarov, who put forward the slogan "Orthodoxy. Autocracy. Nationality," had to engage in a confrontation with the government "liberalism" and interdenominational mysticism, which he pointed to when addressing the emperor in the report "The Decade of the Ministry of National Education. 1833–43."[19] These forces persistently opposed the development of an original national culture.

15. Pypin, *Kharakteristiki*, 93–140.

16. Dement'ev, *Ocherki po istorii*, 354.

17. Kazakov, "Ob odnoy," 5–41; Koshelev, "Slavyanofily," 122–35; Shevchenko, "Ponyatie 'teoriya ofitsial'noy narodnosti,'" 89–104; Kaplin, "Glavnye nachala," 248–55. For brief review of the historiography, see Shevchenko, "Ofitsial'noy narodnosti teoriya," 713–14.

18. Shevchenko, *Konets odnogo velichiya*, 67–77, 97–119.

19. "Naturally, the direction given by Your Majesty to the ministry and its triple formula had to set against it to some extent everything that carried still an imprint of *liberal* and *mystical* ideas. . . . Finally, the word *narodnost'* (nationality) excited in ill-wishers an unfriendly feeling for a courageous statement that the ministry considered Russia mature and worthy to go not behind but at least *alongside* other European nationalities." (Uvarov, "Desyatiletie Ministerstva," 419–20). On the struggle against Uvarov's ideas in the government, see Proskurin, *Literaturnye*, 334–37; Shevchenko, *Konets odnogo velichiya*, 40–41, 93.

III

The main opponent of Uvarov and his "nationality" was the so-called "German Party." Besides cultural and ideological aspects, this conflict also had a political aspect. The development of a national consciousness threatened "Russian foreigners" (such as Count Yegor Kankrin, Count Peter Kleinmichel, Count Ivan Diebitsch or Count Karl Nesselrode) not only with the loss of key positions as the heads of a number of ministries and departments, but also with a blow to a noticeable part of bureaucracy and the unchallenged power of German barons in the Baltic provinces. Therefore, the court upper circle of the "German Party" started a hidden struggle against Uvarov's ideas and aspirations. Explaining the motives of this struggle, Oleg Proskurin writes:

> The "German Party" looked at Russia approximately the same way as European German courts looked at the Slavic population subordinated to them—as a dangerous and hostile "barbaric" force whose movement should be constrained constantly by the cruelest measures. This is the reason for excessive suspiciousness in relation to any manifestations of Russian nationalism, whatever social or political overtones it had.[20]

Besides Proskurin, the collisions with the "German Party" were studied by Svetlana Berezkina in the second half of the 1820s and the first half of the 1830s;[21] Vladimir Shulgin[22] tackled the decades from Nikolay Karamzin to Fyodor Tyutchev and Yuri Samarin;[23] and Aleksandr Shirinyants dealt with the period from the 1840s to the 1880s. Finally, the struggle against it through the nineteenth and twentieth centuries and the very "party" as a peculiar ethno-class was presented by Sergey Sergeyev.[24] However, the latter considers that the "literary process in Imperial Russia (except for administrative measures from above) did not become a field for Russian-German conflicts."[25] On the contrary, Proskurin pointed to uncompromising struggle which the "German Party" launched on pages of Russian literary magazines. Let us note that the "German Party" acted in this struggle rather not as an ethnic group but as an association of figures of the anti-national trend. Certainly, a core of the entire "party" consisted of Baltic Germans

20. Proskurin, *Literaturnye*, 318.

21. Beryozkina, "'Nemtsy' protiv 'Evropeytsa,'" 201–13.

22. Shul'gin, *Russkie svobodnye konservatory*.

23. Shirinyants, "'Vnutrennyaya' rusofobiya," 35–47.

24. Sergeyev, "'Khozyayeva' protiv 'nayemnikov,'" 38–78.

25. Sergeyev, "'Khozyayeva' protiv 'nayemnikov,'" 63.

(and its informal leader till 1828 was Princess Sharlotte Liven, mother of the Minister of National Education, Prince Karl Liven and mother-in-law of Count Aleksandr Benckendorff). However, their interests were shared, for example, by the Poles Fadey Bulgarin and Osip Senkovsky, by the pupil of a Jesuit boarding school and student of the University of Göttingen, Prince Aleksandr Suvorov, and, in the second half of the century, by Peter Valuyev, Aleksandr Timashev and Count Peter Shuvalov. By the way, the latter two, as well as Count Benckendorff, were heads of the Third Department. It is this establishment, which skillfully intimidated Nicholas I with the perceived threat coming from the "Russian Party," that was called a kind of headquarters of the "German Party" by Proskurin.[26]

The "German Party" saw the greatest danger for itself and the sovereign power in Russian nobility and, especially, in nobility by birth. To convince Nicholas I of it was not difficult because representatives of the best noble families were engaged in the plot of 1825.

If to declare "Official Nationality" as a complete theory accepted by the government for execution were an exaggeration, then it would be quite appropriate to speak about an attempt of the Minister of National Education to present "nationality" as a slogan of the development of original national culture. Also, it is impossible to deny the fact that the minister, at least in summary form, managed to express his credo in the well-known "Uvarov's triad." His opponents, on the contrary, not only tried to create an alternative theory in any way, but also an alternative to "Uvarov's formula." Slogans were necessary for the public sphere. Other means were necessary for the activities of the group rallied by caste interests. Nevertheless, the "German Party" showed that even by addressing masses and operating public opinion, it was possible to make do without slogans.

IV

The chief of the Third Department, Benckendorff, understood that one of the most important instruments for influencing society were periodicals. The "German Party" used for its own purposes Bulgarin's newspaper *Severnaya Pchela* and the magazines: *Gretsch's Syn Otechestva*, *Biblioteka dlya Chteniya* (under the editorship of Senkovsky) and Nikolai Polevoy's *Moskovsky Telegraf*. We should add to them Aleksandr Krayevsky's periodicals: *Literaturnye Pribavleniya k Russkomy Invalidu* and *Otechestvennye Zapiski*. Benckendorff, patronizing them, treated Polevoy's "yakobinizm" and Bulgarin's "democratism" with some measure of indulgence. Both of them

---

26. Proskurin, *Literaturnye*, 318.

preached "bourgeois-democratic ideas of the equality of estates, predicting an imminent full degradation of the nobility." Their opponents were "literary aristocrats," who identified themselves with the socio-political interests of "the ancient nobility."[27]

Prince Vladimir Odoyevsky described the situation which developed in journalism between 1836 and 1837 in the following way:

> To hint about the monopoly of *Severnaya Pchela* over political news and a daily appearance was considered as the most reprehensible business. At this time, *Biblioteka Dlya Chteniya*, *Syn Otechestva* and *Severnaya Pchela*, fraternally united, kept everything that did not pander to them in blockade and flagellated mercilessly any periodical daring not to belong to this phalanx. ... In general, the struggle was unequal because then it was considered as the order of the day to suspect the opponent of malevolence, freethinking and other such things.[28]

Uvarov was the only opponent of the "German Party" who concentrated an important "party" resource around himself—a number of periodicals which had different readership audiences. Yet, it is necessary to understand that the struggle between Uvarov and Benckendorff was not total. Nicholas I would not tolerate constant open hostility between the persons in attendance. And sometimes, "friendly" magazines and newspapers *were also reproved* since censorship was a direct business of the minister of national education.

Among the editions patronized by Uvarov were: Nikolai Nadezhdin's magazine *Teleskop* and the supplement to it, the *Molva* newspaper; Mikhail Pogodin and Stepan Shevyrev's magazine *Moskvityanin*; and *Sankt-Peterburgskiye Vedomosti*, the newspaper of the Academy of Sciences. Possibly, handing in 1846 the *Sovremennik* magazine over to Nikolay Nekrasov and the censor Aleksandr Nikitenko, Uvarov expected that it would serve as a counter-measure against *Otechestvennye Zapiski*.[29]

The Magazine of the Ministry of National Education became the first periodical under the direct control of Uvarov. He began to think about establishing it no later than the fall of 1832 when he, being the deputy minister, invited Khomiakov, as the father of the latter recounted, "to be his secretary, not for office work, but to issue the Magazine of the Ministry of

27. For details, see Proskurin, *Literaturnye*, 315–34.

28. Bychkov, "Bumagi knyazya," 47.

29. For more details on the participation of periodicals in this struggle, see Badalyan, "'Nemetskaya partiya.'"

Public Education."[30] And, in its first issue, as it was noted before, the well-known "Uvarov's formula" publicly appeared for the first time, while ideas of nationality were interpreted on the pages of the magazine by Pletnev, Pogodin, Shevyrev, and others.

V

Uvarov was an old acquaintance of the Khomiakovs family, and Alexei Stepanovich Khomiakov probably had an opportunity to share with him his vision of the fundamentals of national ideology. And the minister-to-be could use them and definitely appreciated the similarity of beliefs of his interlocutor. However, Uvarov started to issue the magazine only from 1834, after he had become the minister in charge, and without Khomiakov.[31]

Nevertheless, the fact he had invited Khomiakov is important as an indirect confirmation of the words of his first biographer Peter Bartenev that the founder of Slavophilism and the ideologist of "Official Nationality" were united by similar beliefs right from the very beginning. Publishing in 1863, Khomiakov's poem to which Bartenev gave his own title "A Conversation with Uvarov," he, referring to the minister, noticed: "Perhaps, the conversation with Khomiakov gave him an idea or reinforced his intention to expand the sphere of activities of the Archeological Commission and to establish at Russian universities departments of Slavic languages."[32] Five years later, Bartenev said that "the great symbol," i.e., the slogan "Orthodoxy. Autocracy. Nationality" would take root in Uvarov's mind "owing to conversations with A. S. Khomiakov."[33]

Referring to Bartenev, it is worth emphasizing his awareness. In 1860, he said about Khomiakov: "Over the last eleven years I was lucky enough to see him often; I lived in his house for one year, and, because of my passion for the legends of our old times, I quite often asked him about the past."[34] Even if Bartenev exaggerated Khomiakov's influence on Uvarov, the fact is that, in the late 1830s, he had high hopes for Alexei Stepanovich and cared for his reputation in the eyes of the emperor. Thus, in September, 1839, presenting to Nicholas I the then-unpublished poem "Kiev" by Khomiakov, the minister recommended the author in such words: "Our famous poet Khomiakov who, as it seems to me, is the one who could follow in the footsteps of Pushkin if

30. Mazur, "K ranney biografii," 222, 211.

31. On possible reasons for this, see Badalyan, "Zhurnal'naya bor'ba," 178–88.

32. Bartenev, "Neizdannye stikhi A. S. Khomiakova," 304.

33. Bartenev in Sverbeyev, "Vospominaniya," 989.

34. Bartenev, "Vospominaniya ob A. S. Khomiakove," 452.

he was constantly engaged in the art."[35] Speaking about the poem "Eagle," Uvarov, addressing Nicholas I, emphasized: "In which Khomiakov praised the unity of all Slavic peoples under Russia's banner."[36] In other words, the minister noted the dream of it as a value and expected a similar attitude from Nicholas I. Possibly, at that time, the authorities still treated statements about a future Slavic unity tolerantly.

Later, at the beginning of January 1841, submitting the first issue of *Moskvityanin* to the emperor, Uvarov also drew his attention to Khomiakov's poems.[37] However, at the same time, the overseer of the Kiev educational district, Prince Sergey Davydov, asked for permission to publish Khomiakov's poem "Kiev," where the hope for the reunion with dwellers of Galich and Volhynia (who were the subjects of the Austrian empire) was manifest. Uvarov avoided presenting the poem to Nicholas I as best he could and played for time. He very much did not want to start again a conversation with the emperor on Khomiakov's "Kiev" less than one and a half years later. As before, he supported Khomiakov, but Khomiakov's ideas of the Slavs no longer seemed a suitable subject for a reminder to Nicholas I.

By that time, at first outside and then inside Russia, another myth, "Pan-Slavism," by which the Russian monarch was skillfully intimidated, was adopted. At the very beginning of the 1840s, the German and Hungarian nationalist propaganda put forward the concept of "Pan-Slavism" as a means of compromising the national movements of Slavic peoples, i.e., this term appeared even before the aspiration of Slavs to a unity (rather cultural, than political) reached any serious forms.[38]

The following year of 1842 became the first year of the publicist activities of the Slavophiles and soon, thanks to Belinsky, the nickname "Slavophiles" was branded by the critic on Khomiakov's environment, Pogodin, Shevyrev and scientists close to the St. Petersburg *Mayak* magazine, such as Nikolay Savelyev-Rostislavich and Ivan Sakharov, and started to appear in the press.[39] The years 1842–1848 became the time of publicist activities on the part of Khomiakov as well. However, it is since 1842 that we know no instance when Uvarov tried to present his works to the emperor. The Slavophiles increasingly made themselves and their ideas known, but neither they, nor Uvarov, demonstrated the similarity of views any more. Moreover, the Slavophiles

35. Barsukov, "Zametka ob A. S. Khomiakove," 159.

36. Barsukov, "Zametka ob A. S. Khomiakove," 159.

37. Barsukov, *Zhizn' i trudy N. P. Pogodina*, 6:22.

38. Volkov, "O proiskhozhdenii terminov," 47, 68–69; Myrikova and Shirinyants, "Rusofobskiy mif 'panslavizma,'" 240–44. On the stance that was taken by Uvarov in the 1840s towards Slavs, see Udalov, "Teoriya ofitsial'noy narodnosti," 83.

39. Tsimbayev, *Slavyanofil'stvo*, 31–34.

were often separated from Pogodin who was favored by the minister. Thus, in May, 1848, Khomiakov wrote about the latter to Yuri Samarin: "To regard him as an ally is impossible; he it is too spineless for this, but we have to use him for general benefit, when he accidentally strives for good."[40] Khomiakov avoided the struggle between the party of "Official Nationality" and the "German Party," perhaps more so than other Slavophiles. He did not seek to be and was never under Uvarov's protection.

VI

At the same time, i.e., in the 1840s and 1850s, Khomiakov and the other Slavophiles developed their own concept of nationality which went beyond Uvarov's concept. Their merits in this matter were sometimes recognized by their opponents as well. Thus, the Westerner Vasiliy Botkin in 1847 wrote to Pavel Annenkov:

> Slavophiles uttered one true word: *narodnost, natsionalnost.*
> That is a great merit of theirs. . . . They were the first to indicate
> the need for national development.[41]

In Slavophiles' interpretations, nationality is both an object of cognition (people's everyday life, folklore) and a form of consciousness (a complex of imagery, perception of the world). At the same time, Slavophiles emphasized that Russian nationality is indissolubly connected to the Orthodox Faith. Khomiakov approached nationality not only as a literary criterion, but also as a criterion of art in general. He regarded Mikhail Glinka's music and Aleksandr Ivanov's painting just from this prospective. Finally, in the 1850s, Khomiakov and Slavophiles asserted nationality—just as the form of consciousness—in science. At first, it caused persistent objections.

In 1856, when Slavophiles started the edition of the *Russkaya Beseda* magazine and declared in its program that the task of the magazine is "to promote within our powers the development of the Russian view on sciences and arts,"[42] Moscow and St. Petersburg Westerners initiated a discussion with them. As a result, the dispute on the nationality of science became the brightest and noisiest polemic of the year. Yuri Samarin, Konstantin Aksakov, and Nikita Gilyarov-Platonov participated in it on the part of Slavophiles. Thus Samarin, in response to objections of the *Moskovskiye Vedomosti* newspaper that "sciences and arts allow for only one

40. Khomiakov, "Letter to Yuriy Samarin," 271.
41. Botkin, "Letter to Pavel Annenkov," 271.
42. "Ob izdanii novogo zhurnala," 1.

view—enlightened, and, therefore, universal,"[43] explained that the notion of "nationality" implies not only a subject of study, but also "a property of a comprehending thought," an originality of the outlook on the world which is capable of manifesting itself and manifests itself in the development of sciences "studying man, not nature."[44]

Khomiakov joined in this discussion too. In the philosophical dialogue "A Conversation in Podmoskovnaya," he put into the mouth of one of its characters the following thought of his opponents:

> Nationality is the restriction to the panhuman, and only the panhuman is valuable. The less it is limited in me, the better.[45]

To this, the other character Tulnev, the author's alter ego, objected:

> Of course. The national origin is only the first tutor of a personal mind, and the question has to be raised as follows: does nationality serves as a helper or becomes a hindrance for an individual who perceives the panhuman?[46]

And he himself answered it:

> All true sciences, except twice two is four (burning is the reaction between a combustible and oxygen and so forth), is transferred to us from other people in forms, images, and expressions determined by those nationalities which these people belong to, and, therefore, each nationality is reflected in us. Precisely the same is with our nationality.[47]

The development of nationality, our own original consciousness, is not an impoverishment or a restriction at all, explained Khomiakov. The absence of one's own nationality, according to him, is replaced "not with the panhuman principle, but with the multinationality of Babylon, and a human, without having achieved the impossible honor to be a human unconditionally, becomes only a foreigner in general, and not only in the attitude towards his nation, but also in the attitude towards any other nation or even towards himself."[48]

Continuing this reasoning, Khomiakov began to talk about the possibility (with the reservation "partly") of nationality, i.e., a national outlook in

43. "Literaturnye i drugiye novosti," 106.

44. Samarin, "Dva slova o narodnosti v nauke," 200, 202.

45. Khomiakov, "Razgovor v Podmoskovnoy," 263.

46. Khomiakov, "Razgovor v Podmoskovnoy," 266.

47. Khomiakov, "Razgovor v Podmoskovnoy," 266–67.

48. Khomiakov, "Razgovor v Podmoskovnoy," 268.

exact sciences, be it physics or chemistry, providing as examples the theory of waves of the Swiss Leonhard Euler and the theory of atoms of the Englishman John Dalton.[49] Nobody ventured such statements then, even his friends the Slavophiles (later, in 1869, an extended reasoning on opportunities and features of the Russian national science were offered by Nikolay Danilevsky[50]). However, the twentieth century presented confirmations of it. Let us give only two examples. In 1926–1927, the Eurasianist Peter Savitsky noted the manifestation of a special Russian national tradition in the development of geography (including soil science and forestry) and vice versa—almost the complete borrowing of a tradition in political economy.[51] And, finally, modern historians of science, the American Loren Graham and the Frenchman Jean-Michele Kantor, showed the role of national consciousness in the sphere of exact sciences. In the book *Naming Infinity*,[52] they described how the Russian mathematicians Dmitry Yegorov and Nikolai Luzin, relying on the experience of onomatodoxy (i.e., the mystical and theological doctrine which developed especially just in Russia), discovered the descriptive theory of sets.

However, let us return to 1856, when Khomiakov in his work "A Conversation in Podmoskovnaya" asserted: "Serving nationality is supremely serving the panhuman cause," and, at the same time, "the more a human becomes the servant of the human truth, the dearer is his nation to him."[53] In others words, unlike many contemporaries, he did not oppose the national to the panhuman, and, on the contrary, he declared their antinomic link. And in that, he anticipated Fyodor Dostoevsky's ideas stated in his famous "Pushkin Speech" (yet, it is known that the latter read Khomiakov a lot and with attention).

Let us recall here that in this speech, speaking about Pushkin's "world responsiveness," i.e., about the ability to comprehend and be able to express feelings and experiences of other people, Dostoevsky presented "the nationality in its further development, the nationality of our future, which is already concealed in the present." And "the power of the spirit of the Russian nationality," according to him, lies in "its aspiration (in its ultimate goals) to universality and panhumanism."[54] Summing up his thoughts, Dostoevsky

49. Khomiakov, "Razgovor v Podmoskovnoy," 270.

50. Danilevskiy, *Rossiya i Evropa*, 154–88.

51. Savitskiy, "Ob ekonomicheskoy doktrine," 248–50; "Geograficheskiy obzor Rossii-Evrazii," 272–74.

52. Graham and Kantor, *Naming Infinity*.

53. Khomiakov, *O starom i novom*, 275.

54. Dostoevsky, "Pushkin (Ocherk)," 147.

proclaimed that to become a Russian means "to become a brother of all people, *a universal man.*"[55] It is obvious that such an aspiration to the universal, panhuman unity was tantamount to Khomiakov's *sobornost'*.

Following Khomiakov, Dostoevsky pointed to the indissoluble connection of nationality and the religious feelings feeding it. "He who denies nationality denies faith as well—he emphasized in one of the letters in December, 1880—We have it so because our nationality is based on Christianity."[56]

VII

As for Uvarov it is characteristic that representing the elements of his famous triad, he long spoke very vaguely on "nationality," and it was impossible to understand from his words what content he put in this term. Thus, in 1843, asserting that "the issue of nationality has no unity as the previous ones" (i.e., as "Autocracy" and "Orthodoxy"). Uvarov wrote:

> Regarding nationality, all difficulty was in the agreement of ancient and new notions; but nationality does not force to go back or to stop; it does not demand *immovability* in the ideas. The state structure, like a human body, changes its exterior in process of age: lines change in the course of time, but the physiognomy must not change. It would be inappropriate to oppose to this periodic course of things; it would be enough if we keep the sanctuary of our national notions inviolable; if we accept them as the main idea of the government, especially in respect to domestic education.[57]

In other words, ten years after the minister had uttered the motto "Nationality" for the first time, he had no clear vision what it really was. Uvarov expressed somewhat clearer ideas shortly before the finale of his career, in the circular letter to the overseer of the Moscow educational district as of May 27, 1847. Here he called nationality "a source of national education which should be the guidance when directing the minds of studying youth" and placed it on a par with "the faith of our fathers, language, mores, and

---

55. Dostoevsky, "Pushkin (Ocherk)," 147.

56. Dostoevsky, "Letter to Aleksandr Blagonravov," 236. For more details on Dostoevsky's continuing the ideas of Khomiakov and other Slavophiles, see Badalyan, "A. S. Khomiakov i F. M. Dostoevskiy," 108–11; Badalyan, "Prototipy," 363–71; Gacheva, *Nam ne dano predugadat'*, 460–85.

57. Uvarov, "Desyatiletie Ministerstva," 348.

customs" which are kept by the people.[58] And we might say that in this letter, at least partly, the ideas of Slavophiles had some influence on Uvarov.
However, at the same time, the minister, reacting to the political situation,
scrupulously renounced any solidarity with Slavs.[59]

By this time, Uvarov's reputation in the eyes of the emperor gradually
deteriorated. The Third Department in the annual report of 1843 not only
criticized the minister's activities, but, also, for the first time, openly doubted
the effectiveness of "Uvarov's formula," challenging the progress in educating
the youth "in the spirit of Orthodoxy, Autocracy and Nationality."[60]

Conflict at court made Uvarov more careful, and, out of self-preser-
vation, he was tough on *Moskvityanin* and Slavophiles once again. In the
1840s, he did not try to develop the ideas of the "triad" publicly any more.
Finally, from 1848 and the beginning of "the gloomy seven years," the position of the minister turned out to be especially shaky, and having lost
support of the emperor, under the blows of the "German Party" he resigned
in October, 1849.

If it is right that at the very beginning of the 1830s Uvarov was influenced by Khomiakov, we have to recognize that Khomiakov's ideas
(although not quite developed yet) in Uvarov's interpretation lost much,
became shallow, were narrowed and could not apply nationwide. Possibly
anticipating this, Khomiakov considered it right to separate from the minister and the slogan he put forward.

After that, the Slavophiles preferred for decades not to express their
attitude towards Uvarovs's triad in any way. However, when the last of them,
Ivan Aksakov, began to talk about it in 1884, it was in the sense that Uvarov's
expression "for a long time compromised in the Russian public opinion" the
truth it contained, and, as to the third element of the triad, he said:

> The system laid a claim to "nationality" and justified itself by
> "nationality." The facade of the state building patterned after
> Germany had to be embellished by it. On a deeper interpreta-
> tion of this notion, on the fact that under nationality all content
> of national spirit is understood as expressed externally in the
> history, manners and life of the nation as well as identified in its
> artistic creativity, in its beliefs, expectations and aspirations, on
> the fact that this content of national spirit has a full right for free
> development and for a dominant position in the state which is
> built by this spirit and only by this spirit is kept—on all this, of

58. Uvarov, "Tsirkulyarnoye predlozheniye," 500–501.

59. Uvarov, "Tsirkulyarnoye predlozheniye," 499–500; "Doklad imperatoru,"
494–95.

60. *Rossiya pod nadzorom*, 333.

course, none of official and semi-official adherents of nationality did not even dare to expound at that time.... The St. Petersburg state practice, even unconsciously, was instinctively frightened by genuine Russian nationality—as by an element absolutely non-native to it and, therefore, incompatible with it.[61]

A new stage of opposition to the "German Party" began in the second half of the 1860s. Then, in the pages of the press, the issue of Baltic Germans was seriously brought up for the first time, and not by a government official, but by a number of public figures who started talking about the national interests connected with it. First of all, those were Yuri Samarin and Ivan Aksakov, who were supported by Fyodor Tyutchev. They managed to join in this struggle fully equipped and to appeal to public opinion just because a decade before the ideas of nationality had become deeply ingrained in the mind of Russian society.

Translated by Dmitrii Fedotenko

Bibliography

Aksakov, Ivan. "Chto znachit: vyyti nashemu pravitel'stvu na istoricheskiy narodnyy put'?" In *Otchego tak nelegko zhivetsya v Rossii?*, 358–68. Moscow: Rosspen, 2002.

———. "Pis'mo k izdatelyu 'Russkogo arkhiva'. Po povodu stat'i E. Mamonova: 'Slavyanofily.'" In *Izbrannye trudy*, by Konstantin Aksakov and Ivan Aksakov, 580–96. Moscow: Rosspen, 2010.

Azadovskiy, Mark. *Istoriya russkoy fol'kloristiki*. Vol. 1. Moscow: Uchpedgiz, 1958.

Badalyan, Dmitriy. "A. S. Khomiakov i F. M. Dostoevskiy: K istorii razvitiya 'idei narodnosti' v russkoy kul'ture XIX v." *Vestnik Sankt-Peterburgskogo universiteta. Seriya 2. Istoriya, yazykoznanie, literaturovedenie* 4 (1999) 108–11.

———. "A. S. Khomiakov, S. S. Uvarov i zhurnal'naya bor'ba 1830–1840-kh godov." In *Ostrova lyubvi BorFeda: Sbornik v chest' 90-letiya Borisa Fedorovicha Egorova*, edited by Andrey Dmitriyev and Pavel Glushakov, 178–88. St. Petersburg: Rostok, 2016.

———. "Dva neizvestnykh proizvedeniya ranney publitsistiki A. S. Khomiakova." In *Mir romantizma. Materialy mezhdunarodnoy nauchnoy konferentsii "Mir romantizma,"* 6.30 (2002) 340–48.

———. "'Nemetskaya partiya' protiv 'ofitsial'noy narodnosti': Bor'ba v russkoy zhurnalistike 1830–1840-kh gg." In *Literatura i istoriya*, edited by Ol'ga Fetisenko. Vol. 4. St. Petersburg: Pushkinskiy Dom, forthcoming.

———. "Ponyatiye 'narodnost'' v russkoy kul'ture XIX veka." In *Istoricheskie ponyatiya i politicheskie idei v Rossii XVI–XX veka. Sbornik nauchnykh rabot*, edited by Nikolay Koposov, 108–22. St. Petersburg: Izdatel'stvo Evropeyskogo universiteta v Sankt-Peterburge; Aleteyya, 2006.

61. Aksakov, *Chto znachit*, 361–62.

————. "'Prototipy' idei Pushkinskoy rechi F. M. Dostoevskogo v proizvedeniyakh A. S. Khomiakova, I. V. Kireevskogo i I. S. Aksakova." In *Rossiya i mir: vchera, segodnya, zavtra. Nauchnye trudy Moskovskogo gumanitarnogo instituta im. E. R. Dashkovoy*, 363–71. Moscow: Moskovskiy gumanitarnyy institut, 2003.

Barsukov, Nikolay. "Zametka ob A. S. Khomiakove." *Russkiy arkhiv* 9 (1885) 158–60.

————. *Zhizn' i trudy N. P. Pogodina*. Vol. 6. St. Petersburg: Tipografiya M. M. Stasyulevicha, 1892.

Bartenev, Petr [P. B.]. "Neizdannye stikhi A. S. Khomiakova." *Russkiy arkhiv* 4 (1863) 303–4.

————. "Vospominaniya ob A. S. Khomiakove." In *Dar pesnopeniya. O starom i novom. Tserkov' odna. Truzhenni. Sovremenniki o A. S. Khomiakove. Borets za Svyatuyu Rus'*, by Alexei S. Khomiakov, 452–59. Moscow: Russkiy mir, 2007.

Belinskiy, Vissarion. "Literaturnye mechtaniya (Elegiya v proze)." In *Polnoe sobranie sochineniy: V 13 t.*, by Vissarion Belinskiy, 20–104. Vol. 1. Moscow: Izdatel'stvo Akademii nauk SSSR, 1953.

Berezkina, Svetlana. "'Nemtsy' protiv 'Evropeytsa." *Moskva* 3 (2009) 201–13.

Bogdanov, Konstantin. *O krokodilakh v Rossii. Ocherki iz istorii zaimstvovaniy i ekzotizmov*. Moscow: Novoe literaturnoye obozreniye, 2006.

Botkin, Vasiliy. "Letter to Pavel Annenkov, 14 May, 1847." In *Literaturnaya kritika. Publitsistika. Pis'ma*, by Vasiliy Botkin, 270–73. Moscow: Sovetskaya Rossiya, 1984.

Bychkov, Ivan. "Bumagi knyazya V. F. Odoyevskogo." In *Otchet Imperatorskoy Publichnoy biblioteki za 1884 god. Prilozhenie 2-e*, 1–65. St. Petersburg: Tipografiya V. S. Balasheva, 1887.

Danilevskiy, Nikolay. *Rossiya i Evropa. Vzglyad na kul'turnye i politicheskie otnosheniya Slavyanskogo mira k Germano-Romanskomu*. Moscow: Rosspen, 2010.

Dement'ev, Aleksandr. *Ocherki po istorii russkoy zhurnalistiki 1840–1850 gg*. Moscow: Gosudarstvennoe izdatel'stvo khudozhestvennoy literatury, 1951.

Dostoevsky, Fedor. "Letter to Aleksandr Blagonravov, 19 December, 1880." In *Polnoe sobranie sochineniy: V 30 t.*, by Fedor Dostoevsky, 236–37. Vol. 30.1. Leningrad: Nauka, 1988.

————. "Pushkin (Ocherk)." In *Polnoe sobranie sochineniy V 30 t*, by Fedor Dostoevsky, 136–49. Vol. 26. Leningrad: Nauka, 1984.

Florovsky, Georges. *Ways of Russian Theology: Part Two*. Vol. 6 of *Collected Works*. Vaduz: Büchervertriebsanstalt, 1987.

Gacheva, Anastasiya. *"Nam ne dano predugadat', kak slovo nashe otzovetsya": Dostoevskiy i Tyutchev*. Moscow: IMLI RAN, 2004.

Graham, Loren R., and Jean-Michel Kantor. *Naming Infinity. A True Story of Religious Mysticism and Mathematical Creativity*. Cambridge, MA: The Belknap, 2009.

Kaplin, Aleksandr. "Glavnye nachala—'Pravoslavie, Samoderzhavie, Narodnost': istoricheskiy kontekst, interpretatsii, znachenie." In *Rossiyskaya gosudarstvennost' i sovremennost': problemy identichnosti i istoricheskoy preemstvennosti*, edited by M. B. Smolin, 248–55. Moscow: RISI, 2012.

Kazakov, Nikolai. "Ob odnoy ideologicheskoy formule nikolayevskoy epokhi." In *Kontekst-1989: Literaturno-teoreticheskiye issledovaniya*, 5–41. Moscow: Nauka, 1989.

Khomiakov, Alexei S. "Letter to Yuriy Samarin, May 1848." In *Polnoye sobraniye sochineniy*, by Alexei Khomiakov, 270–74. Vol. 8. Moscow: Universitetskaya tipografiya, 1900.

———. "Razgovor v Podmoskovnoy." In *O starom i novom: Stat'i i ocherki*, by Alexei Khomiakov, 252–77. Moscow: Sovremennik, 1988.

Koshelev, Vyacheslav. "Slavyanofily i ofitsial'naya narodnost'." In *Slavyanofil'stvo i sovremennost': sbornik statey*, 122–35. St. Petersburg: Nauka, 1994.

Kosyakova, Svetlana. *A. F. Merzlyakov—issledovatel' literatury i poyet. Avtoreferat dissertatsii na soiskaniye uchenoy stepeni kandidata filologicheskikh nauk.* Tambov: Izdatel'skiy tsentr Tambovskogo gosudarstvennogo universiteta, 1995.

"Literaturnye i drugiye novosti." *Moskovskie vedomosti* 27 (1856) 106.

Mazur, Nataliya. "K ranney biografii A. S. Khomiakova (1810–1820)." In *Lotmanovskiy sbornik*, edited by Evgeniy Permyakov, 195–223. Vol. 2. Moscow: RGGU, 1997.

"Ministerskiye rasporyazheniya (s 21 marta po 1 sentyabrya)." *Zhurnal Ministerstva narodnogo prosveshcheniya* 1 (1834) xlix–lxxx.

Myrikova, Anna, and Aleksandr Shirinyants. "Rusofobskiy mif 'panslavizma.'" In *Aktual'nye problemy sovremennogo rossievedeniya: Sbornik nauchnykh statey*, 240–44. Moscow: Izdatel' Vorob'ev A. V., 2007.

"Ob izdanii novogo zhurnala v 1856 godu pod nazvaniyem 'Russkaya beseda.'" *Moskovskiye vedomosti. Osoboye prilozheniye* 27 (1856) 1–2.

Proskurin, Oleg. *Literaturnye skandaly pushkinskoy epokhi.* Moscow: OGI, 2000.

Pypin, Aleksandr. *Kharakteristiki literaturnykh mneniy ot dvadtsatykh do pyatidesyatykh godov: Istoricheskiye ocherki.* St. Peterburg: Kolos, 1909.

Rossiya pod nadzorom: Otchety III otdeleniya, 1827–1869. Moscow: Rossiyskiy fond kul'tury "Rossiyskiy Arkhiv," 2006.

Saitov, Vladimir I., ed. *Ostaf'evskiy arkhiv knyazey Vyazemskikh.* Vol. 1. Moscow: Vek, 1994.

Samarin, Yuriy. "Dva slova o narodnosti v nauke." In *Sobranie sochineniy: V 5 t*, by Yuriy Samarin, 200–209. Vol. 1. St. Petersburg: Rostok, 2013.

Savitskiy, Petr. "Geograficheskiy obzor Rossii-Evrazii." In *Izbrannoe*, by Petr Savitskiy, 263–78. Moscow: Rosspen, 2010.

———. "K voprosu ob ekonomicheskoy doktrine evraziystva (V poryadke obsuzhdeniya)." In *Izbrannoe*, by Petr Savitskiy, 243–62. Moscow: Rosspen, 2010.

Sergeev, Sergey. "'Khozyaeva' protiv 'naemnikov': russko-nemetskoe protivostoyanie v imperatorskoy Rossii." *Voprosy natsionalizma: Zhurnal nauchnoy i obshchestvenno-politicheskoy mysli* 3 (2010) 38–78.

Shevchenko, Maksim. *Konets odnogo velichiya: Vlast', obrazovaniye i pechatnoye slovo v Imperatorskoy Rossii na poroge Osvoboditel'nykh reform.* Moscow: Tri kvadrata, 2003.

———. "Ofitsial'noy narodnosti teoriya." In *Bol'shaya Rossiyskaya etsiklopediya*, 713–14. Vol. 24. Moscow: Bol'shaya Rossiyskaya entsiklopediya, 2014.

———. "Ponyatie 'teoriya ofitsial'noy narodnosti' i izuchenie vnutrenney politiki imperatora Nikolaya I." *Vestnik Moskovskogo universiteta. Seriya 8. Istoriya* 4 (2002) 89–104.

Shirinyants, Aleksandr. "'Vnutrennyaya' rusofobiya i 'ostzeyskiy vopros' v Rossii XIX v." *Vestnik Rossiyskoy natsii* 2 (2014) 35–47.

Shul'gin, Vladimir. *Russkie svobodnye konservatory XIX veka ob Ostzeyskom voprose.* St. Petersburg: Nestor-Istoriya, 2009.

Sverbeyev, Dmitriy. "Vospominaniya o Petre Yakovleviche Chaadayeve." *Russkiy arkhiv* 6 (1868) 989.

Tsimbaev, Nikolay. *Slavyanofil'stvo: Iz istorii russkoy obshchestvennoy mysli XIX veka.* Moscow: Gosudarstvennaya publichnaya istoricheskaya biblioteka Rossii, 2013.

Udalov, Sergey. "Teoriya ofitsial'noy narodnosti: mekhanizmy vnedreniya." *Osvoboditel'noe dvizheniye v Rossii: Mezhvuzovskiy sbornik nauchnykh trudov* 21 (2006) 77–85.

Uvarov, Sergey. "Desyatiletie Ministerstva narodnogo prosveshcheniya. 1833–1843." In *Izbrannye trudy*, by Sergey Uvarov, 346–455. Moscow: Rosspen, 2010.

———. "Doklad imperatoru Nikolayu I o slavyanstve." In *Izbrannye trudy*, by Sergey Uvarov, 489–96. Moscow: Rosspen, 2010.

———. "Tsirkulyarnoye predlozheniye popechitelyu Moskovskogo uchebnogo okruga." In *Izbrannye trudy*, by Sergey Uvarov, 497–501. Moscow: Rosspen, 2010.

Volkov, Vladimir. "K voprosu o proiskhozhdenii terminov 'pangermanizm' i 'panslavizm.'" In *Slavyano-germanskie kul'turnye svyazi i otnosheniya*, 25–69. Moscow: Nauka, 1969.

Vyazemskiy, Petr. "Razbor 'Vtorogo razgovora', napechatannogo v 7 nomierie 'Vestnika Evropy.'" *Damskiy zhurnal* 8 (1824) 63–82.

———. "Vmesto predisloviya [k 'Bakhchisarayskomu fontanu']. Razgovor mezhdu izdatelem i klassikom s Vyborgskoy storony ili s Vasil'evskogo ostrova." In *Estetika i literaturnaya kritika*, 48–53. Moscow: Iskusstvo, 1984.

Zorin, Andrey. *Kormya dvuglavogo orla. Literatura i gosudarstvennaya ideologiya v Rossii v posledney treti XVIII—pervoy treti XIX veka.* Moscow: Novoe literaturnoe obozrenie, 2004.

PART III

Influences

10

Slavophile Philosophy of History

From Alexei Khomiakov to Vladimir Lamansky[1]

ALEXEI MALINOV

I

In the history of Russian philosophy and culture, Alexei Stepanovich Khomiakov is highly ranked as one of the leaders of the Slavophiles. Khomiakov's uniqueness is more determined by the scale of his own personality, variety of his talents and diversity of his activity than by the significance of his philosophical works. I suppose that, in this regard, in the history of Russian science and culture Khomiakov is merely comparable with Mikhail Lomonosov and Pavel Florensky. At the same time, Khomiakov's creative work is underestimated. His philosophical works are not being reprinted, and the scope of research literature on Khomiakov can hardly be deemed satisfactory. To some degree, Khomiakov himself is responsible for this situation, as far from being timely published, his philosophical works were even left unfinished. Khomiakov only showed and outlined many of his ideas, while they are not fully reflected in his manuscripts. All of that necessitates the need to apply not only traditional historico-philosophical methods (based on a text as a complete range of ideas) in the research of the legacy of the Moscow Slavophile, but also it would be more appropriate to reconstruct those very ideas, guessing the elements of them which are not clearly and directly shown in his texts. One should elicit something more from Khomiakov's texts than they themselves afford the

1. This research was made with the support of the RFBR: "V. I. Lamanskii and Academic Slavophilism in Russia in the last third of the nineteenth century" (No. 16/03/00450).

reader at first glance. Their reconstruction, including the identification of the essential notions and philosophical concepts, intellectual forms and argumentation, with the subsequent assembly of Khomiakov's thoughts and their completion to create an integral philosophical conception, is a more adequate method. Historical, cultural and polemical contexts (especially for Khomiakov) also play a role in this case.

The fact that, in contrast to many other thinkers, it is impossible to approach Khomiakov unpassionately should be referred to the peculiarities of his perception as a philosopher. Khomiakov's thought demands co-thinking and his ideas need empathy and compassion. It is not worth engaging in the study of Khomiakov's creative work without sympathy to his personality and a love for him. In the case of Khomiakov, historico-philosophical research implies co-thinking with him and after him. And this is not accidental, since Slavophilism as a historico-philosophical phenomenon was the first in Russian philosophy to fully expose the archetypical form of philosophizing as free talk, dispute, etc., i.e., an idle pastime of free people. In contrast to the professional (university) philosophers of their time, the Slavophiles worked under the conditions needed for philosophical creativity—freedom of thinking. Slavophile philosophy was best realized in an oral form. It was "thinking aloud" addressed to other people: either a like-minded person or an opponent. It is no coincidence that the only journal the early Slavophiles published for a long time (when the appropriate conditions appeared) was called *Russkaia beseda* ("Russian Conversation"). The philosophical texts by Khomiakov contain the echo of such conversations and disputes, i.e., they understand their addressee not as a simple reader, but as a participant of the discussion who is ready to grasp Khomiakov's idea and continue it as his own. Slavophile thought demands constant reactualization and vivification in the reader's mind. No doubt that from the point of view of history of philosophy, the absence of the complete doctrine and its dogmatic explication is a disadvantage. Nevertheless, Slavophiles could afford to not compete with their thoughts and or give them a systematic form. The incompleteness of the Slavophile doctrine gives the opportunity to actualize it anew, to recommence "old" disputes and offer "new" arguments. The agonal nature of Slavophile thought is also seen in the fact that, as a rule, the Slavophiles only responded to the criticism against them and, for their part, criticized their opponents. The philosophical phrases the Slavophile often used were reactions and responses, i.e., they were a part of polemics and were not the independent explication of their point of view. Moreover, criticism prevailed even amongst the Slavophiles themselves. They were more eager to criticize their adversaries and clearly showed their own views only in the course of controversy.

The incompleteness and non-dogmatism of Slavophile philosophy is strengthened with its heterogeneity. A narrow understanding of Slavophilism reduces it to the Moscow circle of 1840s–1850s, i.e., so called "early" Slavophilism, which had ceased its existence by the beginning of 1860 when its main adherents had died. From such a point of view, Slavophilism is only interesting as something antique to retrograde-thinking historians of philosophy. The small number of the "Moscow circle" and its weak influence on its contemporaries has caused many to regard Slavophilism as an unviable movement and an unsuccessful Russian reception of European Romanticism and German philosophy (or, if we put it another, a variant of either conservative or liberal ideology). The unproductive doctrine, influentially weak and incapable of further development should undoubtedly be considered either "a dead-end road" or accidental phenomenon in Russian philosophy and culture.

Nevertheless, if we refuse such a narrow understanding of Slavophilism, we will realize that it gave some results and had quite an evident impact on Russian philosophy, science and culture. It is therefore necessary to understand Slavophilism as a form of national self-consciousness and interpret it more broadly as a phenomenon which has its own history and predecessors (at the very least, in the eighteenth century) and can develop, i.e., can change and offer new ideas and conceptions. In this case, the "late Slavophiles" (firstly, Nikolay Danilevsky and Konstantin Leontiev), "pochvennichestvo" (which was close to the "late Slavophiles"), "Academic Slavophilism" of the last quarter of nineteenth century and Neoslavophilism of the beginning of the twentieth century appear to be the intellectual and philosophical heirs of Slavophilism. All these movements continued the polemical line of the "early" Slavophiles, opposing not only their own adversaries, but sometimes also those who were among the originators of the very movement.

Philosophy of history is among those spheres of Slavophile doctrine on which Khomiakov worked. It was a philosophy of history within which Slavophilism fully revealed itself, although we cannot consider it as a united system, but as a number of historico-philosophical conceptions arguing with each other from time to time. To use the example of philosophy of history (or historiosophy as a kind of philosophy of history oriented to religion) it is the best way to trace the evolution of the very Slavophilism. In this case, Alexei Khomiakov and Vladimir Lamansky can be taken as the extreme points. *Semiramis* is the main philosophical creation by Khomiakov on which he had been working since the second half of the 1830s, i.e., in effect, before the appearance of the Slavophile circle; the work was firstly published by Aleksandr Gilferding after the author's death (1860). Lamansky's treatise

Three Worlds of Asia-European Continent (1892) can largely be considered a final Slavophile text showing the ties between Slavophilism and subsequent movements of Russian thought, such as Eurasianism. The basis of the Slavophile philosophy of history was formulated by Konstantin Aksakov in the following works: his short notes published after his death (*Of the Basic Principles of Russian History* and *Of the Russian History*), *Memorandum to Alexander II on the Internal State of Russia* (1855) firstly published in 1881, reviews on the selected volumes of *History of Russia from the Earliest Times* by Sergey Soloviev and Aksakov's response to the article by the same author *Remarks on the Mr. Soloviev' article titled Schlözer and Anti-Historical Movement* (1857) published in *Russkaia beseda*. In the course of the controversy with the historians adhering to the "state school" (Konstantin Kavelin, Sergey Soloviev, Boris Chicherin), Yuri Samarin expressed several important Slavophile ideas about the Russian historical process in some of his articles (*Of the Historical and Literary Ppinions of "Sovremennik"* (1847) and *A Few Words about National Principle in Science* (1856)). Nikolay Danilevsky and Konstantin Leontiev proposed their own version of the philosophy of history in the works *Russia and Europe: A Look at the Cultural and Political Relations of the Slavic World to the Romano-German World* (1869) by Danilevsky and *The East, Russia, and Slavdom* (1885–1886) and *Byzantism and Slavdom* (1875) by Leontiev.

Slavophile philosophy of history is characterized by features such as: a tendency towards transforming it into the philosophy of culture, criticism of Eurocentrism together with establishing of the principle of the civilization diversity and striving to introduce a geographical (natural and climatic) understanding of historical process into the philosophy of history. Within Slavophilism, the religious look at history was gradually replaced with the geographical, even naturalistic approach to history. Nikolai Berdyaev also reproached Khomiakov for the fact that his philosophy had been devoid of eschatological ideas. Slavophile philosophy of history is not pure religious historisophy and the religious understanding of the historical process is poorly presented in Khomiakov and totally absent in Danilevsky and Lamansky.

II

Philosophical reflections upon Russian history and its relation to culture of the Western European nations, which was so sharply outlined by Petr Chaadaev, mostly determined the Slavophile discourse. Among all of the Slavophiles, it was Khomiakov who paid a lot of attention to world history.

However, the same question about the fate of Russia was at the origin of his philosophical discourse. As early as in the report "On the Old and the New," around which there appeared the polemics initiating the very Slavophile circle, he had formulated the main question which provoked the discussion in such a way:

> The question is regarded in complex view and its solving seems difficult. What is better, whether old, or new Russia.[2]

Responding to it, Khomiakov upheld and refuted both parts of the question at the same time. Admitting the necessity of the borrowing of the achievements of Western European Culture, Khomiakov maintained that they should not contradict the principles of Russian historical life. These principles should be preserved, developed and restored by all means. He concluded:

> The ancient Rus' will thus resurrect in enlightened and harmonic sizes, in original social beauty combing the patriarchal lifeway of the regions with deep sense of state showing moral value and Christian identity; it will realize itself, but it will not be accidental, it will be full of living forces and not eternally oscillating between being and death.[3]

Khomiakov intentionally opposed his studies of world history to contemporary historical science, presenting his own historiosophical investigations as a "dilettante" work, i.e., unfinished, unpublished during his lifetime and devoid of scientific rigorousness and form. The task which was also close to Chaadaev—the search not for factual verity, but for reason in the past—lay at the heart of such opposition. Khomiakov maintained: "Wealth and fate of the mankind consists in the point and reason of the earthly world."[4] And he added: "Neither deeds of persons, nor fates of nations, but common task, fate and life of all the mankind form true object of history."[5] History as a common task supplemented world history, as if it were built on nature. It is possible to discover in history an intrinsic regularity, its own "logic" which, nevertheless, does not exclude human responsibility in history. Mankind confronts nature with this point—human freedom. Consideration of history from the point of view of its sense leads to the modernization of past events. The present, i.e., the lifetime of a historian, has priority over that

2. Khomiakov, "O starom i novom," 459.

3. Khomiakov, "O starom i novom," 470.

4. Khomiakov, "Semiramida," 19.

5. Khomiakov, "Semiramida," 39.

which took place in the past. The sense of the past reveals itself by means of the present, i.e., it is seen from the present. That is why Khomiakov holds:

> If you want to get to know something which happened, you should firstly get aware of something which takes place now. The reverse reasoning, i.e., from the present to the past, cannot create history, but it is the only way which can serve as its verification.[6]

The converse is, of course, also true. The present is rooted in antiquity; it grows from the past. However, the past is not completely understandable; therefore, history is the sphere of mystery which is only partially unveiled. It is to be inferred that historical knowledge is fundamentally incomplete, it can never be fully exhausted; and, consequently, the study of history should be oriented not to something factual, but to something sensible. At the same time, the comprehension of the point of history leads to the enlargement of the object of history and its universalization. In Khomiakov's opinion, the true object of history is the common task, fate and life of all the people. The plenitude of sense is dependable on the characteristics of the very object. A greater event has more historical meaning.

A man acting in history is "subjected to the common regulations of the earthly nature."[7] The natural determination of humans entrenches certain characteristics in generations and leads to the formation of several tribes who differ from each other. The entering of the people into a society based on the perception of the profit and good is the other side of human life. The third side of life is spiritual. According to Khomiakov, "faith is the limit of his [man's] inner development."[8] On this basis, Khomiakov makes a threefold division of history (which he himself calls "geographical science," since as early as in the Age of Enlightenment historiography united history with geography, or "world description"): (1) by tribes (nature); (2) by states (society); (3) by faith (spirit). "The notes on the world history" made by Khomiakov are based on the analysis of religious beliefs.

The division into tribes allows us to trace the process of the formation of consciousness. And it is necessary to bear in mind the fact that the Slavophiles considered consciousness to be both a social, collective and generic category. The history of tribes shows "the transition from material world to intellectual one."[9] Language is the main sign of such a transition. Natural

---

6. Khomiakov, "Semiramida," 33.

7. Khomiakov, "Semiramida," 22.

8. Khomiakov, "Semiramida," 22.

9. Khomiakov, "Semiramida," 23.

and conscious components of human existence are combined in the life of tribes. According to Khomiakov, three tribes act in history: the white, yellow and black; olive-colored and red tribes were formed from the essential ones by means of blending.

At the same time, Khomiakov singles out two types of nations in history: tillers-homebuilders and nomads-invaders. The first type shows more universal principles. The nations-tillers are susceptible and tolerant to everything foreign; they sympathize with other tribes, but at the same time, they are devoid of "persistent personal character."[10] The nations-invaders have sense of personal dignity and behave contemptuously toward everything foreign. The tillers bless "every tribe for eternal life and independent development."[11] However, invaders do not have mercy on those whom they have conquered. The clash of these two types in history gradually leads to the fact that nations-homebuilders lose their original features, i.e., their "innate and fundamental principles." The Slavs serve as an example of a nation-tiller in history, while the Germans are as an example of invaders.

Khomiakov pays little attention to the division into states, considering it something which is generally known. On the contrary, the division by faith is the central feature for historiosophy; it splits into polytheism, monotheism and pantheism. The way of "education" and culture of a nation depends on faith. Faith determines the "historical fate" of the nation; that is why the consideration of faith should serve as the starting point of every piece of historical research.

The analysis of religiousness led Khomiakov himself to the identification of two essential types of religious life which can be found throughout human history and, from historiosophical point of view, determine history: *iranstvo* and *kushitstvo*. Khomiakov thought that the specific features of these types can be understood by means of the "categories of will" as freedom and necessity. Khomiakov held: "Freedom and necessity are those principles on which all human ideas concentrate in various forms."[12] *Iranstvo* and *kushitstvo* are two principles, equal in force and shown in history. Of course, this definition of the mentioned forces is metonymical. Each of them (Khomiakov calls them "fundamental principles") has its own characteristics and performs a specific historical role. While *iranstvo* is a creative principle based on freedom and corresponding to monotheism in religion, *kushitstvo* acknowledges "eternal and harmonious necessity," conformity with law and logic order of the world. In the sense of the religious,

10. Khomiakov, "Semiramida," 100.

11. Khomiakov, "Semiramida," 99.

12. Khomiakov, "Semiramida," 188.

kushitstvo is divided into Shaivism ("worship of the reigning element") and Buddhism ("worship of the slave spirit which only finds its freedom in self-annihilation,"[13] i.e., materialism and nihilism). The character of the culture dominating the nation depends on these principles. Thus, *iranstvo* is characterized by literary erudition, vocal written language, simplicity of communal life, spiritual prayer and a contempt for the body. *Kushitstsvo* is distinguished by artistic erudition, relative state institutions, spell-like prayers and a respect for the body. Khomiakov understands *iranstvo* and *kushitstvo* to be such principles each of which is shown in all of the diversity of life of the nation corresponding to it. His historisophy is thus transformed into history and philosophy of culture.

III

The historiosophical and geopolitical conception by Lamansky is mostly expressed in his late work *Three Worlds of Asia-European Continent* (1892), although essential tenets of his doctrine were formed as early as in the middle of 1860s. The works listed below are important to understanding Lamansky's doctrine: the articles *Unresolved question* (1869), his unfinished work *The Outstanding Personalities of the Western Slavic Education in XV, XVI and XVII Centuries* (1875), his doctoral thesis *On the Historical Studies of the Greek-Slavic World in Europe* (1871), his lecture courses *Lectures on the Slavic Dialects* (1880–1881), *Introduction into Slavic Studies* and partially his master thesis *On the Slavs in Asia Minor, in Africa and in Spain* (1859).

Lamansky's doctrine is intimately linked to his professorship. In his historiosophical works, he tried to theoretically realize the problems which were the subjects of his special research. Firstly, it was so called *Eastern Question*, or the question about boundaries of the Slavic and Germanic-Roman worlds. It included the problem of the emancipation of the southern Slavs from Turkish despotism and the very politicized Polish question. The historiosophical treatment of the Polish question resulted in the analysis of the conflict between Orthodox and Catholic cultures, their mutual relations and historical pretensions (the Uniate Churches question etc.). Secondly, it concerned the discussion of the *possibility of a Slavic (common Slavonic) civilization*, the problem of Slavic reciprocity and communication as well as the historical specificity of the Slavic cultures. The belief in the historical and cultural uniqueness of Slavdom considered as something distinct from cultures of Roman and Germanic nations of Europe had brought about the idea of *panslavism*, or the question about the features of the unity

13. Khomiakov, "Semiramida," 442.

of this common Slavonic culture. To acknowledge the reality of panslavism meant to answer the question about the prevalence of the principle of unity over the principle of separation within the Slavic world, or centripetal forces over centrifugal ones. Under such an approach, Russia appeared to be the bearer of the principle of unity and the embodiment of centripetal force, something which demanded the criticism of some other variants of panslavism: Austrian, Illyrian ideas, etc. Panslavism and the idea of a Slavic civilization also included *the question about relation to aliens*, i.e., to non-Slavic tribes who pertained to Slavic cultural and historical community. The admittance of the cultural independence of Slavs and respect for the ethnic and cultural features of other nations led Lamansky to the promotion of the *principle of civilization diversity and cultural equality of nations*. Thirdly, Lamansky was a convinced proponent of the so called St. Cyril and Methodius idea, i.e., he argued for the restoration of the Slavic churches and freedom to worship in Slavic languages, including not only Orthodox Slavs, but also Catholic and Protestant Slavs. Fourthly, the St. Cyril and Methodius idea led to *the question of a common Slavonic language for literature, science and diplomacy*. This question acquired particular significance because of its practical importance. In fact, there is an allegation of the priority of cultural rapprochement over political one. Establishing a common Slavic language as the language of literature would make panslavism a real historical phenomenon. Since the times of Juraj Križanić, several variants of such a common Slavic language were proposed. Lamansky strongly argued for the right of Russian to be the common Slavic language as the language of literature, science and diplomacy.

The justification of the geopolitical role of the Russian language became one of the central topics of both scientific and publicist addresses by Lamansky. To develop and disseminate its language and literature are the first signs of civilizational achievements by a nation in other fields of culture. The educational role of language cannot be reduced to a patriotic conviction. Language serves as an indispensable condition for nation building, and the level of its development is among the features distinguishing a nation from an outcast of "civilization." Lamansky claimed:

> History only deals with the elite. Elevating and distinguishing some of the nations and languages from the other ones which it leaves either for degradation or perishing, history contravene this natural equality. Therefore, the historical, or great nationalities which create great world powers and prolific literature and scholarship are elevated in history. Independent statehood and developed literary language are two necessary features of great historical nationality. While the first feature expresses tangible

power and external unity, the second one serves as expression of internal unity and as its main mean of influencing other nations. To build and maintain a powerful state costs nations high price, expenses and hardship which are only justified with height and greatness of the idea for the sake of which they are suffered.[14]

There is no doubt that from scientific point of view, as Lamansky himself used to put it, "in the opinion of an anthropologist and linguist," all nations are equally valuable and worthy of studying. However, the situation is another from the point of view of philosophy, as its generalizing position allows not only to distinguish historical nations from non-historical, but also to show the conditions under which a folk can evolve into a nation. At first, Lamansky distinguished national independence and developed literature as such conditions (i.e., written language with its prolificacy which corresponds to the social needs and is constantly supported by the demand of the educated public).

To understand Lamansky's views correctly, it is necessary to bear in mind the fact that, in his opinion, a nation is not valuable as itself, but as a bearer of a unique culture and civilization. The transition from a folk to a nation means the development from a tribal and separate culture to a more productive and creative civilization which, as a rule, takes the form of a large and strong state. Contrary to a folk and tribal culture, a civilization and nation implies more creative power and political greatness; the will of state greatness should be demonstrated not in violence and extensiveness of power, but in cultural creativity.

With this idea, Lamansky is for the Slavophile principle: one folk—one state. He thinks that a plurality of small states only produces a plurality of small and weakly developed cultures. A strong culture (in terms of creativity) is an attribute of a great state uniting diverse nations and territories in a single political body. A common language is a necessary condition of a civilized existence and the independent development of every folk. History itself leads to the predominance of one of the dialects to avoid the extremes of language fragmentation and particularization. Lamansky repeatedly pointed at the correlation of political greatness and strong statehood with language predominance. Both of them were evidence of the "centripetal force" of folk.

Those historical conditions under which Russia existed give it the opportunity to develop its distinctive culture. The other Slavic folks were devoid of such an opportunity; that is why their historical future depends on whether they would be decisive enough to join Russia and, particularly, refuse their

14. Lamanskiy, "Vidnye deyateli," 417–18.

national egoism and self-love to adopt the Russian language. Otherwise, they would face historical oblivion and cultural worthlessness. In any case, the only way left for small folks devoid of their own states is to be subject to a more powerful and productive culture and language.

The adoption of the Russian language would only allow Slavic folks to join and share the achievements of world culture and present the results of their cultural creativity to others, at the same time preserving and developing their own culture. Otherwise, their joining to the advances of world culture will be carried out beyond national culture, which means their total assimilation in the long term perspective.

Among foreign languages, Greek, which refers to Antiquity, has priority for the Slavs as the language of culture. Greek indicates the common cultural tradition shared by most Slavic nations and joining them to the common historical past. Indeed, Greek is the past. It is necessary for the Slavs as a cultural background to understand and reactualize tradition. But in the Slavic world, the future belongs not to Greek, but to the Russian language. Russian is fated to become the common Slavic language by history itself. Lamansky thought that the centripetal forces are mostly expressed by the Russian nation; Russians had created a strong state serving as the best guarantor of the successive dissemination of the Russian language. The adoption of the Russian language would primarily be useful to the southern and western Slavs. A common language would help to overcome the split in the Slavic world, to curb egoistic interests, to constrain mutual claims and alleviate old offenses. Only based on Russian language, Slavdom would manage to express itself as "independent historical type," i.e., to move towards independent cultural activity with the achievements which would have a meaning common to all mankind. Lamansky insists that it is impossible to become a nation without common language.

However, the formation of some separate Slavic nations is not the aim Lamanky strives to achieve. Their paucity, political weakness (even with the achievement of state independence) and cultural underproductivity are obvious to Lamansky. Political independence is quite an achievable aim.

Nevertheless, Lamansky's dream was that the Slavs become real and full subjects of the historical process; and it was necessary for them to form "a united global historical nation." Thus, the question about the adoption of the Russian language is not the question about Russian political influence, but the question about civilization priorities of the Slavs and their cultural soundness. What has been achieved by the Slavs in the field of culture is worthy of respect and preservation, but the further activity by the Slavs is impossible beyond reliance on Russian language. The question is not whether it is worth adopting Russian, but whether Slavdom has capacity for further creative development and is able to be preserved as a national-cultural unity. Assimilation, denationalization and then historical oblivion would be the alternatives to the adoption of Russian. The Slavs themselves should realize this fact and acknowledge Russian as a common Slavic diplomatic, scientific and literary language willingly.

The time when some individual nations and the states formed by them played a global historical role is disappearing in the past. The time has come for the languages to acquire a global historical role; so does for the nations united by them. Three Romance languages (French, Italian and Spanish) and two Germanic languages (English and German) are predominant among other modern European languages; they "achieve more or less universal historic significance." The old Eastern European nations, such as the Greeks, Armenians and Georgians who have rich cultural traditions, are now not only very small in number, but also weak politically and culturally. Nowadays, only Russian could take on the civilizing role of uniting the Eastern European nations; and thus acquire a global historical role.

Uniting nations and territories, language not only has a communicative and cultural function, but also becomes a political, or more precisely, geopolitical force. Lamansky is even ready to explain the geopolitical role of language by means of historical law. According to him,

> there is the law formulated by means of historical observations which reads that the more the folks and territories feeling a demand for adoption of some foreign language are distant, diverse and different from each other, the more this language acquires universal and world meaning. This world character of the language does not depend on the fact that, for example, each Spaniard is better than a Frenchman and an Englishman, or each Russian is better than a Czech or a German. No! It is formed by the forces which are beyond the individual will of man, namely by geographical circumstances, space of country, quantity of population feeling the demand for the adoption of language and how much free space is available to some people, i.e., how many conditions there are for the development of language.[15]

The pretensions of the Russian language to world historical significance are proved with by the course of the historical and cultural development of Slavdom. In this regard, Russian appears to be a successor of the Greek and All-Slavian written language created by St. Cyril and Methodius. It has no competitors in Eastern Europe. The opposite trend took place in Europe, where French, Spanish, Italian, German, and English were fighting

15. Lamanskiy, *Lektsii*, 62.

one another. Lamansky thought that the outcome of this battle was prede-termined; in future, the meaning of German and French would only be pre-served in Europe, while the meaning of Spanish and especially English would increase because of the vast colonies of Spain and England. The historical future belongs to these languages. The Russian scholar supposed that even the Spanish colonies in South America would eventually come under the con-trol of the Anglo-Saxons. The leadership of the English language in America would result in the fact that the center of the West would shift to the New World. The old European culture would yield to America (the US).

However, the Russian people and Slavdom are merely the prevailing part of a more significant civilizational unity. From the ethnographical and historical-cultural point of view Lamasky distinguished three parts, or "independent and unique worlds" of Eurasia: 1) properly Europe, 2) properly Asia, 3) the Middle world. In most of his works Lamansky called the Middle world "Greek-Slavic," or the "Russian cosmos." It was called "Greek" because of the prevalence of the Orthodox faith (the Greek faith) and was called "Slavic" because of the numerical superiority of the Slavs. On the one hand, the Slavic element links the Middle world with the heri-tage of Antiquity; on the other hand, it makes the Middle world the succes-sor to the idea of the Empire. Lamansky understood the idea of a Christian Empire as the "pure moral" and

> inner belief of the Eastern Christian nations, regardless of the tribes, in necessity and eternity of the united Christian king-dom on the Earth, including all the diversity of the nations and countries with their own governments, rulers, župans, princes, voivodes, kings and tsars. Just as the dissimilarity of the languages in worship as well as the dissimilarity of the rites and customs of the local churches in no way contradicted the unity of Church, and, on the contrary, was compatible with it, so the diversity and blend of the tribes, countries and directions did not hamper them make a single Christian kingdom, or a united Empire.[16]

The idea of the united Christian Empire was usurped by the West dur-ing the reign of Charles the Great and distorted by the principles of violence and intolerance. At the same time, Russia inherited the idea of Empire from the Byzantine Empire in a more "pure" form and preserved it for the whole Middle world.

The Middle world is *geographically* distinguished from Europe with the "poverty of the coastline," i.e., it is of a land character with the plains only constrained by the mountains on the periphery and with moderate,

16. Lamanskiy, "Vidnye deyateli," 465.

or even harsh climatic conditions. From the ethnographical point of view, the Middle world includes a plurality of various folks with the prevalence of the Slavic population uniting this world into a single entity. "Ethnographical forces" of the Middle world include Greeks, Albanians, Romans (Romanians, Vlachs), Germans, Latgalians (Lithuanians, Latvians), Iranic (Armenians, Kartvelians, Ossetes, Kurds), Finnish, Mongolian, Turkish and Tatarian tribes. The boundaries of the Middle world in the South, in the East and in the North-East largely coincide with the frontiers of the Russian Empire, while western boundary of "this specific historical word" touches those territories of the Eastern Europe which are mostly populated by the Slavs. The unity of the European and Asian Russian was fundamental to Lamansky's conception. He wrote:

> Russia's Asian dominions are sharply distinct from so called European Russia, forming an indissoluble and territorial integrity with it. Strictly speaking, from the geographical, ethnological and historical point of view, there are no definite and sharp differences and contrasts between, on the one hand, the Eastern and Southern peripheries of Russia and, on the other hand, Western and North-Western peripheries of Asian Russia.[17]

The unity of the Greek-Slavic world can be seen in the fact that "within European Russia, as well as in our East, land dominates over shore, the protective and conservative character of its population dominates over a thirst for something new, the overactive, anxious and restless spirit of coastal residents."[18]

During its historical development, the Middle world experienced a range of influences, such as the Byzantine and Eastern Christian, Mongolian and Modern European. Now it was time for the nations of the Greek-Slavic World to show their cultural uniqueness again in order to successfully oppose the pressure of Western Civilization.

IV

Despite the criticism over eurocentrism, Slavophilism should not be understood as an ideology of confrontation. Given all the acuity of its political opinion, even Danilevsky's conception of cultural-historical types is an example of the doctrine of the diversity of manners of civilizational development; and Europe only appears to be a cultural-historical type for such a

17. Lamanskiy, *Tri mira*, 8.
18. Lamanskiy, *Ob istoricheskom izuchenii*, 35.

development. Panslavism was not a predominant ideology for Slavophilism as well. This fact is essentially correct when speaking about Khomiakov and early Slavophiles. I suppose the Panslavic motifs can only be found in the poetry of Khomiakov, while they are not well presented in Khomiakov's philosophy of history. The Slavophiles never denied the need to study European science and culture; they both knew and liked it. For instance, Lamansky pointed out the similarity between the historical and cultural origins of Roman-Germanic and Greek-Slavic Worlds (Christianity, Antique heritage, including the idea of Empire). Moreover, Khomiakov was a notable anglophile, although he predicted the fall of British might in his poem "An Isle"; Lamansky, for instance, foresaw the growth of Anglo-Saxon influence and Anglo-Saxon historical predominance in a world whose center would shift to the New World. "The Rotting West" was only a metaphor used by Slavophiles in their dispute with Westernizers. Danilevsky used this expression as a title for one of the chapters of his book *Russia and Europe* having put a question mark at the end of the phrase. Responding this question, Danilevsky acknowledged that the European civilization was finishing its blossoming period and its future decay was inevitable. However, neither to hasten the decay of Europe, nor to diagnose the processes of degradation which could be found in European culture was an aim the Slavophiles strived towards; their aim was to address the Russian people and the Slavs to move towards independent cultural and philosophical creativity, "to cease to seem and to become to exist," i.e., not to imitate Roman-Germanic civilization thoughtlessly, but to create an independent culture.

Pan-Slavism was not a dominant idea for Slavophilism, so the very term *Slavyanophilstvo* was not the name chosen for itself by this movement of Russian thought. Considering folk culture as an alternative to the total imitation of European culture, the Slavophiles urged recourse to the folk foundation for culture. They saw their aim in the returning of the Russian educated stratum back to the folk principles in order to stop the multiplication of cosmopolitan intellectuals who disdained everything Russian and Slavic. It is no coincidence that the publication *On the Folk Principle in Science* by Samarin, which provoked the expected polemics, had become required reading for the Slavophile journal *Russkaia beseda* ("Russian Conversation"). Danilevsky formulated the Slavophile attitude to the folk principle very well: one folk—one state. According to Danilevsky, "every folk has the right to its independent life insofar as it itself realize it and pretend to it";[19] and from political point of view, the Slavic cultural-historical type should be either a federation, or a union of states (All-Slavic Union).

19. Danilevsky, *Rossiya i Evropa*, 20.

However, Lamansky did not agree with him and thought that a united form of civilization should also imply a great united state oriented to the ideal of Christian Empire. A developed and fruitful culture is impossible beyond large political form.

The Slavophile philosophy of history had been presented from these worldviews. According to the cultural and historical topology outlined by the Slavophiles, the problems of the philosophy of history were concentrated on the relations between Russia and the West. However, cultural and historical dualism also implied the methodological features of Slavophile philosophy of history. The Slavophile philosophy of the history is schematic. It boils down to oppositions and binary models: Russia and Europe, the Greco-Slavic world and the Germanic-Roman world, Iranian and Cushitic, farmers-homebuilders and nomadic conquerors, Land and State, Germanic and Roman (Romance) Europe, etc. Early Slavophiles considered faith as the basis of the historical process, although they did not give any substantiated conception of the religious philosophy of history, criticism existed, for example, Nikolai Berdyaev, prejudging Khomiakov on the measure of the "new religious consciousness" of the twentieth century evading pseudo- and even anti-Christianity. The heirs of the early Slavophiles proposed a more developed philosophical-historical doctrine, developing not religious, but naturalistic (organicist) potencies inherent in Slavophilism. Thus, in addition to religion, Konstantin Leontiev pointed out that the state was the basis for civilizational development. Danilevsky talked about four aspects of the cultural-historical type: religion as people's view of the world, then state-political structure, economy and culture (scientific, technical and artistic activities). Lamansky believed that an original culture could not arise until a rich literary language is developed and a strong state is formed. However, in addition to them, geographical conditions are important for the formation of civilization (Lamansky referred his doctrine to the field of political geography, and not the philosophy of history), which complicated the theoretical construction itself. Along with Europe and Asia, the Middle (Greco-Slavic) world declared its right of cultural-historical independence. Khomiakov started the *Semiramis* (at least in the layout of the material that was offered by the publisher) with arguments about the importance of geography for history. In the same situation, and more reasonably, Lamansky was completing the circle of philosophical and historical theories of the Slavophiles, and simultaneously opening up new perspectives of the Slavophile doctrine which was implemented in the twentieth century by Eurasianism.

Bibliography

Danilevsky, Nikolay Y. *Rossiya i Evropa. Vzglyad na kul'turnye i politicheskie otnosheniya slavyanskogo mira k germano-romanskomu.* St. Petersburg: Glagol', 1995.

Khomiakov, Alexei S. "O starom i novom." In *Sochineniya v dvukh tomakh,* by Alexei Khomiakov, 456–74. Vol. 1. Moscow: Medium, 1994.

———. "'Semiramida' (Issledovanie istiny istoricheskikh idey)." In *Sochineniya v dvukh tomakh,* by Alexei Khomiakov, 15–446. Vol. 1. Moscow: Medium, 1994.

Lamanskiy, Vladimir I. *Lektsii po slavyanskim narechiyam, chitannye professorom S.-Peterburgskogo universiteta V. I. Lamanskim za 1880–81 akad. god.* St. Petersburg: n.p., 1881.

———. *Ob istoricheskom izuchenii Greko-slavyanskogo mira v Evrope.* St. Petersburg: Tipografiya Maykova, 1871.

———. *Tri mira Aziysko-Evropeyskogo materika.* St. Petersburg: Tipografiya A. I. Transhelya, 1892.

———. "Vidnye deyateli zapadno-slavyanskoy obrazovannosti v XV, XVI i XVII vekakh. Istoriko-literaturnye i kul'turnye ocherki." *Slavyanskiy sbornik* 1 (1875) 413–584.

11

The Echoes of Alexei Khomiakov's Theological Views in the Literary Works of Nikolai Leskov

Marta Łukaszewicz

The journalistic and artistic work of the Russian writer Nikolai Leskov (1831–1895) is evidence of his vivid interest in religious and ecclesiastic issues. The writer's father was the son of a rural clergyman, but after finishing the theological seminary, he refused to become a priest and chose the career of a clerk. Thus, he acquired hereditary nobility but, according to Leskov's *Autobiographical Note*, preserved some of the habits of his former estate, such as singing liturgical chants at home. Aside from that, he was not especially religious in a conventional way, i.e., he rarely attended church services, did not believe in miracles and rituals but preferred solitary personal prayer before the icon of Christ. Ironically, it was the writer's mother and grandmother who passed to him his traditional Orthodox piety, including the *molebens* and visits to monasteries.[1] Another important influence on Leskov's spiritual development was that of his uncle (the husband of his mother's elder sister) Alexander Scott, a Russified Scotchman and probably a Nonconformist by religion.[2] He also had contact with Old Believers and members of several religious movements and sects who inhabited surroundings of Orel, Leskov's birthplace. Numerous trips throughout Russia during his work for the trading company "Scott and Willkins" in the second half of the 1850s also promoted acquaintance with different beliefs, while

1. Leskov, "Avtobiograficheskaya zametka," 11.
2. Edgerton, "Nikolai Leskov," 34. John Muckle clarifies that Scott most likely belonged to the Presbyterian Church (Muckle, *Nikolai Leskov*, 142).

his business trips to Riga and Pskov in 1863 gave him the opportunity to examine Old Believers' living conditions and the organization of the educational process of their children.

At the same time as studying the diversity of religious experience, Leskov demonstrated a deep interest in the Orthodox tradition and the problems of the Orthodox Church in the Russian Empire in the epoch of the Great Reforms introduced by Alexander II. In his articles, the writer touched upon numerous issues which were widely discussed at the time in the lay and church press: the quality of clerics' preparation for the pastoral ministry, parish priests' living conditions, the position of the Orthodox Church in the state system of the Russian Empire, etc. It is worth noticing that his approach to the ecclesiastical issues of the 1860s and 1870s has a lot in common with the position of the Slavophiles. Namely, those were such matters as the financial situation of the parish clergy and the possibility of introducing the regular state salary for them; the position of the Ortho-dox Church in the Russian Empire or the problem of religious tolerance and freedom of conscience. Both the Slavophiles and Leskov underlined the necessity of a rapprochement between the clergy and the laity for joint participation in overcoming the challenges faced by Russian society in the epoch of reforms; they criticized the subordination of the Church to the state and demonstrated the necessity of the restoration of its independence and exemption from state custody. They also had similar views on the ide-als of religious tolerance, although some Slavophiles, such as Ivan Aksakov, opposed the idea that any Christian confession or even any religion would have the equal and unlimited possibility to spread their teaching on the ter-ritory of Russian Empire, while for Nikolai Leskov, freedom of conscience was one of the main human rights.

Leskov's interest in ecclesiastical problems was not limited to acute, topical ones but also covered the areas of Church history, Biblical studies and even—to some extent—dogmatics. The writer followed new publications on these issues, which is evidenced by his correspondence, press reviews and mentions in his literary works. In particular, he reviewed such books as *Se-lected Works* by Archbishop Innocenty (Borisov), *History of Russian Church* by Metropolitan Macarius (Bulgakov), historical articles by Philip Ternovskiy, works about Old Believers written by Pavel Mullov, translation of John Bu-nyan's *Pilgrim's Progress*, etc. Among authors named in Leskov's letters and literary texts one can find those of Rev. Ioann Bellyustin, Metropolitan Phil-aret (Drozdov), Evgeny Golubinskiy, Ernest Renan, Eugène Bersier, Jacques-Bénigne Bossuet and, last but not least, Alexei Khomiakov.

Leskov did not know Khomiakov personally but was familiar with the philosopher's works and which is confirmed, for instance, by his letter of

23 December 1874 to Ivan Aksakov, where he mentioned the intention to use Yuri Samarin's foreword to the second volume of Khomiakov's *Collected Works* in his essay about the Stundists. Khomiakov's name can also be found in another letter to Aksakov, dated 29 July 1875, where Leskov wrote about Russian books—including Khomiakov's—in Marienbad, and in the letter of 15 September 1884 to Alexei Suvorov.

One can also find references to Khomiakov in Leskov's literary works. For instance, in the story *Laughter and Grief* (published in 1871) one of the narrator's interlocutors, the constable Vasilyev, admitted that he was persuaded to convert to Orthodoxy by "unapproved writings of Innocenty and prohibited theological works of Khomiakov, written, by the way, in the strictly Orthodox spirit."[3] He called them powerful propaganda in favour of Orthodoxy and evidence of its inner truth. Ironically, the crucial arguments for Vasilyev's decision were those of the essentially free nature of Church unity and the principle of the non-interference of state in matters of faith, which turned out to be only declarations which did not have much in common with the actual position of Church in the Russian Empire. This contradiction between the ecclesiastical ideal and the harsh reality leads to the frustration of the hero and his conclusion about the falsehood of the Orthodox theology.

Alexei Khomiakov is also mentioned in another of Leskov's stories, *The Co-functionaries* (*Sovmestiteli*, 1884), and he is treated as a symbol of the sublime needs fashionable among aristocracy in 1830s–1840s, together with Vissarion Belinskiy, Nikolai Polevoy and Archbishop Innocenty (Borisov). The philosopher's name is used here not without irony and the effect is reached by invoking in one phrase the abovementioned thinkers and omnipresent bribes. Another ironical reference to Khomiakov presents him as a standard of Russianness and Orthodoxy: "Cancrin, when signing the documents . . . quite unexpectedly for people who surrounded him, made the sign of the cross in Russian manner, just like Khomiakov himself."[4]

Finally, in several short articles in *Birhevye vedomosti* from 1869 (no 141, 305) and literary works, such as *No Way Out* (*Nekuda*) and *Dwellers in God's House* (*Bozhedomy*), Leskov quotes shorter or longer excerpts from Khomiakov's poem *To Russia* (1854). It is very significant that in all four cases he chooses verses exclusively from the fourth stanza, being the only fully critical one in the poem, which on the whole conveys the idea of Russian messianic closeness:

3. Leskov, "Smekh i gore," 490.

4. Leskov, "Sovmestiteli," 430.

Smeared with dark injustice in the law courts,

And branded with the mark of slavery:

Full of godless flattery, foul lies,

Of deadly apathy and vice,

And every other known depravity![5]

This stanza is preceded in the poem by others which emphasize the view of Russia being chosen by God, and is immediately followed by an apostrophe to the persona's fatherland: "Oh, unworthy to be chosen / Yet you were chosen!" This context completely disappears in Leskov's texts and consequently the excerpts he quotes express only the idea of the ill-being of Russia in the period of the "dark seven years" (1848–1855), just before the Crimean war.

However, for our purpose it is much more important to trace the way Khomiakov's theological (mainly ecclesiological) views are echoed in Leskov's opinions about the Church. Several similarities between them may be noticed in the writer's journalistic and literary works, especially those written in the 1870s. One of the most important is the fundamental significance of the free unity which constitutes the Church. He begins his famous work *The Church Is One* (published for the first time with the title "On the Church" in the journal *Orthodox Review* in 1864 and then in the second volume of his *Collected Works* (1867) with the title *A Catechetical Exposition of the Doctrine of the Church*) with a categorical statement:

> The unity of the Church follows necessarily from the unity of God. . . . The unity of the Church . . . is not illusory: it is not metaphorical but true and essential, like the unity of the numerous members of living body.[6]

According to Khomiakov's concept, the free unity of the Church is organic in nature as Church's members form together the Body of Christ and are connected with each other by bonds of love. The philosopher is amplifying here the ideas of St. Paul expressed in the First Letter to the Corinthians: "For just as the body is one and has many members, and all the members of the body, though many, are one body, so it is with Christ" (1 Cor 12:12–27). He is also actualizing the patristic testimony of the Church being an organism animated by the Holy Spirit,[7] and emphasizing the interconnection between the clergy and laity, complementary to

---

5. Translation of the poem taken from Christoff, *A. S. Xomjakov*, 106.

6. Khomiakov, "Church Is One," 31.

7. Kozłowski, *Rosyjska eklezjologia*, 79.

each other and only together constituting the Church. This statement distinguishes his ecclesiological views from the theses of scholastic theology, with its strict division into pastors and flock.[8]

The unity was one of the fundamental values for Leskov, too. The writer repeatedly and bitterly underlined the dissociation of Russian society, which he called *russkaya rozn'*. He used this collocation in particular in the title of the collection of eleven stories and essays published in 1881, where he depicted the reality of a chaotic Russia, unable to find consent. Bjela Leonova qualified the collection as a kind of anthology of the masks of this great division, which, however, demonstrates at the same time the hope for unity, reflections of Leskov's social and ethical ideal.[9] It was precisely in overcoming social disunity where the writer saw the way to resolve modern Russia's problems.

Leskov also perceived the Church as a unified organism and hoped for the incarnation of this unity on the parochial level, by means of rapprochement between the clergy and the laity. For instance, in the article "Some Words on the Note of the Metropolitan Arseniy about Dukhobors and Other Sectarians" he stressed that the pastor and the flock should be united; in the essay entitled *Diocesan Justice* the writer recalled once more that the Church consists not only of clergy but it is rather a congregation of people connected by a unity of spiritual interests. In two short notes for the newspaper *Novosti i Birzhevaya gazeta* "About the Aristocratism of the Clergy" and "The Correction to the Reference" he pointed out the negative tendency present in numerous parishes to emphasize the distance between the priest and the ordinary parishioners, especially those belonging to the lower strata of the society. He also underlined once more the necessity of a rapprochement between the clergy and all parish members, regardless of their social status.

It should be noted that the idea of unity and understanding the need to gather together different members of society was quite characteristic of the period of the 1860s. When applied to the ecclesial discussion, they were expressed mostly in debates around parishes and brotherhoods. For the Slavophile journalists, the parish reform should have initiated the rebirth of Russia and truly Russian values, as the parochial community should consolidate people belonging to different classes, creating between them bonds of love and mutual help. Another form of including laity in church activities was an attempt to revive brotherhoods, especially in the Western dioceses of Russian Orthodox Church. These aspirations inspired many priests who were

8. Kozłowski, *Rosyjska eklezjologia*, 68.

9. Leonova, *Zhanr memuarnogo ocherka*, 40–41.

organizing parochial communities and brotherhoods with the main focus on charity and the education of the poorer. One of the most famous among them was Rev. Aleksandr Gumilevsky who served in Saint Petersburg in the 1860s and succeeded in setting up a shelter for orphans, free Sunday lunches for beggars, a parish library and choir, etc. At the end of the nineteenth century, charity work became an important element of the ministry of Rev. Ioann Sergiev, better known as St. John of Kronstadt.

In several of Leskov's literary works, one can also find the incarnation of the ecclesial ideal and human unity. For instance, members of the Old Believers' community depicted in the story *The Sealed Angel* flock together according to their own will and choice, and their free, organic unity is perceived as one of the higher values. In the chronicle *The Cathedral Clergy* the heroes are presented as living together and caring about each other: "All these people . . . more or less, bore one another's burdens and provided the scanty variety of life for one another."[10] In the story *The Unbaptized Priest* the accent is put, on the one hand, on Rev. Savva's concern to maintain unity and solidarity between the members of the parish and, on the other, on the parishioners' loyalty to their pastor, their readiness to support and protect him from slander and accusations. On the contrary, in Leskov's understanding, internal disconnection is among the main evils in the church and for the church. For instance, in the series of sketches *The Trifles from the Life of Archbishops* he wrote a lot about inaccessibility of bishops, their separation from ordinary believers and simple priests.

For Alexei Khomiakov, love, free consent and truth were the cornerstones on which the spiritual building of the Church is erected. In his work *The Church Is One*, the philosopher called love "the crown and glory of the Church,"[11] which creates the unity of believers. Referring to another fragment from the First Letter to the Corinthians (1 Cor 13:13), Khomiakov writes about the three gifts of the Holy Spirit—love, faith and hope—calling love the greatest of them and reminding the reader about different forms of its expression, such as works, prayer and spiritual song. Also, in Leskov's opinion, mutual love is the foundation of both the ecclesial and human community and should precede the formation of any union. Such a belief is expressed in the novel *At Daggers Drawn* by Rev. Evangel Minervin who emphasizes that unanimity is reached through constant efforts and active love for the other person, patience for their peculiarities and drawbacks, so that it comes as a final result of such life. To express his idea, the priest uses a phrase taken from the Orthodox liturgy of St. John Chrysostom,

10. Leskov, *Cathedral Folk*, 11.
11. Khomiakov, "Church Is One," 34.

pronounced just before the Symbol of Faith: "Let us love one another that with oneness of mind we may confess."

According to Leskov, active love for the neighbor is the main human virtue and the most important vocation of a Christian. It becomes the most characteristic feature of righteous men depicted in a writer's works, such as Golovan (*Deathless Golovan*), Sheramur (*Sheramur*), Konstantin Pizonskiy (*The Cathedral Folk*), soldier Postnikov (*The Sentry*), etc. As Valentin Khalizev and Olga Mayorova noted, the behavior of these characters is the result of their constant readiness to provide help to those who need it, regardless of any ideological attitudes or the consequences of a choice made.[12] Needless to say that such approach is founded on the principles of Christian ethic, i.e., the teaching of Christ, even if it is not openly declared by the hero, as in the case of Sheramur. The dedication and the disregard of oneself demonstrated by the righteous applies not only to the field of their earthly life (e.g., Golovan helping infectious patients during an epidemic despite the threat to his life; the soldier Postnikov leaving his position to save a drowning man and thus exposing himself to corporal punishment) but also to the salvation of their souls. The most striking examples of the last are found in Leskov's Prolog tales (short stories based on the narratives taken from an old Russian compendium of religious writings from various ancient sources) where several characters renounce seclusion and a prayer-oriented way of life, choosing the secular life and "ungodly" activities in order to have more opportunities to help other people. For instance, the main hero of the story *Pamphalon the Entertainer* gives away all money he has earned as a ransom for a hapless woman and her children to save them from slavery while the title character of the story *Beautiful Aza* sells all her belongings to help a poor family and becomes a prostitute to earn her living.

Freedom was for Khomiakov an indispensable component of the Church unity. The philosopher stressed this in his polemical work *On the Western Confessions of Faith*: "The unity of the Church was free; more precisely, the unity was freedom itself, the harmonious expression of inner agreement."[13] Such an understanding of unity leads to the denial not only of any external compulsion but also of any authority: "the Church is not an authority, just as God is not an authority and Christ is not an authority."[14] In Khomiakov's concept, they are replaced by the activity of the Holy Spirit, God's grace and love.

12. Khalizev and Mayorova, "Leskovskaya koncepciya pravednichestva," 201.

13. Khomiakov, "Western Confessions."

14. Khomiakov, "Western Confessions."

The principle of religious freedom was one of the most important for Leskov, too, as was the idea of an individual spiritual experience being the only basis of deep faith and true unity deriving from inner calling, and not from external circumstances. He defended this position in all his journalistic and literary works, especially in ones devoted to the situation of Old Believers in the Russian Empire. In the article "Is Religious Censorship Possible and Rational?" the writer stressed the critical significance of spiritual quests and the free development of religious thought. He demonstrated that only such freedom guarantees the open discussions which make religion unimpeded by superstitions and formalism, and promote the development of theological thought. To deprive believers of such a possibility means to contribute to their loss of living religious feeling and to replace it with external forms.[15]

Thus, freedom turns out to be inseparably linked with the problem of the limits of religious searching and the question of *truth*. Khomiakov demonstrates their connection with the life of the Church expressed primarily in prayer and love; only the Church as a whole contains the truth and is able "to contemplate the grandeur of heaven and penetrate its mystery."[16] At the same time, the philosopher underlines that the search of truth is a sign of a living faith and an inalienable right or even the obligation of every member of the Church: "the apostles permitted free investigation, even made it an obligation . . . free investigation, understood in one way or another, constitutes the sole basis of true faith."[17] And, in conclusion, he indicates the paradox that the Church contains at the same time both the universality of the truth already known and the search for the truth. The first element belongs to the Church as a whole while the second one is the property of its members.

Leskov's position, although to some extent seemingly similar, turns out to be quite different. The writer was fond of people who believed, as Sergey Durylin put it, in a peculiar and poignant way; many of his "righteous men"—such as Rev. Savely Tuberozov from *The Cathedral Clergy*, Rev. Cyriak from the story *At the Edge of the World* or Aleksandr Ryzhov from *Singlemind*—defend their right to have an opinion of their own and, as a result, their faith is perceived as "questionable." According to Khomiakov, such an approach does not exclude them from the ecclesial community, although in the unique historical conditions of nineteenth-century Russia it caused many problems (Tuberozov's suspension, the authorities' suspicious

15. Leskov, "Vozmozhna li," 3.
16. Khomiakov, "Western Confessions."
17. Khomiakov, "Western Confessions."

attitude towards Ryzhov, etc.). However, the aspiration to stand apart, to underline the disaccord of his own position as well as the position of his characters with the official church teaching becomes increasingly significant for Leskov. Hence the facetious signature "humble heresiarch Nikolai" used by the writer in his personal letters and dedications from the second half of the 1880s. It is connected with the concept of heresy which was crucial for his self-determination, expressing for him an idea of the freedom of religious search, independence of thinking and ethical maximalism. In his famous letter of 29 July (10 August) 1875 to Petr Shchebalskiy, Leskov opposes the so-understood heresy to the official Orthodox Church:

> In general, I have become a "turncoat" and no longer burn incense to many of my old gods. Above all, I have broken with clericalism ... had I read all the many things I have now read on this subject and heard all that I have now heard, I would not have written *The Cathedral Folk* as I did write it. . . . Instead, I am itching now to write about a Russian heretic—an intelligent, well-read, and free-thinking *spiritual Christian*, who has passed through all doubts for the sake of his search for Christian truth and has found it only within his own soul. I would call this story *Fornosov the Heretic*.[18]

This opposition would become aggravating with time, leading the writer to deny Orthodoxy the right to see itself as the genuine Christianity, as it was demonstrated by Irina Dolinina in her analysis of the linguistic representation of these two concepts.[19] As for Khomiakov, he linked heresy primarily with a lack of love, an unwillingness to reconcile one's private opinion with the position of the Church, and ascribed such an approach mainly to Protestant theologians, some of whom were, as it is known, familiar and appealing for Leskov.

One more problem which was exceptionally important for the writer was that of the boundaries of the Church, both visible and invisible, and the possibility of salvation for non-Christians. In his work *A Few Words of the Orthodox Christian about Western Denominations Apropos Different Latin and Protestant Works About the Subjects of Faith*, Khomiakov underlined that the mystery of the bonds between the earthly Church and the rest of mankind is inaccessible for people and therefore they do not have right to presume that all those outside of the visible Church would be condemned, especially since such an assumption would contradict the Divine Mercy. Moreover, according to the philosopher, every person who

18. Translation of the letter taken from Edgerton, "Leskov and Tolstoy," 533–34.

19. Dolinina, "Dikhotomiya khudozhestvennogo koncepta," 236.

loves truth, acts morally and performs acts of charity in fact worships Christ, even if they do not know him and cannot bless his name. He was convinced that truth, compassion, love, self-sacrifice, beauty are just different forms of the name of the Savior.

Khomiakov's views were amazingly similar to those expressed by Nikolai Leskov in his story *On the Edge of the World*. The bishop who is the narrator in the story recognizes that the unbaptized savage who has selflessly saved his life in the snowy desert is probably closer to Christ than the baptized one who has abandoned him to his fate:

> It's not for me to put a shackle on his feet and persecute his ways, when He Who Is wrote the commandment of love in his heart with His finger. . . . Abba Father, make Yourself known to him who loves You . . . and may You be blessed to the ages—to me and to him and to everyone—to each whom You allow by Your goodness to comprehend Your will. There is no more trepidation in my heart: I believe that You revealed Yourself to him according to his need, and he know You as everything know You.[20]

Sergey Durylin, in his reflections on Leskov's religiosity, praised as deeply Orthodox the writer's conviction that every human truth and good has Christ as their original source. He considered this belief to be the foundation of one of his legends—a legend about "Christians without Christ," righteous men who do not know the roots of their righteousness. We can perceive Leskov as one more link in the chain of theologians and Church writers who dwelled upon the idea of the Gospel parable of the Sheep and the Goats (Matt 25:31–46) where the criterion of the separation into the saved and the condemned is the good done to another person. We can mention such names as Clement of Alexandria or Justin the Martyr who were convinced that in the works of non-Christian philosophers one can find some ideas of Christian Revelation. They believed in the existence of the germs of truth scattered in all philosophical systems, and appreciated ancient culture and literature. Another modification of this idea may be seen in the concept of *apocatastasis* developed by Origen, teaching about salvation as a result of a long-term nurturing process, in which Christ persuades man to voluntarily turn to the good and, in effect, to reach plenitude, i.e., to return to the unity with God.[21] The concept of *apocatastasis* was not officially condemned by the Orthodox Church but until the end of the nineteenth century was considered a heretical one and, as such, attracted Leskov's attention. In the writer's letters of the 1870s, one can find Origen's

20. Leskov, *On the Edge*, 104.
21. Tofiluk, "Koncepcja apokatastazy," 27.

name and ideas while in his works of the 1880s there are several reference to philosopher's treaty *De principiis*.[22]

To summarize, let us underline that the question of the relation between Leskov's position and opinions about Church issues and Khomiakov's ecclesiological ideas remains a complex one. The writer was familiar with his works, appreciated and respected him, although in some of his statements one can see slight irony at play, which is a result of discrepancies between the Church ideal depicted by the philosopher and the actual situation of the Orthodox Church in the state system of the Russian Empire. However, there are several similarities between Leskov's and Khomiakov's ecclesiological views, the most important of which was perceiving the Church as a free unity of the believers based on their mutual love. Their opinions about religious searching, the boundaries of the Church and the possibility of salvation outside its visible limits were relatively close, too. But one cannot definitely assess whether these similarities are caused by the influence of Khomiakov's views on Leskov's opinions or whether they are the typologically close results of the tendencies and atmosphere of the epoch or the personal spiritual experience of both of them. It should be stressed that the ideas of unity, love, free religious search and choice became very popular in the nineteenth century among educated people, thus creating the basis of modern religiosity. Moreover, it is known that Leskov was familiar with numerous works of European and Russian theologians of the eighteenth and nineteenth centuries, such as Jules-Ernest Naville, Ernest Renan, Roger Hollard, Gregory Skovoroda or Archimandrite Feodor (Bukharev). Thus, some of their ideas could have had a certain influence on the writer's religious opinions, too.

One of the main differences in the ecclesiological views of Khomiakov and Leskov seems to be the distinct attitude of both writers to the problem of truth and the necessity of reconciling one's private opinion with the position of the Church. Khomiakov perceived it as a demonstration of freedom and love, while Leskov manifested himself as an individualist who, with time, appreciated or even boasted his divergence from the Church doctrine more and more and relished the title of "heretic." This attitude can be treated as an important symptom of modern religiosity with its tendency to shift faith from the doctrinal and ethical contents of religious systems to the private sphere of personal choices. Thus in Leskov's works we may observe how some of the ideas of Khomiakov's ecclesiological concepts are put into a new context and re-interpreted by the writer. This process may be evaluated both as a distortion of a certain intellectual reality and as an enrichment

22. Maksimkin, "Leskov i Origen," 29–32.

and creative development of the original system. In both cases, it is still underexplored and deserves further research.

Bibliography

Christoff, Peter K. *A. S. Xomjakov.* Vol. 1 of *An Introduction to Nineteenth-Century Russian Slavophilism.* The Hague: Mouton, 1961.

Dolinina, Irina V. "Dikhotomiya khudozhestvennogo koncepta 'khristianstvo' na 'istinnoe khristianstvo' i 'pravoslavie' v diskurse tsikla N. S. Leskova 'Melochi arhiereyskoy zhizni.'" *Vestnik gumanitarnogo fakul'teta IGHTU* 9 (2009) 236–41.

Edgerton, William B. "Leskov and Tolstoy: Two Literary Heretics." *American Slavic and East European Review* 4 (1953) 524–34.

———. "Nikolai Leskov: The Intellectual Development of a Literary Nonconformist." PhD diss., Columbia University, 1954.

Khalizev, Valentin, and Ol'ga Mayorova. "Leskovskaya koncepciya pravednichestva." In *V mire Leskova,* edited by Viktor Bogdanov, 196–232. Moscow: Sovetskiy pisatel', 1983.

Khomiakov, Alexei S. "The Church Is One." In *On Spiritual Unity: A Slavophile Reader,* edited and translated by Boris Jakim and Robert Bird, 31–53. Translated by Robert Bird. Hudson: Lindisfarne, 1998.

———. "On the Western Confessions of Faith." *Archangels Books.* Translated by Asheleigh E. Moorhouse. http://www.archangelsbooks.com/articles/east_west/WesternConfessions_Khomiakov.asp.

Kozłowski, Rościsław. Rosyjska eklezjologia prawosławna w XIX–XX wieku. Warszawa: Chrześcijańska Akademia Teologiczna, 1988.

Leonova, Bela. *Zhanr memuarnogo ocherka v tvorchestve N. S. Leskova 1880-kh godov.* Orel: Izdatel'skiy dom "Orlik," 2005.

Leskov, Nikolay S. "Avtobiograficheskaya zametka." In *Sobranie sochineniy v 11 t,* by Nikolay Leskov, 7–15. Vol. 11. Moscow: GIKhL, 1958.

———. *The Cathedral Folk.* Translated by Isabel F. Hapgood. New York: A. A. Knopf, 1924.

———. *On the Edge of the World.* Translated by Michael Prokurat. Crestwood: St. Vladimir's Seminary Press, 1992.

———. "Smekh i gore." In *Sobranie sochineniy v 11 t,* by Nikolay Leskov, 382–570. Vol. 3. Moscow: GIKhL, 1957.

———. "Sovmestiteli." In *Sobranie sochineniy v 11 t,* by Nikolay Leskov, 399–431. Vol. 7. Moscow: GIKhL, 1957.

———. "Vozmozhna li i racional'na li chisto duhovnaya cenzura?" *Birzhevye vedomosti* 111 (1870) 3.

Maksimkin, Vladimir A. "N. S. Leskov i Origen: k rekonstruktsii opyta vzaimodeystviya i ottalkivaniya." *Ural'skiy filologicheskiy vestnik* 5 (2014) 26–34.

Muckle, John Y. *Nikolai Leskov and the "Spirit of Protestantism."* Birmingham: University of Birmingham, 1978.

Tofiluk, Jerzy. "Koncepcja apokatastazy ks. Sergiusza Bułgakowa." *Roczniki Teologiczne* 50 (2003) 23–42.

12

A Possible Filiation Between Alexei Khomiakov and Lev Karsavin

FRANÇOISE LESOURD

K homiakov exerted a certain influence on Lev Karsavin, one of the lead-ing Russian philosophers of religion of the twentieth century. The latter was born in Saint Petersburg in 1882. His family belonged not to the intel-ligentsia, but to the artistic milieu: his father was principal dancer at the Mariinsky Theatre, the Saint Petersburg opera house, and his sister Tamara Karsavina became a famous ballerina and went on to dance with Nijinsky.[1] Karsavin himself studied at the Faculty of History and Philology under the distinguished professor Ivan Mikhailovitch Grevs, and was to become one of the most outstanding historians of the St. Petersburg school, and a specialist on medieval Western spirituality. Karsavin's principal research interests during this period led to two theses: *Essays on Religious Life in Italy in the Twelfth and Thirteenth Centuries*[2] (1912) and *The Foundations of Medieval Spirituality*[3] (1915).

Although he was hostile to the Bolshevik revolution, he decided to collaborate loyally with the newly-established Soviet authorities. He participated in the great publishing enterprises initiated by Gorki.[4] Yet he was expelled from the USSR in 1922, along with a swathe of leading Russian intellectuals, and settled in Berlin where, shortly afterwards, he was contacted by the founders of the Eurasianist movement and asked

1. Karsavina, *Theatre Street.*
2. Karsavin, *Ocherki religioznoj zhizni.*
3. Karsavin, *Osnovy srednevekovoy religioznosti.*
4. For example, he published *Otkroveniya blazhennoy Andzhely* for the collection "Biblioteka mistikov" and the treatise *Katolichestvo* for the collection "Mirovye religii."

to become the ideologist of this political movement, which aimed to re-establish links with Soviet Russia and develop an alternative ideology that could take the place of communism after the end of what they expected to be a short-lived Soviet era.

Karsavin had never accepted his émigré status, but was gradually obliged to recognize that the Soviet regime was probably going to remain in place for a considerable time, and was forced to admit that: "we will probably never go back to Russia." Nevertheless, he reframed Eurasianist ideology, which was set out in several pamphlets, in particular: *The Foundations of Politics*[5] and *A Phenomenology of Revolution,*[6] in both of which a Slavophile influence can be felt. In fact, the notion of Eurasia was of little importance to him: it was Russia that really interested him. As he wrote in 1923: "Do they [the Eurasianists] really think that all things 'European' and 'Russian' should be eliminated, and replaced by something that is 'Eurasian' (whatever that might be)?"[7] He goes on:

> I am Russian, and I prefer to die along with my Russian fellow countrymen. It is not in times of trial and tribulation that one should renounce one's language and one's country.[8]

However, he endorsed the Eurasianist attempt to re-establish links with the new—Soviet—reality of Russia.

In 1926 he moved to Paris, where the core of the movement was based, but left it after little more than a year, not only because of his disagreements with the "right-wing" Eurasianists, who were unwilling to recognize the Soviet authorities, but also because of the opacity of its funding (it was suspected that the movement was financed in part by the Soviet secret services), and above all because he had been invited to take up the chair of world history at the University of Kaunas, the then capital of newly-independent Lithuania. From 1928 on, his destiny was linked to that of his Lithuanian university; within a few months he was lecturing in Lithuanian, and it was in this language that he wrote his monumental *History of European Culture.*[9]

At the end of the Second World War, when Lithuania became a Soviet satellite, he was encouraged to leave, as it was dangerous for someone forced into exile in 1922 to find himself in Soviet territory again. But he

5. Karsavin, "Osnovy politiki."

6. Karsavin, "Fenomenologiya revolyutsii."

7. Karsavin, "Evropa i Evraziya," 298.

8. Karsavin, "Evropa i Evraziya," 298.

9. Karsavin, *Europos kultūros istorija.*

wished "to be re-united with Russia,"[10] and was convinced that the Soviet authorities "had changed"; he therefore decided to stay, but in the course of time, despite his loyal co-operation, he was obliged to give up his position at the university, and was later forced out of his post as director of the Vilnius Museum of Fine Arts. In 1949, he was arrested and incarcerated in the city's prison for a year, during which the first signs of tuberculosis became apparent. Karsavin died of the disease in the summer of 1952 in the Abez prison camp (located south of Vorkouta), where he was serving a ten-year sentence.[11]

It was more especially after the revolution that the links between his philosophy and Khomiakov's thinking emerged and the importance of the latter's thought for an understanding of Russia's historical destiny in the twentieth century came to be recognized. But in fact, even in Karsavin's youth, when his attention was particularly focused on St. Bernard of Clairvaux, Abelard, and St. Francis, etc., he had already published an article (on the papacy) that demonstrated a certain kinship with Khomiakov.[12] Moreover, this closeness was intentional: he claimed (probably wrongly, however) to be related to him through his mother.

This paper, written in 1910, addressed a subject dear to the Slavophiles: the birth of the papacy as an institution and the specificity of the Roman Church. It is a scholarly study, without any obvious polemical intent yet the influence of Khomiakov is clearly perceptible: the "democratic" spirit of the nascent Roman Church is clearly underscored, the "charismata" are seen, at that time, as involving all the faithful, whereas they subsequently went on to become the preserve of the few, the "pastors," whose role, moreover, is justified by the importance of the Eucharist in worship. Furthermore, the choice of the word "pastor" (*presviter*) is significant, as it indicates the type of relationship between the faithful and the leaders of the early church, and is a term often used by Khomiakov.

In this article, the influence of Khomiakov is unexpectedly intertwined with that of Vladimir Soloviev. In his treatise, *The Great Controversy and Christian Politics*,[13] the latter author admits that papal authority could be justified by the part played by different Popes—as guardians of Church doctrine in the struggle against heresy—at a dangerous time, that of Marcion, the Gnostics, etc.

---

10. Unpublished letter to Elena Skržinskaja.

11. Vaneev, "Dva goda v Abezi."

12. Karsavin, "Rimskaya tserkov."

13. Solov'ev, *Velikiy spor.*

After the 1917 revolution, the influence of Khomiakov took on a new dimension, and he came to be seen as the veritable prophet of the Russian catastrophe. Karsavin's pamphlet *East, West and the Russian Idea*[14] portrays the revolution as a "second period of rampant Westernization"[15] after that of Peter the Great. In this document, Khomiakov's ideas on the Westernization of Russia and its damaging consequences are melded with what is peculiar to Karsavin himself: a particularly profound knowledge of medieval Western spirituality and the concept of a "dualism of religious consciousness" (that is, two contrary orientations: the one directed towards the world and good works, in order to attain salvation, and the other towards contemplation and prayer; the idea of a complete break between God and the world, or that of possible access to the Godhead). This opposition between the two types of spirituality is reminiscent, to a certain extent, of Khomiakov's distinction between what he calls the "Persian" and the "Cushitic" principles,[16] which he, however, used to distinguish between two main types of culture. For Karsavin, it is the type of spirituality that defines the type of culture. His understanding of the notion of "faith" is so broad as to be almost synonymous with the concept of "mentality." From Karsavin's perspective, as can be seen in *East, West and the Russian Idea*, Russia occupies an intermediate position: for him, its type of religiosity is "Eastern," but he conceives it as belonging within an overall European framework. Both thinkers attach fundamental importance to the question of the *filioque*. But whereas Khomiakov simply considered the matter as a "crime" perpetrated by the West against its Eastern brothers, Karsavin emphasizes the consequences of this change in dogma upon people's worldview. The insertion of the *filioque* introduces into the Trinity a sort of second unit, comprising the Father and the Son. It reduces the part played by the Holy Spirit and renders impossible "the manifestation of God within the created world,"[17] because of the sharp break thus introduced.

The Russian catastrophe, he continues, is due to the imposition of a foreign, Western, ideal of exclusively earthly happiness, involving "both the refusal of an inaccessible heavenly life, and an ideal of empirical prosperity presented as an absolute," on a country whose religious consciousness was of a different (passive, contemplative) type. Yet Russia, he writes, needs to carry through to its conclusion the trial imposed upon it in order to realize

14. Karsavin, *Vostok, zapad*.

15. Karsavin, *Vostok, zapad*, 105.

16. Especially in his *Zapiski o vsemirnoy istorii*, published for the first time in 1860 (in the review *Russkaya Beseda*).

17. Karsavin, *Vostok, zapad*, 108.

its full potential and truly become itself through the demise of the old world (the old regime). Karsavin's ontology can be summed up, therefore, in the expression: "Life through death."

Some time later, however, his closeness to Khomiakov was explicitly manifested when Eurasian Book Publishers in Berlin republished the latter's essay, *The Church is One*, with a preface by Karsavin entitled "On the Church."

Judging by the title, one might expect Khomiakov's essay to target Western Christian confessions, considered as heretical, and cut off from the ecumenical Church. On first sight, this in fact seems to be an incorrect impression: Khomiakov speaks of the oneness of the church visible and invisible, and the grace which reaches out to all men, at all times.

In Khomiakov's *Collected Works*, its full title is: "A Catechetical Exposition of the Teaching of the Church." At first sight then, it is simply a catechism. It may appear strange, to Western eyes, that a secular author should write a "catechism." Yet in Russia, on the other hand, it represented a major innovation. I refer readers here to the article by Antonella Cavazza,[18] in which she admirably demonstrates the novel character of this initiative (a point of which Westerners would otherwise be unaware). This typically Russian tradition—the elaboration of theology by secular authors—which Karsavin, moreover, went on to continue, may strike us as surprising. But there was none other.

As is well known, the Orthodox Church confined itself exclusively to Holy Scripture and the first seven ecumenical councils. Exegesis was not allowed, and there was no other text. The very first catechism, produced by Peter Mohyla in the early eighteenth century, remained largely unknown. That of Metropolitan Philaret appeared shortly before Khomiakov's essay.

Khomiakov set out the fundamental truths of faith in straightforward contemporary language. This corresponded to a pressing need, as certain accounts evince. However, his essay was regarded with suspicion by the religious authorities, who were apprehensive about even a simple presentation of the truths of faith, when produced outside the Church, whereas Khomiakov himself considered that he had helped the Russian Church by filling a gap. For, by refusing to accept a modern formulation of the truths of faith, it was depriving itself of a means of countering the influence of the Western churches.

The essay consists firstly of a systematic presentation of the principal religious truths: religious life is grounded in Holy Scripture, good works, and tradition; their authenticity flows from the person of Christ, who is the

18. Cavazza, "Sources de l'essai."

foundation of doctrine as a whole; religious truths cannot be rationally demonstrated; the creed, which occupies a central place, sets out mysteries that are inaccessible to reason. Next come the enumeration and explanation of the theological virtues and all the sacraments, and then the essay deals with the Last Judgment, and the Resurrection, just as in an ordinary catechism. It offers an answer to a frequently asked question on the value of the sacraments administered by unworthy priests: the value of such sacraments is not lost as, in each instance, the rite is performed by the whole Church.

But in fact, we very quickly discover there is a polemical intention hidden beneath each point dealt with in the presentation. The Church as a unified body possesses the truth, whereas an individual person may fall into error. The Church "cannot acknowledge that any particular private individual or bishop or patriarch or their successors are immune from succumbing to error in doctrine and that they are protected from error by some special grace."[19] Clearly Khomiakov's target is papal infallibility.

"The Church," writes Khomiakov, "belongs to the whole world, and not any locality."[20] The fact that "Rome" has become the symbol of ecumenism in the minds of some people should not disguise the fact that Rome is no more than an insignificantly small territory on a terrestrial scale. What is accepted by the Church is that which is "proclaimed by a General Council and common agreement,"[21] and not by the will of a single individual (the Pope). In Western cultures, the desire to prove the existence of God is fairly widespread, but this only demonstrates "the pride of reason and unlawful power."[22]

But the worst sin of all consists in adding to the canonical texts. And this, of course, alludes to the *filioque*, which introduces a sort of new dogma into the teaching of the Church: "the addition of the word *filioque* contains some illusory dogma unknown to any of the God-pleased writers, bishops, or apostolic successors in the first centuries of the Church; nor was it spoken by Christ the Savior."[23] As regards the Eucharist, the Catholic term of "transubstantiation" is not rejected, but the Holy Church "does not ascribe to it the material sense attributed to it by the teachers of the churches that have fallen away,"[24] as it represents a drift towards magic. Ritual is one of the foundations of the life of the Church, but if the importance attached to it becomes exclusive, it distances man from God: such is the case of the "ritualism" of the

19. Khomiakov, "Church Is One," 33.

20. Khomiakov, "Church Is One," 33.

21. Khomiakov, "Church Is One," 33.

22. Khomiakov, "Church Is One," 38.

23. Khomiakov, "Church Is One," 38.

24. Khomiakov, "Church Is One," 42.

Catholic Church. Thus, what might at the outset have appeared to be a simple catechism ultimately turns out to be a polemical essay.

While Karsavin prolongs the tradition of theological elaboration by secular writers, he adds new dimensions, because of the new historical situation. For him—and this is already visible in his earliest historical studies, and even more so towards the end of his life, in his dialogues with Vaneyev—dogma needs to become (or once again become) the object of intellectual attention, in order to respond to the modern-day secularization of culture.

Karsavin's introduction to *The Church is One* is a veritable apologia for Khomiakov. It demonstrates the relevance of his thought just as the Bolshevik revolution was confirming the validity of his vision of the evolution of Russian culture, and the impasse into which it had been drawn by one-sided Occidentalism (Karsavin mentions Khomiakov's curious lightheartedness at the time of the siege of Sebastopol). He points out that Khomiakov had practically no readers in Russia, and suggests that it may be for this reason that he wrote his essays in various foreign languages.

Karsavin underscores the fact that Khomiakov neither refused the idea of progress, nor rejected the contribution of Peter the Great, and he cannot be considered to be a chauvinistic nationalist (on the contrary, he never ceased to emphasize the running sores of life in Russia). Herzen rightly said of the Slavophiles: "The importance of their outlook, what was true and essential in it, lay not in Orthodoxy and not exclusive nationalism, but in those elements of Russian life which they unearthed from under the manure of an artificial civilization."[25] These particular "elements" (*stikhii*) has very little to do with the "people," which is a notion invented by the intelligentsia (the "ruling layer of society" which has lost its "organic character," as Karsavin points out in *A Phenomenology of Revolution*[26]).

What gives particular relevance to Khomiakov's ideas is the fact that the end of the First World War revealed the bankruptcy of European values, all across Europe, but more especially in Russia. Indeed, it was precisely because of the catastrophe of the revolution that the country became involved in the common destiny of Europe. It was at this time that certain Russian intellectuals turned away from Europe, and began to look "towards the East." Not so Karsavin, who stressed that, despite everything, Russia is inconceivable outside Europe as a whole.

Karsavin's preface demonstrates not only common thinking with Khomiakov, but also a kinship of sensibility: the latter warns against an abstract

25. Herzen, *My Past and Thoughts*, 2:512.
26. Karsavin, "Fenomenologiya revolyutsii," 19.

understanding of Christianity ("it is not without the body that we shall be resurrected"[27]). Incarnation is the core of the Christian idea, Karsavin underlines, and abstraction is harmful. During this period he even wrote an article entitled: "On the Dangers of Abstract Christianity and How to Overcome It."[28] More importantly, his attitude towards emigration can also be explained in part by his refusal of abstraction, highlighting a new aspect of the Westernization of Russia, the loss of the concrete: "what is foreign is only concrete in its place of origin, and is only assimilated in an abstract form."[29]

The idea of the Church is inseparable from Khomiakov's idea of *sobornost'*, but the latter concept takes us well beyond ecclesial life *stricto sensu*. It is an idea that is very close to Karsavin's idea of the "symphonic person," and is linked to his very individual ontology, which comes from Nicholas of Cusa (and his *est/possest* distinction) and Hegel.

The concept of the symphonic person can be briefly summed up as follows: all reality is made up of a multiplicity of collective (symphonic) persons. These represent a sum of potentialities and hence are in retraction. At a given point in time, one of these potentialities separates from this sum of elements in retraction, undergoes a transition from a state of potentiality to one of reality, and is individuated, acquiring certain precise concrete qualities (*kachestvovanie*). Some time later it is, as it were, annihilated: it then goes back towards the center and resumes its status of potentiality. But it does not disappear entirely and can later be realized once more as a new, concrete, individual realization of the higher symphonic person: in sum, a sort of metaphysics of the circle. Its center brings together, in a reduced concentrated form, all the potentialities, and its circumference is made up of the infinite number of their possible realizations. This conception is reminiscent of the well-known Renaissance representation of God: a sphere whose center is everywhere and whose circumference is nowhere.

The fact that, sooner or later, the person comes back to the center is what Karsavin calls "ontologically necessary death."[30] But the person in question may also voluntarily give up his individuality for the benefit of others: hence self-sacrifice lies at the center of this fundamentally Christian conception. The complete realization of one's "self" supposes a willing acceptance of death, on behalf of another (a fellow being, or a higher "symphonic person").

27. Khomiakov, "Church Is One," 42.
28. Karsavin, "Ob opasnostyakh."
29. Karsavin, "Fenomenologiya revolyutsii," 17.
30. "Ontologicheski neobkhodimaya smert'" (Karsavin, *Filosofiya istorii*, 80).

In this interpretation, Khomiakov's *sobornost'* acquires new, darker characteristics, but at the same time it becomes an organic component of an overall world vision and a whole conception of existence. It is complemented by a philosophy of self-sacrifice that also impinges on the political domain. The type of society to which Karsavin aspires, and which he defines in his writings on Eurasianism, supposes on the part of each individual "constant live communication with other like persons."[31] Communication between people involves self-denial, indeed this is even its main feature (as can be seen, in particular, in his *Poem of Death*). As he writes in *The Foundations of Politics*:

> At the root of communication between people lies love, once again empirically expressed by the idea of service for the individual and collective benefit of others, which is ontologically equivalent to the mutual gift of self.[32]

Orthodoxy is particularly well suited to expressing the Christian idea of self-denial, because it is unaffected by the *filioque* heresy, and has kept the primitive tradition intact. It encapsulates Russia's past and its future. But Karsavin's reflections on the essence of Orthodoxy were accompanied by very real pain at the risks to the Russian Orthodox Church during the Soviet era. As the threat to the Russian Orthodox Church increased and the prospect of his being able to return to Russia receded even further, his articles became increasingly polemical. This was doubtless coherent with the spirit of Khomiakov's thinking, but at the same time the polemical aspect of both authors' writings went together—surprisingly—with a desire for dialogue.

Khomiakov's son, Dmitrii, once wrote to André Gratieux, the author of a dissertation on his father[33]:

> Essentially, nothing is more harmful to a desirable union than when both parties are unable to clearly recognize the differences that separate them; and for this reason, I have always considered my father's theological writings to be not so much polemical as 'irenical,' because in their author's mind their—positive— aim was to clarify respective positions, and not to crush his adversaries.[34]

31. Karsavin, "Osnovy politiki," 24.

32. Karsavin, "Osnovy politiki," 25.

33. Gratieux, *A. S. Khomiakov*.

34. Dmitrii Khomiakov's letter (in French) to André Gratieux: "Rien n'est au fond plus nuisible pour une union désirable que quand les deux partis ne se rendent pas nettement compte de ce qui les sépare; et pour cette raison j'ai toujours regardé les écrits théologiques de mon père comme beaucoup moins polémiques qu' 'iréniques,' parce

The same can be said of Karsavin, only more so: his religious positions are hard to define clearly. He was considered to be a staunch defender of Orthodoxy and an enemy of Catholicism (in Lithuania, he had only been very reluctantly accepted by the Catholic hierarchy), yet the Orthodox authorities regarded him with suspicion (Semen Frank wrote of him in a letter that he enjoyed "sowing the seeds of heresy").

On this point, perhaps what was most characteristic of him was his correspondence with Father Wetter. When Gustav Wetter first contacted Karsavin, he was a youthful Jesuit priest planning to write a dissertation on the Orthodox conception of the Trinity. They very soon began discussing the subjects closest to their hearts. Their correspondence[35] offers a unique example of a particularly intense inter-faith dialogue on topics of Christian metaphysics. Initially, Karsavin stated that he had always been "at war" with Catholicism (which is rather surprising when one thinks of his early work, his edition of Angela of Foligno's mystical illuminations in *The Revelation of the Blessed Angela*, or his treatise on *Catholicism*). But at the same time he wrote to Father Wetter:

> Catholicism differs from Orthodoxy in that it is a rigorously and precisely formulated system that sets out the limits to individual philosophical reflection. But the metaphysics that I myself defend does not, I fear, fit entirely within the framework of traditional Orthodoxy.[36]

This, then, is where Karsavin's profound kinship with Khomiakov lies; for him, true dialogue is not so much compromise as a deepening of the understanding of one's differences as part of an authentic quest for truth.

Bibliography

Cavazza, Antonella. "Sur les sources de l'essai d'A. S. Khomiakov 'L'Église est une.'" *Slavica Occitania, Toulouse* 41 (2015) 177–89.

Gratieux, Albert. *A. S. Khomiakov et le mouvement slavophile*. Paris: Cerf, 1939.

———. *Le Mouvement slavophile à la veille de la révolution*. Paris: Cerf, 1954.

Herzen, Alexander. *My Past and Thoughts*. Translated by Constance Garnett. 4 vols. London: Chatto and Windus, 1968.

Karsavin, Lev. *Europos kultūros istorija*. Vol. 5. Kaunas: V. D. Universiteto Humanitarinių mokslų fakultetas, 1931–1936.

———. "Evropa i Evraziya" *Sovremennye zapiski* 2/25 (1923) 297–314.

qu'ils avaient dans l'esprit de l'auteur le but positif d'éclaircir la situation réciproque, et non celui de pourfendre les adversaires" (Gratieux, *Le Mouvement slavophile*, 60).

35. Karsavin, "Perepiska A. Vettera s L. Karsavinym," 104–69.

36. Karsavin, "Perepiska A. Vettera s L. Karsavinym," 109.

————. "Fenomenologiya revolyutsii." *Evraziyskiy vremennik* 5 (1927) 58–74.

————. *Filosofiya istorii.* Berlin: Obelisk, 1923.

————. *Katolichestvo.* Moscow: Ogni, 1918.

————. Letter to Elena Skržinskaja. In *Lietuvos Ypatingasis Archivas.* P. 11972 LI. No. 16416.

————. "Ob opasnostyakh i preodolenii otvlechennogo khristianstva." *Put'* 6 (1927) 32–49.

————. *Ocherki religioznoj zhizni v Italii XII–XIII vekov.* St. Petersburg: Tipografiya M. A. Aleksandrova, 1912

————. "Osnovy politiki." *Evraziyskiy vremennik* 5 (1927) 185–239.

————. *Osnovy srednevekovoy religioznosti v XII–XIII vekakh.* Petrograd: Tipografiya "Nauchnoe delo," 1915.

————. *Otkroveniya blazhennoy Andzhely.* Moscow: Izdatelstvo G. A. Lemana, 1918.

————. "Perepiska A. Vettera s L. Karsavinym." *Simvol* 31 (1994) 104–69.

————. "Rimskaya tserkov' i papstvo do poloviny II veka." *Zhurnal ministerstwa narodnogo prosveshcheniya. Novaya seriya* 11 (1910) 73–97.

————. *Vostok, zapad i russkaya ideya.* Petrograd: Academia, 1922.

Karsavina, Tamara. *Theatre Street. The Reminiscences of Tamara Karsavina.* London, 1948.

Khomiakov, Alexei S. "The Church Is One." In *On Spiritual Unity: A Slavophile Reader*, edited and translated by Boris Jakim and Robert Bird, 31–53. Hudson, NY: Lindisfarne, 1998.

————. *Zapiski o vsemirnoy istorii.* Vols. 5–6 of *Polnoe sobranie sochineniy Alekseya Stepanovicha Khomiakova*, by Alexei S. Khomiakov. Moscow: Tipo-litografiya T-va I. N. Kushnerov, 1904.

Solov'ev, Vladimir. "Velikiy spor i khristianskaya politika." In *Sobranie sochineniy Vladimira Sergeevicha Solov'eva*, by Vladimir Solov'ev, 3–114. Vol. 4. St. Petersburg: Prosveshchenie, 1914.

Vaneev, Anatoliy A. "Dva goda v Abezi. V pamyat' o L. P. Karsavine." Bruxelles: Zhizn' s Bogom, 1990.

13

Alexei Khomiakov, Pierre Teilhard de Chardin, and Ladislav Hanus

Three Points of View on Faith and Church in Human Life[1]

ZLATICA PLAŠIENKOVÁ, PETER RUSNÁK, AND LUCIO FLORIO

Introduction

In the introduction to our paper we would like to emphasise that three notable authors, namely the Russian philosopher, Slavophile and lay theologian Alexei S. Khomiakov, the French scientist, philosopher and priest, the Jesuit Pierre Teilhard de Chardin, and the Slovak culturologist, philosopher and priest Ladislav Hanus belong to three different cultural-religious contexts: the Eastern Orthodox (Khomiakov), Western Catholic (Teilhard de Chardin), and Central-European (Slovak in particular) Catholic context (Hanus). In spite of this different contextual anchoring, several overlapping ideas regarding the issue of the understanding of faith and the Church can be identified in the discussed authors.

Our starting point is represented by the conception of the Church orthodoxy (and a broader understood identity of man in the environment of love) that was introduced by the Russian philosopher Alexei S. Khomiakov. His reflections on faith and the Church serve as a basis also for the comparison with the opinions on faith and the Church in the work of Teilhard de Chardin, who incorporated them in the understanding of evolution of the entire universe. According to this conception, he interprets the Church as a biological *phylum* of Christ, and at the same time, as a unity of God

1. This contribution was supported by VEGA: "Man within the Profane and the Sacral in Russian Thought of the Twentieth Century" (No. 1/0375/16).

and man. It is a unity that is constantly formed and matures over time. The central unifying force of this unity is love.

Reflections on the issue of the unity of God and man are typical of the spiritual legacy of Ladislav Hanus. This unity is mostly expressed in Hanus's philosophical-personalistic anthropology, in which he emphasises the meaning of spiritual life of man and society against the background of Christian humanism.

Concerning the ideological legacy of the analyzed authors, we focus on the comparison of several specific ideas. Foremost, it is the perception of the Church in connection to the term *sobornost'* by Khomiakov in comparison with the understanding of the unity of the Church by Teilhard de Chardin. At the same time, we note the interpretation of the Church as a living organism as well as a cultural phenomenon whose manifestation is the culture of a man as indicated by Hanus in particular. Our attention is also focused on the role of love which plays a central role in the understanding of the Church as a community of believers. Besides love, it is also the faith of man itself that is crucial, not only in the life of man as an individuum but also at the level of their institutional life in the Church community. It regards both the Orthodox and the Catholic Church. The last aspect we would like to point out in this study is the very understanding of man as a being that is manifested both as a reasonable being and believing being. The unity of reason and faith is then also demonstrated in the field of cognition and the search for truth.

Khomiakov and His Reflection on Faith and the Church

The Russian philosopher Khomiakov is considered to be a thinker who had an immense impact on discussions in the field of the understanding of Russian culture, philosophy, and theology. Nikolay O. Lossky, in his work *History of Russian Philosophy*, even states that the Slavophile Khomiakov, together with Kireevsky, may be considered thinkers who represent the beginning of the Russian philosophical thinking of the nineteenth century:

> The beginnings of independent philosophical thought in Russia date back to the Slavophiles Ivan Kireevsky and Khomiakov. Their philosophy is an attempt to overcome the German type of philosophizing on the strength of the Russian interpretation of Christianity based upon the Works of the Eastern Fathers and nourished by the national peculiarities of Russian spiritual life. Neither Kireevsky nor Khomiakov worked out a system of

philosophy, but they set out the program and established the
spirit of the philosophical movement which is the most original
and valuable achievement of Russian thought. I mean the attempt of the Russian thinkers to develop a systematic Christian
world conception.[2]

The noted originality of the thought was manifested in the understanding
of human knowledge, national identity and the Church in connection to the
term *sobornost'*.[3]

The term *sobornost'*[4] is likely to be best understood at present against
the background of two opposing interpretations: individualism and collectivism. While individualism prefers the priority of individual freedom, personal sovereignty and responsibility that has to be respected in members of
a specific community, collectivism, on the contrary, prefers group integrity,
sovereignty and collective fate to an individual. However, *sobornost'*, in a
certain meaning, transcends both understandings: both the understanding
of individualism and the understanding of collectivism. *Sobornost'* is more
than just a "community" linking several individuals together. *Sobornost'* as a
dynamic principle does not so much describe the individual's merging with
or absorption by collectivity. Although this collectivity in Khomiakov's view
is still analogically associated with the Russian *obschina* (the *obshchina* as a
peasant community), more importantly, according to him, *sobornost'* is an
organic, living unity, the origin of which lies in the divine grace of mutual
love.[5] Let us add that it is also a mystical unity of God and man. It is an
invisible Church, a spiritual unity, not only a social unity.

Khomiakov's treatise *The Church is One* (*Tserkov' odna*),[6] in which he
formulated the basic credo—*Confession of Faith* (*Symbol of Faith*), is the

---

2. Lossky, *History of Russian Philosophy*, 13–14.

3. From the etymological point of view, the term *sobor* comes from the root of the
word *sobirat'*, which means to put together, summon, gather. In the Slavic church, it had
three meanings: council, cathedral, and gathering of people. Modern Russian uses it in
the first two meanings. The general gathering—Catholic (Greek *katholikos*, i.e., general,
universal) is neglected here. See Ambros, "Učitel církve?," 29.

4. There is no literal English translation for *sobornost'*, but its meaning could be
paraphrased with words such as "community," "togetherness," or "collegiality."

5. Let us recall here that Khomiakov used the adjective *sobornyy* (as multitude in
one) rather than the substantive *sobornost'*. This term has been assigned to him by later
translations and elaborations of his works. For a detailed analysis, see Riasanovsky,
"Khomiakov on Sobornost."

6. The work was published for the first time only after Khomiakov's death, in 1864.
Several years later, it was published in Prague under the editorship of Yuri F. Samarin
(a friend and younger Slavophile) and with a foreword by the same. It was a translation
from French that was a part of the collection of works published in Prague in 1868, even

most inspiring work for us in the submitted study. It is the first and most significant theological essay by Khomiakov. He attempts to justify the unity and uniqueness of the Church in a brief and metaphorical form.[7] Khomiakov holds by it a free unity of members of the Christian Church in the understanding of Divine truth and common salvation based on the common love of God—the Godman Christ.[8] In him (in Christ) the world can unify and not divide. In Christ, there is only the undivided and complete truth for which all those who live in the Church and for the Church are bound. Also, the fullness of Christ is to be sought for in a community of those who believe in this only truth, while "the unity of the Church follows necessarily from the unity of God."[9]

Let us note that it was precisely Khomiakov who sought an appropriate term to express wholeness in regard to the unity of the Church. He was looking for a word that would capture the organic unity of the Church, or the idea of its ideal image. Therefore, the word *sobornaya* or *sobornost'* should be a more adequate and dignified expression than the one used by the Roman Church, that is just the word Catholic or universal, general.[10] In a sense, the origin of the word *sobornyy* was derived from a council meaning, a gathering without the need to summon anyone. In this context, Tomas

---

though the year 1867 is stated on the cover of the book. However, it has to be noted that in this edition, "The Church is One" is found in the contents of the book under a more general title: "Opyt katikhizicheskago izlozhenia uchenia o Tserkvi."

7. It is known that Khomiakov would let the people read the work as a work by an unknown old Orthodox author that was found accidentally by his nephew. His main intention was probably to discover people's attitudes and opinions on the given subject as well as his fear of censorship.

8. Nikolay Lossky adds to the understanding of *sobornost'* (commonalty) in Khomiakov the following: "*Sobornost* is the free unity of the members of the Church in their common understanding of truth and finding salvation together—an unity based upon their unanimous love for Christ and Divine righteousness" (Lossky, *History of Russian Philosophy*, 35).

9. Khomiakov, "Church Is One," 31.

10. See Ambros, "Učitel církve?," 8. Let us make a further comment that Khomiakov does not reject the word "Catholic" and "universal," however, he puts them in brackets while defining the Church. In paragraph 4, Khomiakov writes: "The Church is called *one, holy, sobornyj* (catholic and universal), and *apostolic* because she is one and holy; because she belongs to the whole world and not any locality; because she hallows all humanity and all the earth and not one particular nation or one country; because her essence consists in the harmony and unity of the spirit and life of all her members who recognize her over the entire earth; and because finally all the fullness of her faith, her hopes, and her love are contained in Scripture and apostolic teaching" (Khomiakov, "Church Is One," 33–34).

Spidlik quotes Khomiakov's words according to which the Christian people living their faith are a hidden council to themselves.[11]

Let us add that this term meant a kind of a distance from the formal authority of the Catholic Church (including the authority of its Pope) for Slavophiles and, at the same time, a distance from Protestant individualism.[12] In Slavophile thought (and in Khomiakov's in particular), *sobornost'* became an ideal model of the natural coexistence of not a single nation or state but all people with a shared faith who form one organic whole.[13]

In this connection, let us recall here the words of Khomiakov's friend, Samarin, which he wrote in the introductory foreword to the Russian edition of the second volume of his writings in Prague. These words were devoted to a characterisation of the personal relationship of Khomiakov to the Church. Samarin writes:

> For him the Church was a living center in which all his thoughts originated and to which they all returned. He stood before the face of the Church and judged himself with an inner judgment according to her law. All that was dear to him he held dear in relation to the Church.[14]

Teilhard de Chardin and His Reflections on Faith and the Church

Reflections on the Church representing one organic whole were also developed in the work of the French thinker, Pierre Teilhard de Chardin.[15] Unlike Kho-

11. See Spidlik, *L'idée russe*, 126.

12. Khomiakov's criticism of the Catholic and Evangelic Church obviously corresponds to the entire criticism of the superficial "rationalistic" Western world, which disables the accomplishment of the complexity of the truth by its violent intervention in the natural structures. According to the author, only "the Orthodox Church remained the 'true' Church; not because of proud claims but due to remaining compact, i.e., *sobornaya*" (Ambros, "Učitel církve?," 31). The critical attitude of Khomiakov to Catholicism and Protestantism related to his understanding of *sobornost'* as the harmony of unity and freedom is also expressed in the opinion that Catholicism represents unity without freedom and Protestantism represents freedom without unity, as pointed out by Lossky: "In Catholicism, he finds unity without freedom and in Protestantism freedom without unity. In these denominations only external unity and external freedom are realised" (Lossky, *History of Russian Philosophy*, 35).

13. For more on the meaning of Khomiakov's teaching and his persona as a teacher of the Church in the context of the Russian Orthodoxy, see Ambros, "Učitel církve?"

14. Samarin, "Theological Writings," 162–63.

15. Teilhard, like Khomiakov, held it important that the Church was for him personally also a divine environment that he could not secede even if his relationships with

miakov, he associated the understanding of the Church as an organic whole with the teachings on evolution. Teilhard de Chardin was also a scientist, not only a theologian and a priest, and throughout his life, he attempted to carry out a "synthesis of science and religion," a synthesis—as he often stressed—of the "religion of the Earth" and "religion of Heaven."

This is also suggested by his reflections on the understanding of the Church and faith, which he interprets in a broader and not strictly religious meaning. Besides the faith in God and personal Jesus (who has, at the same time, a cosmic character and is Pantocrator), it also regards, for example, faith in man, in evolution, in science and progress, in increase of spirituality on Earth and final completion of Evolution of the Universe in the Omega Point.[16]

His personal credo, which he published as a motto in his work in 1934 entitled *Comment je crois* (*How I believe*), sounds like this:

> I believe that the Universe is an Evolution. I believe that Evolution proceeds towards the Spirit. I believe that the Spirit is fully realized in a form of personality.[17] I believe that the supremely Personal is the universal Christ.[18]

Christ is, for Teilhard, the saviour of both the idea and the reality of evolution.

It may be appropriate to note that the Pastoral Constitution on the Church in the Modern World *Gaudium et spes* (1965) pointed out precisely to the need to grasp the active role of man and humankind in the context of the modern and evolving world, precisely such a world as Teilhard de Chardin described.

The Pastoral Constitution is a revolutionary work due to several reasons; in the context of our ideas, a statement in point 5 is of particularly great importance:

> The human race has passed from a rather static concept of reality to a more dynamic, evolutionary one. In consequence there

---

the authorities were rather tense. However, Teilhard not only considered the Church as a divine environment, but the Universe, too. For more ideas on the subject, see Plašienková and Kulisz, *Na ceste s Teilhardom de Chardin*, 133–34.

16. For a detailed interpretation of the Omega Point from the biological and ecological perspectives, see Florio, "Omega Point."

17. In 1950, Teilhard de Chardin clarified this sentence as follows: "I believe that *in Man*, Spirit is fully realized in Person." And he continued with a note: "It is only an added touch, but it allows us to emerge unequivocally from metaphysics and move into the historical, the biological—the planetary" (Teilhard de Chardin, *Heart of Matter*, 78).

18. Teilhard de Chardin, "How I Believe."

> has arisen a new series of problems … calling for efforts of analysis and synthesis.[19]

Teilhard de Chardin had dealt with these issues much earlier in his work.

In order to understand Teilhard`s intention of clarifying the position and meaning of the Church in the history of humankind and in the context of the modern world better, interpretations and characterisations of the Church itself are briefly indicated further.

If we assume that in the history of Christianity, and especially in its periods of crisis, the Church has always sought adequate formulations and images to bring man closer to their mission as well as the role of the Church itself, it is self-evident that within this historical context and many "historical turning points" we can also find various characteristics and definitions of the Church itself: from the apostles of Paul, Peter, John through the Church Fathers to the Tübingen School, especially the theologian Johann Adam Möhler, who, thanks to a new analysis of the images of the Holy Scripture and the interpretation of the Church Fathers, paved the way for a deepened view of the Church. He influenced many theologians of the nineteenth century, as well as some opinions expressed in the scheme of the Church at the First Vatican Council (though these were later rejected because of their ambiguity). The following period connected to the "crisis of modernism" brought new challenges for any understanding of the essence of the Church; and eventually, the Second Vatican Council, after a deeper examination of the mystery of the Church, communicated its mission in the world in a new spirit, too.

Within these important approaches to the understanding of the Church, we can find characteristics that define the Church as: the community of believers, the Body, the Bride of Jesus Christ (St. Paul), the living body of Christ (St. Peter and St. John), people united through the unity of the Father, the Son and the Holy Spirit (St. Cyprian), spiritual Israel, the family of people glorifying God, the house of Israel, the people of God, the vineyard of the Lord (the Fathers of the Church), and so on. It should be noted that within these characteristics, the mystery of the community of the Church with which man is connected is also emphasised. It is not an accidental connection but a unity with God, which is constantly being realised in the Church and through the Church. It follows that this unity is not predetermined and ready, but it is realised through the Church and thus, it also becomes its mission. It is therefore to "mature in time," which ultimately emphasises the very need to get to know this world and its expectations (the Second Vatican Council).

19. See Paul VI, "Gaudium et spes."

The history of the Church demonstrates, in a plastic manner, how the mission of the Church was understood within the Church itself and within the period's conditionality and it points out the difficulties the Church encountered. The Eastern and later Western Schism within the Church meant that theological reflection placed an emphasis on the visible, organisational and legal (for instance, hierarchy in the Church) features of the Church so that the borders between the Orthodox, Protestant and Catholic Church were determined.

A major change occurred especially after the First World War when the Church began to be spoken of as a community created by the Holy Spirit (and not by law). Teilhard de Chardin belonged to the theologians of this period. He wanted to point out the unique role and mission of the Church and its place in the world in a new way.

Although Teilhard has not left a systematic explanation of his ecclesiology, we can find such statements in his work that allow us to create an image of the Church as a whole; a whole that is in line with his evolutionary image of the world. Therefore, Teilhard's aim was to give a new meaning to the dogmas of the Catholic Church in accordance with some concepts of the theory of evolution. He held an interesting position that, since religion and science are inextricably linked together, they form two phases of a cognitive act that captures the image of the past and of the future and points to the evolutionary completion of the entire Universe. Teilhard is also aware of the fact that the evolution of our planet Earth is linked to the development of thought and a constantly increasing concentration of the human spirit that gradually creates the "spirit of the Earth." This spiritual cover is called the noosphere.

However, this is not the final developmental actuality. This is the unification of the spiritual center of the entire Universe that is a meta-intellectual center, independent of its material bearer. This center is called the final Omega Point.[20]

And just like the evolution of the Universe leads to an increasingly greater organisation and concentration, the development of thought leads to a deeper spirituality. The unification of all of the elements of the spirit of the Earth provides, according to Teilhard, a basis for the second coming of Christ, that is Parousia.[21] Through these ideas, Teilhard reaffirms the need for the synthesis of science and religion.

---

20. From the religious perspective, the Omega Point is actually the Cosmic Christ.

21. Teilhard develops these ideas in a work written in 1927 entitled "Le Milieu Divin" (Teilhard, *Divine Milieu*). For new inspirations from this work in the field of the understanding of the spirituality at present, see Savary, *Divine Milieu Explained*.

Teilhard's effort to point out the role of Christianity in evolutionary development, and above all, the function of "its heart," which is the Catholic Church, resulted in the implementation of biological concepts in the field of religion. These basic concepts include: *phylum* and *axis* (*l'axe*). The Church represents a biological *phylum*[22] and at the same time, it is an *axis* of the universal, cosmic convergent development heading toward the Omega Point.[23]

According to Teilhard, this convergence needs to be carried out on the *Christian axis*, in faith in Christ. In him the other Creeds find the just expression of what they have been looking for in their movement towards the Divine.

From the biological point of view, the Church represents a "living branch," collective and well-developed. It is associated with those characteristics that apply to every biological *phylum*, that is, polymorphism and elasticity. They are manifested in the richness of individuals within the same species and in the ability to adapt to the environment, which proves dynamism within new life conditions.[24]

Based on these observations we discover that *phylum*, despite the constant development and multitude of different individuals, creates unity. Thanks to it, the given species differs from other forms of life. According to Teilhard, every religion has the properties of the biological *phylum*, however, the fullness of spiritual content is revealed only in the Christian *phylum*.[25] This view of religion as such (that is, a view through the prism of the biological *phylum*) enables Teilhard to discover, in the multitude of religions, a new meaning for religion.

It has to be noted here that not all religions as *phylum* have been equally important in the history of humankind. Teilhard presents a comparison with the animal realm. Not all of the animal species (*phyla*) evolved immediately toward the origin of man, likewise, not all religions had the same value. Biological species, however, were necessary so that the "tree of life" could develop. Similarly, in the development of religion, a "place" emerged which a little strand of spiritual life grew towards, creating a space in which the mystery of incarnation, and divinisation of the world, should take place.[26] This strand was a place for the personal encounter of God with

22. Phylum is a taxonomic rank at the level below Kingdom and above Class in a biological classification, especially of animals.

23. Teilhard de Chardin, *Phenomenon of Man*, 257–64.

24. See Plašienková and Kulisz, *Na ceste s Teilhardom de Chardin*, 171.

25. Teilhard discusses this issue in an important essay, written in 1933, entitled "Christianisme."

26. Teilhard, "Christianisme," 144–45.

man, it was the hearth of love that emerged in the heart of Christianity—in the Church. And this burning hearth starts in Jesus. Teilhard believed that it is the Roman Church that is the biological *phylum* of Christ. In the Church, Christ actualises his salvation power and develops his total personality in the world. The Church, according to the author, is also a place in which God reveals himself as Father to humanity through Jesus.

Finally, it can be added that love is the inner quality, the spiritual energy that penetrates and forms the physical unity of the Christian phylum. Thanks to it, the state of a specifically new consciousness appears in the Church and through the Church in the world. Therefore, Teilhard says that the Church is a "phylum of love in nature," and thus, he compares the Church—a community formed by love—to a living organism that is revived by the power of the risen Christ. In him we are connected in one. If the love of God in the soul of the believers vanished, the whole Church would disintegrate.

It can be seen that reflections on the Church and the meaning of love connected to the faith in Christ are typical not only of Teilhard, but—as it has been already demonstrated—they were also present in Khomiakov's reflections. As it is demonstrated further, certain parallels can also be found in another author whom we would like to introduce briefly—the Slovak philosopher and priest Ladislav Hanus.

Ladislav Hanus and His Reflection on Faith and the Church

Reflections on the Church representing an organic whole were also developed in the work of the Slovak philosopher and theologian Ladislav Hanus.[27]

27. Prof. Ladislav Hanus (1907–1994), a philosopher of culture and dialogue, Slovak philosopher of *sobornost'*, prominent Slovak theologian and philosopher of the twentieth century, famous for brilliant analyses of Slovak society and culture. Ladislav Hanus was born in Liptovský Mikuláš, studied philosophy and theology in Spišská Kapitula, continuing his studies in Innsbruck, in Germany, Switzerland and Italy. He attended the lectures of Peter Lippert and Romano Guardini (Werkwoche, Rothenfels an Main); he devoted an individual monograph to Guardini (1944). In 1938, he became a professor of morality at Vysoká škola bohoslovecká in Spišská Kapitula. He was the chief editor of the journal of the Slovak Christian intelligentsia *Kultúra*, the avantgarde journal *Obroda* and the journal *Verbum*. The school was disbanded in 1950. In 1954, Hanus was sentenced to 16 years imprisonment for treason, which he served in Czechoslovak prisons and forced labor in mines in Jáchymov. After his release, he worked as a stoker and gave lectures at private philosophical and cultural symposiums held in Bratislava, known as the "underground university." Despite many years spent in the worst communist prisons, he maintained his human and moral integrity and managed to continue his violently interrupted philosophical and theological work. He died

He understood culture as an element of the spiritual life of an individual and community which alone could prevent an acutely threatening dehumanisation of society. Similar ideas are also found in Khomiakov. As with Khomiakov's conception of *sobornost'* and statements on the importance of the community and the Church, Hanus concentrates on the value of human life, the human individuum as a spiritual being and at the same time a social being.[28] Hanus emphasises the importance of culture in the shaping of society and points out the threat of the devastation of spiritual values in competition with other values (totalitarianism and its forms such as Fascism and communism). In Hanus's understanding, culture is a personal feature of man, an essential way of existence, a higher spiritual quality, an inner norm of thinking, acting and decision-making. Culture is a spiritual habitus of the individual and society too; a habitus that the individual and the whole society approach through a persistent, intentional and demanding work on their own improvement, while they gradually shape their spiritual substance and leave a shape in it. Culture, similarly to Khomiakov's *sobornost'*, is a manifestation of the effort of generations, where the defining element of the acquisition of culture is tradition. Tradition is like a river that makes its way either as a dominant current of the period, or as an "undercurrent" in the bowels of the world.[29] For Hanus, Europe was primarily the culture of order, of standard of thought and acting in the unity of spiritual affinity. In *Rozprava o kultúrnosti*, Hanus suggested seven principles of culture that communicate closely with Khomiakov's concept of *sobornost'*. They include: diligence, opinion, breadth, nature, piety, goodness, human relations. Culture, according to Hanus, is definitely not a natural gift, nor a talent. Without effort, a shape will not originate even from natural assumptions.

> The resultant of indifference is shapelessness. The noble essential form is achieved only in a tedious effort and is proportionate to exerted efforts.[30]

---

in 1994 and some of his works were published after his death. Hanus's work consists of the following monographs: *Rozprava o kultúrnosti* (1991), *Romano Guardini. Mysliteľ a pedagóg storočia* (1994), *Princíp pluralizmu* (1997), *Človek a kultúra* (1997), *Umenie a náboženstvo* (2001), *O kultúre a kultúrnosti* (2003), *Princípy kresťanskej morálky* (2008). Hanus belongs to the most important personalities of European culture and European philosophical thought.

28. In his reflections on the spirituality of man and humankind, Hanus is also inspired by Teilhard's conception of the noosphere. See Hanus, *Človek a kultúra*, 217.

29. Let us add that this telluric flow of the spirit in the world and the society is also highlighted in the work of Pavel Florensky.

30. Hanus, *O kultúre a kultúrnosti*, 57.

Hanus comes to realise that culture is essentially a moral property that a man acquires already in childhood through education in a family environment and later at school. The sacrificed generation brings values for other successor generations, which can then create a cultural humus which permits the cultivation of a precious form of life, create a lifestyle, refine the spirit, unwind from the earthy, original simplicity. However, while diligence is a voluntary law, the thesis represents a synthesis of will, moral character and cognition. Culture begins with cognition, which is a complex process, claiming the whole of man and their life consequences. The cognised represents a challenge for man—it puts them in front of a choice and asks for a decision, that is, an opinion. Cognition itself is merely a formal ability, the content and importance are given to it by a moral decision. However, for Hanus, a man becomes a cultivated person when their opinion has "breadth" and openness. Hanus warns against narrowness, limitedness, flatness, restriction of the view. The breadth, this openness to the truth, requires significant effort—fanaticism does not demand effort, it is carried away by spontaneity, by "natural gravity." Limited persons only acclaim the existence and value of what they see, what they immediately understand and they put their circle of knowledge in place of reality.[31] However, the result of cultural diligence is a person whose characteristic is nobleness, which is a human work, but also the work of the mysterious action of the divine. It is the willingness and openness of man to the action of transcendence, that is, something that transcends them and promises the fulfilment of their deepest aspirations. In Christianity, God approaches man to raise man over their naturalness, drawing him into the inner circle of God's life. Devotion, according to Hanus and Khomiakov, is essential to man: it creates order in them, stimulates cultural performance, presents goals, encourages building, elevates them toward ideas, unifies personality, connects personal history with human history, inspires accomplishments in culture, art and social engagement, even heroics.[32] Devotion to religion is the main nerve of cultures and the uplifting of nations.

Ladislav Hanus sees a natural piety in Slovak nature, but points out that it is necessary to cultivate a conscious religious culture so that it reaches a higher, noble form. Besides piety, goodness is the second source of nobleness, and it is an effective determination for the good. According to Hanus, goodness springs in the contemplation of beauty, in love of life, in gratitude (Khomiakov). It is a substantial overcoming of selfishness in respect to reality, to the order of the world. The basic disposition of goodness is to help this

---

31. See Hanus, *Princíp pluralizmu*, 31–33.

32. See Hanus, *Romano Guardini*, 18–20.

truth, and in the effort to confirm it, it is based on itself, it actively interferes and does not remain passive. Goodness is the moral dimension of the truth, it is the fate of the absolute.[33]

Human relationships—life space, household, society, lifestyle—grow out of the above-mentioned factors of culture. Human relationships are a manifestation of the nature of man. A man leaves the loneliness of their life, and proceeds to the world of faces. At first, they are the faces of strangers, material, non-disturbing faces with no demands. Only after the first contact do the faces cease to be things, they start to disturb, make demands. The community, however, interferes with the innermost personal sphere, in which a man is alone with himself and with his God—only there does the face, its depth and spirituality call.[34] Hanus notes that with the onset of liberal society, a prerequisite for individual self-actualisation was created, which led to the decline of the depth of interpersonal relations as a social phenomenon. Hanus thus anticipates the fate of mankind, which later atomised, where contemporary man is often an essentially lonely individual. The utilitarian understanding of man marked the whole culture of humanism. This applies equally to the postmodern age and it seems to be the case for contemporary post-secularism, too. Even in this, Ladislav Hanus was a great prophet of Slovak history, which he had to experience so painfully himself.

Conclusion

To conclude, it may be stated that all of the analyzed authors, despite living in different historical and social conditions and representing three different cultural-religious traditions, thought rather similarly in regard to the issue of faith and the relationship of man to God and the Church. Thus, several overlapping ideas and parallels in defining the meaning of spiritual life of a man and society in the context of the individual and social life of the Church can be found in their works. Besides the intellectually critical attitude of all the authors (Khomiakov, Teilhard, Hanus) to the totalitarianism and ideological manipulation of their time, they are connected by the quality of their Christian education and formation in their childhood, where the emotional and intellectual influence of their mothers was of immense importance.

33. On the relationship of good will as a disposable openness to the truth, the spiritual truth in particular, see Rusnák, *Pravda, veda, symbol*, 87–92.

34. See Hanus, *Človek a kultúra*, 23–26.

Bibliography

Ambros, Pavol. "Alexej Stěpanovič Chomjakov—učitel církve?" In *Jedna církev*, by Alexej S. Chomjakov, 5–40. Translated by Petra Otýpková and Pavol Ambros. Olomouc: Refugium, 2006.

Florio, Lucio. "The 'Omega Point' Revisited from the New Tree of Life and the Ecological Crisis." *Studia Aloisiana* 7.3 (2016) 31–40.

Guardini, Romano. *Mysliteľ a pedagóg storočia*. Bratislava: Lúč, 1994.

Hanus, Ladislav. *Človek a kultúra*. Bratislava: Lúč, 1997.

———. *O kultúre a kultúrnosti*. Bratislava: Lúč, 2003.

———. *Princíp pluralizmu*. Bratislava: Lúč, 1997.

———. *Princípy kresťanskej morálky*. Bratislava: Lúč, 2008.

———. *Rozprava o kultúrnosti*. Bratislava: Lúč, 1991.

———. *Umenie a náboženstvo*. Bratislava: Lúč, 2001.

Khomiakov, Alexei S. "The Church Is One." In *On Spiritual Unity: A Slavophile Reader*, edited and translated by Boris Jakim and Robert Bird, 31–53. Translated by Boris Jakim and Robert Bird. Hudson, NY: Lindisfarne, 1998.

Lossky, Nikolai. *History of Russian Philosophy*. London: George Allen and Unwin, 1952.

Paul VI. "Gaudium et spes." December 7, 1965. http://www.vatican.va/archive/hist_councils/ii_vatican_council/documents/vat-ii_const_19651207_gaudium-et-spes_en.html.

Plašienková, Zlatica, and Józef Kulisz. *Na ceste s Teilhardom de Chardin*. Trnava: Dobrá kniha, 2004.

Riasanovsky, Nicholas V. "Khomiakov on Sobornost." In *Continuity and Change in Russian and Soviet Thought*, edited by Ernest J. Simmons, 183–96. Cambridge, MA: Harvard University Press, 1955.

Rusnák, Peter. *Pravda, veda, symbol. Úvod do myslenia P. A. Florenského*. Trnava: FF TU, 2008.

Samarin, Jury. "On the Theological Writings of Aleksei Khomiakov." In *On Spiritual Unity: A Slavophile Reader*, edited and translated by Boris Jakim and Robert Bird, 160–83. Translated by Boris Jakim and Robert Bird. Hudson, NY: Lindisfarne, 1998.

Savary, Louis, M. *Teilhard de Chardin—The Divine Milieu explained. A Spirituality for Twenty-first Century*. New York: Paulist, 2007.

Spidlik, Tomas. *L'idée russe. Une autre vision de l'homme*. Troyes: Fates, 1994.

Teilhard de Chardin, Pierre. "Le Christianisme dans le Monde." In *Science et Christ*, by Pierre Teilhard de Chardin, 129–45. Paris: Éditions du Seuil, 1965.

———. *The Divine Milieu: An Essay on the Interior Life*. Translated by Bernard Wall. New York: Harper and Row, 1960.

———. *The Heart of Matter*. Translated by René Hague. New York: Harvest, 2002.

———. "How I Believe." In *Christianity and Evolution*, by Pierre Teilhard de Chardin, 96–132. Translated by René Hague. New York: Harcourt, 1971.

———. *The Phenomenon of Man*. New York: Harper and Row, 1959.

14

Pitirim A. Sorokin

A Successor to the Slavophiles

Frederick Matern

"Slavophile" is a label which hides as much as it reveals. For a student of intellectual history, representatives of a movement with such a title are bound to be of concern only to those who deal with Slavic nations, particularly Russia, or with Orthodox Christian theology. But the name would seem to point away from any universal concept. At best it would seem a relic of the nineteenth century; at worst, a potential catalyst for ugly forms of nationalism in the twenty-first. There is, however, at least one "unofficial" modern Slavophile who lived in the twentieth century and wrote primarily in English for a Western audience, but whose thoughts about society and culture clearly show at least indirect influence from the early Slavophile movement, including Khomiakov's philosophy of history, even if no direct credit is given. That "modern Slavophile" was Pitirim Sorokin (1889–1968). Sorokin represents an interesting and unique phenomenon in the history of social thought. The background of this sociologist and the circumstances that brought him across the Atlantic from Russia and, intellectually speaking, from nineteenth century through the pivotal and disruptive years of the Russian Revolution to the burgeoning American society of the twentieth century make him, in a sense, a bridge across space and time, between two very different cultural worlds.

Slavophilism seems by its very name to be firmly localized and temporized, belonging only to one place and period of history: Russia of the nineteenth century. As Nikolai Berdyaev states, "the controversy between the Slavophils and the Westernizers was a dispute about the destiny of

Russia and its vocation in the world."[1] Such a controversy would seem to exclude the interests of anyone not willing to dispute about Russia. Yet the early Slavophiles, including Alexei Khomiakov, often called upon transcendent principles in their defense of the idea of Russia. Philosophically, these early Slavophiles were remarkably cosmopolitan in their approach to such problems as those posed by the philosophy of history. These transcendent principles forming the basis of a Russian mission can be seen later in the nineteenth century, in the writing of Soloviev and Dostoevsky. It is in this vein—philosophical and cosmopolitan—that Sorokin seems to bring such clear notes of Slavophile thought into his sociology, a sociology that matured during his long career in the United States of America, not in isolation from, but in dialogue with other American practitioners of sociology (and it is worth noting that the vast majority of Sorokin's scholarly output was originally in English). This chapter will demonstrate that Sorokin's philosophy of history displays signs of being a development of Khomiakov's philosophy of history; at the very least, it will be seen that Sorokin can be regarded as a twentieth-century Slavophile, but it will also illustrate the idea that Khomiakov's Slavophilism is compatible with a pluralistic, even cosmopolitan worldview such as Sorokin's. This view is compatible with a view of the Slavophile movement that was not merely a localized debate at a particular time in history, but the wellspring of a number of "indirect successor" schools of thought.[2]

Sorokin was a sociologist and, during his early career, a political activist. He was born in 1889 in the village of Turya, then the Vologda Governorate, now the Komi Republic, to a Russian icon-painter and an ethnic Komi mother who died when he was three years old.[3] As a child, the young Pitirim wandered from village to village with his elder brother and his alcoholic father. His younger brother was raised by an aunt and uncle. As a boy Sorokin learned his father's icon-painting trade while beginning to read and write. After a violent drunken outburst by his father during his youth, he and his elder brother set off to live on their own, making a living in their father's trade while studying sporadically. His father died a

1. Berdyaev, *Russian Idea*, 39.

2. Walicki, *Slavophile Controversy*, 473. It is also worth remembering that the original sense of "Slavophile" was one of valorizing what was seen as the indigenous, "Slavonic" elements of Russian culture, as against perceived striving towards assimilation with the West. See Berdyaev, *Russian Idea*, 495. Furthermore, Prince Eugene N. Trubetskoy held that the main error of the Slavophiles—such as Kireevsky and Khomiakov, as well as of the early Soloviev—was to conflate universal moral principles with the mission of Russia. See discussion in Trubetskoy, *Mirosozertsanie Vl. S. Solovyeva*, 1:50–72.

3. Sorokin, *Long Journey*, 11.

year after their separation and both of his brothers died in the aftermath of the Russian revolution.[4]

Despite this, Sorokin went to a teachers' seminary (where he befriended Nikolai Kondratiev, an economist who later became well-known around the world for his theory of business cycles[5]) and became politically active in the Socialist Revolutionary (SR) party. This association is of note due to the philosophical differences Sorokin found between this party and the Marxists. In Sorokin's words, "Unlike Marxist materialism and the economic interpretation of man and history, the philosophy and sociology of the Social-Revolutionary Party were much more idealistic or integralistic. They emphasized strongly the role of creative ideas, voluntary efforts."[6] Thus in spite of the shift from his early traditional world-view to a socialist one, he tended to reject materialism and positivism, which became an important theme in his later intellectual life.

Sorokin continued his studies in St. Petersburg, where he studied sociology and criminology. He remained active in the Social-Revolutionary Party. After the February Revolution in 1917, Aleksandr Kerensky, premier of the Provisional Government, chose Sorokin to be his secretary.[7] Sorokin was arrested after the Bolsheviks came to power. After some six weeks in prison, in line to be executed, he was released.[8] After his release he was able to teach at university and published his *System of Sociology,* and continued to teach and publish critical notes about the new regime.[9] But by 1922 the regime decided that he and a large number of other intellectuals must leave Russia, and he became part of that well-known community of exiles. After some time in Europe he went to America, and found a job teaching at the University of Minnesota. During his six years there, he published some studies that would be considered more mainstream (and highly-regarded) sociological fare in the American context (for example, *Hunger as a Factor in Human Affairs*). He then received the call from Harvard to chair that university's new Department of Sociology. It was here, during the Great Depression, that he received a large grant to work on his *Social and Cultural Dynamics,* a publication which would prove very controversial in his

4. Sorokin, *Long Journey,* 26.

5. Sorokin, *Long Journey,* 61.

6. Sorokin, *Long Journey,* 44.

7. Sorokin, *Russian Diary,* 73.

8. Sorokin, *Russian Diary,* 8.

9. See, for example, his speech to the teachers and students on the day of the anniversary of the founding of Petersburg University, delivered February 21, 1922, in Sorokin, "Rech' P. A. Sorokina."

professional community and marked a turning point in his career.[10] Three
volumes were published in 1937 and a final one, introducing his idea of integralism, was completed in 1941. This publication led to his marginalization
from mainstream sociology, but he was able, through a grant from Eli Lilly,
to further his work in the study of altruism as a possible solution to the
crisis he identified in the *Dynamics* and other publications, and he remained
popular as a public intellectual throughout his retirement.

In his methods, the various scholars who have studied him have
found him to be a disciple of behaviorists such as Pareto[11]; of positivism
and Comte[12]; or even of St. Thomas Aquinas[13]; while he himself has written
about his own affinity to the Christian anarchism of Tolstoy,[14] which indicates a Slavophile influence. Lawrence T. Nichols has made a more direct
link to the primacy of his Russian religious philosophical heritage, showing affinity with Nikolay O. Lossky, Vladimir S. Soloviev, and, of interest
in the present context, the Slavophiles Ivan Kireevsky and Aleksei Khomiakov.[15] This affinity is in despite of some of the only direct commentary
Sorokin made on the Slavophiles, unfavorably comparing their messianism
with that of the Bolsheviks in 1917, when he was politically active in the
Provisional Government and writing editorials for the newspaper *Volya
Naroda* (*The People's Will*).[16] Nichols argues that Sorokin's marginalization
in American social science was the result of a lack of understanding of the
socio-political, intellectual and cultural formative context of his early life
and career, and pointed to the early Slavophile philosophy of Kireevsky and
Khomiakov as being characteristic of Sorokin's work in the last phase of
his career, beginning in 1937 with the publication of *Social and Cultural
Dynamics*, where the concept of "integralism" first began to be developed
in Sorokin's sociology.[17] A couple of interesting points stand out from Nichols's reviews of Sorokin in the context of his Russian heritage. The first is
that Sorokin, who was encyclopedic in his citations of many hundreds of
thinkers of the past, pays scant or no attention to the early Slavophiles in
his works. In one of his late works on creative altruism, he relies heavily

---

10. Johnston, *Pitirim A. Sorokin*, 124.

11. See Simpson, "Pitirim Sorokin and his Sociology."

12. Timasheff, *Sociological Theory*, 31.

13. Jeffries, "Foundational Ideas," 26.

14. See Jaworski, " Sociological Anarchism."

15. Nichols, "Russian Intellectual."

16. Nichols, "Science, Politics," 144. The column referenced by Nichols was entitled
"Slavophilism Inside-Out."

17. Nichols, "Russian Intellectual," 378.

on Soloviev; and as regards Nikolay Lossky, Sorokin collaborated with him in the research on the *Dynamics*, and maintained an amicable relationship with his fellow exile.[18] The second is that the one other successor of the Slavophiles that Sorokin devotes considerable attention to in a number of works is Nikolay Danilevsky, rather than figures who would appear to be more intellectually aligned such as Khomiakov or Kireevsky. Sorokin saw Danilevsky as a direct influence on Spengler.[19]

The prominent place of integralism in Sorokin's epistemology is indeed a similarity with the philosophy of Kireevsky, as Nichols has pointed out.[20] There are, nonetheless, striking features of Sorokin's work that recall Khomiakov's philosophy of history and society more than, perhaps, any other single predecessor. There are three major themes in Sorokin's work that can, in a broad sense, Khomiakov. First, unlike Kireevsky, both Khomiakov and Sorokin developed a philosophy of history that was based on the succession of broad cultural systems where basic world-views (in Khomiakov's parlance, faith) change over time. Second, Sorokin's tendency, in a way similar to Khomiakov's, was to regard the West (that is, "Europe and a Europeanized America") as worthy of deep respect, but now in a phase of senility or decay, which would ultimately lead to the ceding of place to emerging cultures from the East (or, as Sorokin stated, "Afro-Asian cultures and peoples"[21]). Third, the principle of altruistic love developed by Sorokin as the means to integrate society compares well with Khomiakov's development of the concept of *sobornost'*.

According to Sorokin,[22] the central claim of his sociology is that sociocultural reality is a complex manifold, with inexhaustible modes of being which the human mind is unable to grasp in its totality, but can gain partial access to via three forms or differentiations, which require three distinct epistemological bases and therefore three differing types of methodologies. There is, first, its *empirical* aspect, which must be studied through sensory, empirical methods. These methods are appropriate to discovering what Sorokin calls "the truth of the senses." The subject matter of the truth of the senses is mainly the world of sensory perception, such as the phenomena studied in the natural sciences. This worldview tends to reduce phenomena of culture, psychology and values to their sensory or material forms. There is, next, what Sorokin refers to as a *logico-rational* aspect, "the truth

18. Lossky, *Vospominaniya*, 235.

19. Timasheff, *Sociological Theory*, 271n.

20. Nichols, "Russian Intellectual," 390.

21. Sorokin, *Basic Trends*, 63.

22. Sorokin, "Integralism is My Philosophy," 180–89.

of reason," which can be apprehended through the discursive logic of human reason, including mathematical, deductive and inductive reasoning.
Finally, there is what Sorokin refers to as *supersensory, superrational* or
"metalogical" reasoning. By the first two designations, Sorokin means that
major religions, ethical norms and fine arts cannot be reduced to a complex
of sensations or to rational or logical propositions. The truth proposition is
the "truth of faith," which is perceived as a mystical or metalogical intuition.
Mystic experience provides the ultimate foundations of the great systems of
art, ethics and religion. Mystical, or metalogical, intuition will normally be
the foundational on which a logico-empirical structure of a cultural super
system is built.[23] It is necessary, according to Sorokin, to use all of these
different ways of knowing in order to grasp the truth. None of these three
systems is, on its own, sufficient to grasp reality.[24]

Cultures, according to Sorokin, tend to build the frames through
which they view reality primarily through only one of these three aspects,
and cultural phenomena of all sorts tend to be built around these primordial frames. Sorokin's observation about cultures is that they tend to be a
system of meanings and values, rather than a "dumping ground" of unre-
lated phenomena. Whole systems of belief about the world, with concomitant reflections in a culture's dominant systems of philosophy, ethics, law,
science, art, politics, and so on, tend to be integrated to a great extent. It is
the dynamics of these systems of thought that form the basis of the major
developments in history.

The driving force identified by Sorokin bore itself out in systems based
on the culture's perception of reality and derivation of truth. Other cultural
elements, whether fine arts, laws, morals, ethics, systems of government, are
dependent on the major premise of the prevailing worldview. Worldviews
are never in a full equilibrium, as they are part of a living social system that
cannot be static. "Sensate" worldviews derive their truth from the senses.
Cultures exhibiting this major premise will tend to produce works of philosophy, art, science, literature that reflected this bias towards the senses.
This tendency will also be seen in the systems of law, government and ethics
that predominate these cultures. In time, such a culture inevitably reaches
a limit and is pushed towards a worldview, which has, as its major premise,
a super-sensory "truth of faith." Sorokin called this kind of supersystem
"ideational." Finally, between these two integrated forms, there can be any
number of "mixed" forms of culture, but Sorokin reserves a special place
for a culture where a system of truth that integrates, in a harmonious way,

23. Sorokin, *Social and Cultural Dynamics*, 4:752.
24. Sorokin, "Integralism is My Philosophy," 181.

empirical systems of truth with the supersensory, calling this mixed form "idealistic." Its premise is truth of both faith and the senses, moderated by our faculty of reason.[25]

Sorokin's study of history, based on these categories, showed that Classical and Western culture moved from an idealistic phase in classical Greece during the time of Plato and Aristotle, though a sensate phase during the Hellenistic (the dominance of Epicureanism being characteristic of the sensate worldview). This was followed by an ideational phase during the period we call the "Dark Ages," but the High Middle Ages represented a mixed system, that is, an idealistic phase coinciding with scholasticism. Since then, a long growth of sensate culture has been characteristic, reaching what Sorokin found to be an extreme level even by the early twentieth century, characterized by logical positivism, scientism in the social sciences, atomized individualistic society, art preoccupied with sex and criminality and also the brutal First World War and even more brutal and bestial Second World War.

Taken in isolation, Sorokin's worldview seems inconsistent, and the three labels of "sensate," "idealistic," and "ideational" have been misread as an ascent or descent through stages, as in the philosophy of Comte.[26] Sorokin in fact saw Comte's theory, along with other "linear" conceptions of social and historical change, as eschatological and fallacious.[27] Sorokin's view of history was not linear at all, but rather described fluctuations in the dominance or preponderance of the basic sociocultural types over long timescales. As regards the apparent similarities to Vico, Sorokin clearly admired the Italian's philosophy of history, and was indeed a proponent of a cyclical theory of the history of society. It is very tempting to draw a parallel between Sorokin's ideational, idealistic and sensate phases and Vico's repeating ages of gods, heroes and men, which correspond to similar periods in history. However Sorokin is clear that while there is inevitability to the oscillation between sensate and ideational culture types, the exact path of points in between can vary and the advent of the idealistic type is not a certainty.

Also, the ideational and sensate poles are ideal types of complex integrated systems and, empirically speaking, no culture is likely ever to have been "purely" ideational or sensate. At the same time, the idealistic system only exists as an integration of the sensate and ideational systems, which is likely the reason why, starting with the last volume of the Dynamics,

25. See Sorokin, *Social and Cultural Dynamics*, 1:67.

26. One example of the propagation of this error from a textbook of social theory: "Sorokin modified Comte's law of three stages—distinguishing ideational, idealistic, and sensate stages—and saw these defining a series of cyclical transformations that produce the historical succession of human civilization" (Scott, *Social Theory*, 46).

27. Sorokin, *Contemporary Sociological Theories*, 728.

Sorokin began to use the word *integral* to describe this particular integrated culture. This disconnection between Sorokin's developing epistemological position and his philosophy of history causes confusion among even the most supportive students of Sorokin. Colbert Rhodes,[28] for example, is of the view that Sorokin's philosophy of history is built around three types of integrated culture, each built around one of the systems of being and of knowing that Sorokin enumerated later in his career.[29] It may well be that Sorokin had begun to form his epistemological system in parallel with his philosophy of history, even if it only began to be clearly articulated late in his life.[30] It was, however, the view of a sufficiently mature Sorokin in his *Dynamics* that "many systems of logically integrated culture are conceivable, each with a different set of major premises but consistent within itself."[31] He goes on to say that few of these conceivable integrated systems will be reflected in cultural systems that have in fact existed in history; and that the "idealistic" culture was one of a number of "mixed" supersystems, albeit the only logically integrated one.[32] But the main premise of Sorokin's philosophy of history is that cultures oscillate over time between two profoundly different ideal types, and may, in the right circumstances, settle for a time on an idealistic type that combines the best features of the two polar types. In a tradition of Russian social criticism dating back to Vladimir Odoevsky and the early Slavophiles, Sorokin saw Western civilization of the present day as having exhausted the possibilities of the sensate cultural system. Sensate Western society had reached its internal limits, and was now undergoing a profound shift, a disintegration of that form of culture that would be succeeded by a reintegration into a different form of culture, with its concomitant meanings, norms and values.[33]

Sorokin's philosophy would therefore seem more consistent when viewed as a development of the Slavophile outlook. Khomiakov, in his philosophy of history outlined in the *Notes on Universal History*, also sees history as a movement between two main ideal types. In Khomiakov's version, these types are based on a voluntaristic typology of religion, based on the religion's relationship to the categories of freedom and necessity.[34] Sorokin's types are centered on a unity created by an adherence to a fundamental

28. See Rhodes, "Promise of Integralism," 25.

29. See Sorokin, "Reply to My Critics," 373–80.

30. See Sorokin, "Integralism is My Philosophy."

31. Sorokin, *Social and Cultural Dynamics*, 1:66.

32. Sorokin, *Social and Cultural Dynamics*, 1:75.

33. See Sorokin, *Crisis of Our Age*.

34. Walicki, *Slavophile Controversy*, 209.

axiological principle, where all facets of a culture articulate the same basic value.[35] Furthermore, for both Khomiakov and Sorokin, social and cultural systems are prone to change, and this change is not exclusively due to external forces acting on social and cultural groups. Khomiakov writes in his essay *On Humboldt* that

> Societies do not collapse because of some great cataclysm, or in consequence of some struggle—they fall even as old trees which have lost all their vital sap but still have just recently withstood a severe storm sometimes fall, thundering and booming, on still night when there is not movement enough in the air to stir a leaf on the healthy trees; they die as old men die who, as the people say, are *tired of living.*[36]

Sorokin's view of societal change is not very different, although shows a characteristic search for a golden mean. Against "externalistic" theories of sociocultural change, which look for causes or forces outside of the socio-cultural system itself, Sorokin places theories of "immanent change," that change is a property of the system itself, and sides with that view, with the proviso that external or cosmic factors can influence change in such as system.[37] Thus, like Khomiakov, he is of the opinion that change is immanent, like the tree that has lost its sap; external forces like the storm can nonetheless force change on the system.

Furthermore, Khomiakov's philosophy of history, as expressed in his *Notes,* contains not only a dialectic of sorts, with an oscillation over historical time of two value-principles (labelled by Khomiakov as Kushite and Iranian, but really in essence the principle of determinism and that of freedom);[38] there is also an attempt to reconcile opposing principles of unity and freedom using the idea of *sobornost'*, linking the Slavophile ideal in history to a kind of integralism (to use Sorokin's preferred term). Thus, in Khomiakov's view, the Roman world saw unity and freedom as opposing forces and regarded unity as superior. This disposition expressed itself in a tendency toward hierarchy, the subordination to the Pope, militant monastic orders and universal use of Latin. The Germanic world favored, in his scheme, the opposite view, in the reaction that led to the Reformation, which sacrificed unity for freedom, a tendency that led Protestantism into philosophic skepticism.[39] Only in Orthodoxy, for Khomiakov, can be

35. Sorokin, *Crisis of Our Age,* 17.

36. Khomiakov, "On Humboldt," 211.

37. Sorokin, *Social and Cultural Dynamics,* 4:600.

38. See, for example, Khomiakov, *Zapiski o vsemirnoy istorii,* 5:235.

39. Khomiakov, "On Humboldt," 213.

found the reconciliation of these principles. This theme was later taken up by a young Soloviev in his lecture on "Three Forces,"[40] but this time the history of religion was supplanted by national principles, defined in part by religion, where throughout history a centrifugal force acts to subordinate humanity to one ruling principle; a centripetal one which asserts the primacy of the atomized individual; and finally a third, integral, unifying principle, where the nation would be called upon not only to reconcile up uplift the opposing principles as an intermediary between the world and a revealed, divine, transcendent world. For Soloviev, the three principles were embodied in the Muslim Ottoman Empire, the nations of the West, and the Slavic world, particularly the Russian Empire, respectively. Khomiakov and Soloviev's conceptions can be seen as the start of a trend that culminates in Sorokin's study of changes between ideational, sensate and idealistic or integral cultural supersystems.

What Sorokin shares with his two predecessors is not so much agreement on exactly how or what changes in the course of history, but the value placed on the *integral* as the supreme and universal ideal of historical balance. Compared to Khomiakov and the early Soloviev, Sorokin is more willing to look for this ideal in different cultures and places. Thus, the systems of Plato, Aristotle, Albert the Great and Aquinas are all supreme examples, for Sorokin, of an attempt to embrace "in one organic whole divine as well as sensory and dialectic truth."[41] In his approach to accessing knowledge of this truth, Sorokin places himself together with a large current of Russian philosophy post-dating Khomiakov, in the camp of ontologism in epistemology, which Zenkovsky identifies as a characteristic of Khomiakov's epistemology and trend in Russian philosophy generally.[42] Specifically, Sorokin identified intuition with a direct knowledge of Being, an identification of subject and object.[43] In *The Ways and Power of Love*, Sorokin explains how this supra conscious intuition of Being provides access to the highest forms of creative love, which, for him, is humanity's only real hope to avoid catastrophe.[44] Khomiakov's epistemology led him, much earlier, to similar universalistic conclusions, of the ability of faith and love, as against reason, to bring one into contact with reality, with the truth, where other, external ways of knowing can only lead to an imperfect

40. Soloviev, "Three Forces," 24–25. See also a précis of that lecture in Lossky, *History of Russian Philosophy*, 114.

41. Sorokin, *Crisis of Our Age*, 102.

42. Zenkovsky, *History of Russian Philosophy*, 194.

43. Sorokin, *Modern Historical and Social Philosophies*, 308.

44. Sorokin, *Ways and Power of Love*, 142.

knowledge of reality.[45] The living knowledge of faith and love, and their precedence over the incomplete knowledge of reason, are an integral part of Khomiakov's conception of *sobornost'*.[46]

Given the profound influence of Khomiakov on Russian social thought, and the depth to which Sorokin was steeped in the ideas of his country of birth, there is a case to be made that Sorokin's body of work represents an inheritance of Khomiakov and Slavophile thought more generally in the English-speaking world and beyond. While the philosophy of history expounded in the *Dynamics* did not leave a deep imprint in the Western practice of sociology, it may merely be a matter of time before conditions will be ripe for a revisiting of Sorokin's theories of cultural change, as well as for further development of the *sobornost'*—like theory of altruism that Sorokin began to develop a century after the Slavophiles. Due to his tremendous popularity in mid-twentieth-century America, there is an extensive availability of Sorokin's vast output to draw from for scholars willing to explore this work. It is quite possible that the work of another post-Slavophile, the panslavist Danilevsky, has already had a profound influence on early twenty-first-century social and political thought, since it remains possible that Danilevsky was one of the influences on Spengler and Toynbee, who in turn inspired Samuel Huntington's *Clash of Civilizations*. The availability of so many copies of Sorokin's works may indeed prove to be a bridge for the more universalistic aspects of Slavophile thought into the twenty-first century.

Bibliography

Berdyaev, Nicolas. *The Russian Idea.* Translated by R. M. French. London: G. Bles, the Centenary, 1947.

Christoff, Peter K. *A. S. Xomjakov.* Vol. 1 of *An Introduction to Nineteenth-Century Russian Slavophilism: A Study in Ideas.* The Hague: Mouton, 1961.

Jaworski, Gary Dean. "Pitirim A. Sorokin's Sociological Anarchism." *History of the Human Sciences* 6.3 (1993) 61–67.

Jeffries, Vincent. "Foundational Ideas for an Integral Social Science Private in the Thought of St. Thomas Aquinas." *Catholic Social Science Review* 6 (2001) 25–40.

Johnston, Barry V. *Pitirim A. Sorokin: An Intellectual Biography.* Lawrence, KS: University Press of Kansas, 1995.

Khomiakov, Alexei S. "Essay on the Unity of the Church." In *Russia and the English Church During the Last Fifty Years,* edited by William John Birkbeck, 192–222. Vol. 1. London: Rivington, Percival, 1895.

———. "On Humboldt." In *Russian Intellectual History: An Anthology,* edited by Marc Raeff, 209–29. Atlantic Highlands, NJ: Humanities, 1978.

45. Khomiakov, "Essay on the Unity of the Church," 199.

46. Christoff, *A. S. Xomjakov,* 159.

————. *Zapiski o vsemirnoy istorii*. Vols. 5–6 of *Polnoe sobranie sochineniy Alekseya Stepanovicha Khomiakova*, by Alexei S. Khomiakov. Moscow: Tipo-litografiya T-va I. N. Kushnerov, 1904.

Lossky, Nikolai. *History of Russian Philosophy*. New York: International Universities Press, 1951.

————. *Vospominaniya. Zhizn' i filosofskiy put'*. Moscow: Russkiy Put', 2008.

Nichols, Lawrence T. "Science, Politics and Moral Activism: Sorokin's Integralism Reconsidered." *Journal of the History of the Behavioral Sciences* 35.2 (1999) 139–55.

————. "Sorokin as Lifelong Russian Intellectual: The Enactment of an Historically Rooted Sensibility." *The American Sociologist* 43.4 (2012) 374–405.

Rhodes, Colbert. "The Promise of Integralism." In *Renewal: The Inclusion of Integralism and Moral Values into the Social Sciences*, edited by Colbert Rhodes, 21–42. Lanham, MD: Rowman and Littlefield, 2017.

Scott, John. *Social Theory: Central Issues in Sociology*. London: Sage, 2006.

Simpson, Richard L. "Pitirim Sorokin and His Sociology." *Social Forces* 32.2 (1953) 120–31.

Soloviev, V. S. "Three Forces." In *Enemies from the East? V. S. Soloviev on Paganism, Asian Civilizations, and Islam*, edited and translated by Vladimir Wozniuk, 24–33. Evanston, IL: Northwestern University Press, 2007.

Sorokin, Pitirim A. *The Basic Trends of Our Times*. New Haven, CT: College and University Press, 1964.

————. *Contemporary Sociological Theories*. New York: Harper and Row, 1928.

————. *The Crisis of Our Age*. New Haven, CT: College and University Press, 1964.

————. "Integralism is My Philosophy." In *This is My Philosophy*, edited by Whit Burnett, 179–89. New York: Citadel, 1957.

————. *Leaves from a Russian Diary—And Thirty Years After*. Boston: Beacon, 1950.

————. *A Long Journey. The Autobiography of Pitirim A. Sorokin*. New Haven, CT: College and University Press, 1963.

————. *Modern Historical and Social Philosophies*. New York: Dover, 1963.

————. "Rech' P. A. Sorokina na torzhestvennom sobranii prepodavateley i studentov v den' 103-y godovshchiny so dnya osnovaniya Peterburgskogo Universiteta." In *"Ochistim Rossiyu Nadolgo": Repressii Protiv Inakomyslyashchikh. Konets 1921—nachalo 1923 g. Dokumenty*, edited by Andrey N. Artizov and Vasiliy S. Khristoforov, 40–43. Moscow: Materik, 2008.

————. "Reply to My Critics." In *Pitirim Sorokin in Review*, edited by Philip J. Allen, 371–496. Durham, NC: Duke University Press, 1963.

————. *Social and Cultural Dynamics*. Vols. 1–4. New York: American Book, 1937–1941.

————. *The Ways and Power of Love*. Philadephia: Templeton Foundation, 2002.

Timasheff, Nicholas. *Sociological Theory: Its Nature and Growth*. New York: Random House, 1967.

Trubetskoy, Evgeniy N. *Mirosozertsanie Vl. S. Solovyeva*. Vol. 1. Moscow: Put', 1913.

Walicki, Andrzej. *The Slavophile Controversy: History of a Conservative Utopia in Nineteenth-Century Russian Thought*. Translated by Hilda Andrews-Rusiecka. Oxford: Clarendon, 1975.

Zenkovsky, Vasilii V. *A History of Russian Philosophy*. Translated by George L. Kline. Vol. 1. New York: Columbia University Press, 1953.

15

"Our Slavic Pope"

The Mission of Slavs according to John Paul II[1]

Paweł Rojek

In a homily delivered on Lech's Hill in Gniezno during his first pilgrimage to Poland, on the 3 June 1979, Pope John Paul II said:

> Is it not Christ's will, is it not what the Holy Spirit disposes, that this Pope, in whose heart is deeply engraved the history of his own nation from its very beginning and also the history of the brother peoples and the neighboring peoples, should in a special way manifest and confirm in our age the presence of these peoples in the Church and their specific contribution to the history of Christianity? Is it not the design of Providence that he should reveal the developments that have taken place here in this part of Europe in the rich architecture of the temple of the Holy Spirit? ... Yes, it is Christ's will, it is what the Holy Spirit disposes.[2]

The Pope evidently believed that his calling to the See of Saint Peter also entailed in some way the calling of his nation, and even the whole family of

1. This publication was generously supported by a grant from the National Science Center, Poland (No. 2014/15/B/HS1/01620).

2. John Paul II, *Return to Poland*, 43, 45. This edition contains the official English translation of the papal homilies, sermons and speeches delivered in Poland in 1979, but does not include the additions made by John Paul II to the previously prepared texts, which were subsequently authorized by the Pope and embedded into the Polish editions. In case of such additions, I refer to the original Polish text.

Slavic nations with which he felt connected. The Holy Spirit, directing the election of the Pope, also indirectly pointed to the special mission of Poland and the whole of Slavdom. This belief, however, assumes a view that nations and their families in general have a special contribution to make to the community of the Church, which may prove especially valuable in certain circumstances. Hence, the Church is not only comprised of particular individuals and families, but also nations and even broader cultural communities. The first idea is the foundation of the specific Slavic missionism of John Paul II, the second view is the basis of his general theology of nation.

In this chapter I would like to take a closer look at both thoughts. First, I will address the general theology of the nation. I will try to outline the personalistic concept of nation adopted by John Paul II, according to which a nation is nothing but a whole made up of individuals which nevertheless constitutes the very identity of its members. The papal concept is significantly weaker, and so less controversial, than some theories developed in the so called Polish school of theology of the nation, founded by Father Czesław Stanisław Bartnik. Second, I will present some of the fundamental principles concerning the place of particular nations in the Universal Church, referring mainly to the *Slavorum Apostoli* encyclical. Then I will pass to the specific papal missionism. On many occasions, John Paul II suggested that Poland and other Slavic nations, including Russia, had a special role to play in the modern world. Poland was to become, as the Pope jocularly said in an improvised dialogue during the visit in 1979, "a theological society," that is a society whose entire social economic, and eventually also political order is based on the principles of Christianity.[3] His election as Pope could be seen as a kind of proof that a special time had come for the Slavs. I think that John Paul II's statements gain their proper meaning when placed in the context of his previous literary output. Before the Second World War, the young Karol Wojtyła prepared a collection of poems entitled *Renaissance Psalter (Slavic Book)*, where he formulated a vision of "Slavic soul," gravely influenced by Slavic Messianism.[4] This specific Slavic Christianity was, according to the young Wojtyła, a synthesis of two earlier epochs: gothic and renaissance, just as, many years later, when he had become Pope, Poland's experiences was thought to be a new combination of religion and modernity. The Pope remained interested in the Slavic world. Reading a book by his friend and fellow student, the Slavist Maria Bobrownicka, who wrote about the place of Slavdom in European culture, induced him to devote one summer symposium

3. See Jan Paweł II, *Pielgrzymki do Ojczyzny*, 28. For the idea of "theological society," see Rojek, "Społeczeństwo teologiczne."

4. Wojtyła, *Poezje, dramaty, szkice*, 27–76

in Castel Gandolfo to this issue.[5] Until the end of his life, the Pope also believed in the special destiny of Poland and other countries of Central and
Eastern Europe, which can be seen in his interviews and speeches addressed
to Poles. Like Father Richard Neuhaus, he thought that "if not in Poland,
then nowhere," although certainly the hopes of the Polish Pope significantly
exceeded the estimations of American neo-conservatives.

There are striking analogies between the Slavic ideas of Karol Wojtyła
and John Paul II on the one hand, and the various versions of Russian Slavophilism on the other. The underlying idea of integral Slavic Christianity
corresponds to Alexei Khomiakov's vision of the special status of Orthodoxy. The Papal theological appraisal of nations, which build the fullness
of Church, might be compared with the Slavophile teaching on *sobornost'*.
Finally, the belief in the special Slavic mission places the Polish Pope close to
a number of Russian thinkers, starting at least from Khomiakov, and ending
with Alexandr Solzhenitsyn and Patriarch Kirill. These analogies, however,
can hardly be explained by the direct influence of Russian religious thought
on Karol Wojtyła. He had formulated his views long before his acquaintance
with Russian thinkers, although we have evidence that he read in his youth
Nikolai Berdyaev's *New Middle Ages*, published in Polish in 1936.[6] The striking parallels between Wojtyła's Slavic idea and Russian religious thought
derived rather from the same religious, intellectual and social sources: a deep
Christian vision of the world, the general influence of romantic thought, and
the common situation of the Slavic nations in world history.[7]

The Theology of the Nation

The theology of the nation is presumably one of the most original elements
of John Paul II's teachings. According to Dorian Llywelyn, a contemporary
Jesuit researcher into the Catholic theory of nationality, it was precisely
John Paul II who "of all the popes of the twentieth century . . . insisted
most on the spiritual role of the nation."[8] In the papal theology of the nation, it is also most easy to see the influences of the Polish experience,
which the Pope never hid. During his first pilgrimage to Poland, he admitted: "For us, the word 'motherland' has a meaning, both for the mind and
for the heart, such as the other nations of Europe and the world appear not

5. Bobrownicka, *Narkotyk mitu*; Jan Paweł II, "Przemówienie inauguracyjne."

6. See, for instance, Wojtyła, "Listy," 304.

7. For the relations between John Paul II and Russian thought, see Valitskiy, *Rossiya*;
Przebinda, *Większa Europa*; Pshebinda, *Russkaya ideya*, 261–335.

8. Llywelyn, *Theology of Nationality*, 12.

to know."[9] Indeed, in many countries, the development of the national idea resulted in conflict with Catholicism, unlike in Poland, where national identity endorsed the religious one, and religion empowered the nation. Moreover, the Polish experience, comprising the long loss of an independent national state, clearly showed that the most important factor for a nation's existence is culture, not politics. "It is decisive for us throughout the course of history, more decisive even than material power. Indeed, it is more decisive than political boundaries."[10] The Pope contributed to the teachings of the Church not only the Polish experience, but also the Polish theological reflections on the nation, from Piotr Skarga through the Polish romantic messianists, redemptorists, ending with Cardinal Stefan Wyszyński. According to Father Mirosław Kowalczyk, in papal homilies from John Paul II's first pilgrimage to Poland,

> the vision of homeland and nation reached summits of mysticism and gained something from universal primatial perspective. In this way the whole Polish theology of nation received a lot from the new universal Christian perspective.[11]

Finally, papal teachings about the nation became a tremendous impulse for the development of an original Polish school of the theology of the nation, cautiously referring to the legacy of Polish romanticism.[12]

The foundation of John Paul II's theological reflection is his personalistic concept of the nation. Karol Wojtyła dealt with the nation's way of being in his lectures in Catholic social teaching, delivered in the fifties at the seminary of the Archdiocese of Krakow. The script of these lectures, recently published in Polish, says that "a nation exists 'through' persons, individuals, and so exists also 'for' them."[13] Hence, for Wojtyła, a nation was not a substantial being, something beyond and above individuals, but merely an accidental unity of many particular individuals. In his famous homily on Victory Square in Warsaw, John Paul II outlined a dialectical dependence between individuals and nation. A nation indeed is made up of particular individuals, but participation in the nation is constitutive for them, for it is the participation in their nation's culture that creates the deepest identity of

---

9. John Paul II, *Return to Poland*, 21.

10. John Paul II, *Return to Poland*, 47.

11. Kowalczyk, "Z teologii historii narodu," 245.

12. See Bartnik, "Problematyka teologii narodu"; "Sakrament pojednania"; *Teologia narodu, Idea polskości*; Buczek, *Teologia narodu*. See also Strzelczyk, "Kłopoty z teologią narodu"; Popiołek, "Poza narodem nie ma zbawienia?"; "Polska szkoła teologii narodu"; Gałkowski, "Naród i Objawienie."

13. Wojtyła, *Katolicka etyka społeczna*, 164.

each man. The Pope said that, on one hand, "it is right to understand the history of the nation through man," namely through "each human being of this nation," while on the other hand, "man cannot be understood apart from this community that is constituted by the nation" for "it is a special community . . . the most important for the spiritual history of man."[14] The same thought was later expressed by the Pope in his encyclical *Laborem Exercens*, where he indicated that, although a nation is primarily "a great historical and social incarnation of the work of all generations," it secondarily influences people, becoming "the great 'educator' of every man, even though an indirect one," as a result of which, "that man combines his deepest human identity with membership of a nation."[15] Hence, nation is on one hand a historical product of individuals, and on the other maintains towards them relative independence thanks to which it can influence them and constitute their identity. Therefore, John Paul II could write that "it is people and not nations who have to face God's judgment, but in the judgment pronounced on individuals, nations too are in some way judged."[16] Nations are judged as creations of community that subsequently form future generations. The dialectic vision of the nation by John Paul II, adopting both its individual and collective aspects, causes many problems to interpreters. A substantial, and quite risky, interpretation of this concept predominates in the Polish school of the theology of the nation. According to Father Czesław Bartnik, John Paul II ascribed the identity of nation "the rank of quasi-personality, some communal personality,"[17] and according to Father Jerzy Buczek, a nation in the Pope's vision was "a nation of people, and had some personality like that of a human being."[18] Unfortunately, the problem is that the nature of this supposed "personality" of nation is unknown. Ambiguity in this key point is manifest in Father Bartnik, who says for example that the nation admittedly, "is not a 'person' in the sense of an individual" but "has something of personality," which leads it to possess something "as if personal subjectivity," and is "as if 'a person,'" and that, although the nation's soul is being discussed "as some metaphor," yet it is not "fictitious."[19] This fundamental ambiguity of the Polish theology of the nation provokes well-founded charges of

14. John Paul II, *Return to Poland*, 28.

15. John Paul II, *Laborem Exercens*, 10.

16. John Paul II, *Memory and Identity*, 86.

17. Bartnik, "Sakrament pojednania," 318.

18. Buczek, *Teologia narodu*, 179.

19. Bartnik, *Idea polskości*, 143.

unjustified "hypostatization" of the nation.[20] However, I do not think this criticism has any bearing on John Paul II's dialectic vision.

The anniversary of Saints Cyril and Methodius's mission in 1985, honored by the Pope with his *Slavorum Apostoli* encyclical, was an occasion to discuss the papal theology of the nation more broadly. *Slavorum Apostoli* was, according to Llywelyn, "one of the most personal encyclicals of the Polish Pope."[21] It is notable that the reflections on theology of nation were again placed in the broader Slavic context, and not only the Polish. Clearly, the Pope, as usual, wanted to avoid raising suspicions of Polish particularism. He first recalled that the Church's mission is naturally universal and exceeds all national limitations. The Church's task is

> the proclamation of the eternal message of salvation, peace and mutual concord among peoples and nations, beyond all the frontiers that yet divide our planet, which is intended by the will of God the Creator and Redeemer to be the common dwelling for all humanity.[22]

At the same time, Christianity does not require the faithful to renounce the cultural experience of their nations. On the contrary, national differences enrich the content of the Church's universality. For "catholicity," as the Pope reminded,

> is a symphony of the various liturgies in all the world's languages united in one single liturgy, or a melodious chorus sustained by the voices of unnumbered multitudes, rising in countless modulations, tones and harmonies for the praise of God from every part of the globe, at every moment of history.[23]

The differentiation of nations, as of individuals, ultimately stems from God's will. To express this idea, John Paul II used the evocative metaphor of a mosaic:

> The Church is catholic also because she is able to present in every human context the revealed truth . . . in such a way as to bring it into contact with the lofty thoughts and just expectations of every individual and every people. Moreover, the entire patrimony of good which every generation transmits to posterity . . . forms as it were an immense and many-colored collection of tesserae that together make up the living mosaic of

20. Strzelczyk, "Kłopoty z teologią narodu," 40.

21. Llywelyn, *Theology of Nationality*, 160.

22. John Paul II, *Slavorum Apostoli*, 16

23. John Paul II, *Slavorum Apostoli*, 17.

the Pantocrator, who will manifest himself in his total splendor only at the moment of the Parousia.[24]

The Church, therefore, as a living icon of Christ, is made not only of particular people or families, but also of varied national cultures.[25] Hence, every nation is an irreplaceable individual, indispensable for the full realization of God's plan for the world. If any of the nations were missing, Pope suggested, the image of Christ would be incomplete. As he continued: "all individuals, all nations, cultures and civilizations have their own part to play and their own place in God's mysterious plan and in the universal history of salvation."[26] The fundamental claim of missionism could not have been formulated more clearly. Nations differ from one another, and although they all participate in the growth of God's kingdom on Earth, they may have various functions in different times. Obviously, the Slavs are also a special part of this divine mosaic. John Paul II ended his encyclical with the following prayer:

> The whole Church thanks you, who called the Slavic nations into the communion of the faith, for this heritage and for the contribution made by them to the universal patrimony. The Pope of Slav origin in a special way thanks you for this. May this contribution never cease to enrich the Church, the Continent of Europe and the whole world! May it never fail in Europe and in the world of today! May it never fade from the memories of our contemporaries! We desire to accept in its entirety everything original and valid which the Slavic nations have brought and continue to bring to the spiritual patrimony of the Church and of humanity.[27]

However, the encyclical does not explain precisely the contribution that Slavs made to the legacy of the Church and humanity. It is only known to be specific, yet its content is not revealed. I think that some light may be thrown on this issue by the Polish homilies of 1979, read in the perspective of pre-war poems by the man who would become Pope.

A Slavic Pope

John Paul II very emphatically introduced the Slavic theme in his speeches during his first pilgrimage to Poland. He referred to himself as the "Slavic

---

24. John Paul II, *Slavorum Apostoli*, 18.

25. Llywelyn, *Theology of Nationality*, 161.

26. John Paul II, *Slavorum Apostoli*, 19.

27. John Paul II, *Slavorum Apostoli*, 31

Pope" many times,[28] and often addressed the Slavic "related peoples" and "nations."[29] Everyone in Poland read these words as a clear allusion to the poem "Our Slavic Pope" written by Juliusz Słowacki in 1848, which gained a broad circulation at that time. Słowacki speculated long before John Paul II's election on the papacy of the new epoch of the Spirit and supposedly predicted the first Slavic Pope.[30] In fact, however, the Pope also implicitly referred to other poems of which he was author. The volume *Renaissance Psalter (Slavic Book)*, completed in the spring of 1939, is his earliest preserved work. These poems, not included in the first Polish collection of Wojtyła's poetry published in 1979, appeared in two different versions as late as 1996 and 1999.[31] At the time that John Paul II delivered his Slavic speech on Lech's Hill, they could have been known to no more than a few people in Poland. Yet it seems that precisely these early poems are the key to understanding the mystery of the Slavs in the teachings of John Paul II. The young Karol Wojtyła hoped for the coming of a Slavic era which would unite the greatest values of the gothic and the renaissance; years later, John Paul II officially inaugurated in the Church an age of the Slavs, who were to show how to combine traditional religion and secular modernity.

John Paul II must clearly have been greatly concerned by his election to the See of Peter. During his first pilgrimage to Poland he repeatedly emphasized that his choice was the "inscrutable design of Providence."[32] The Pope saw in it a special sign of choice, not only of himself, but also of his local church and nation. "Since thou, Lord Jesus, have taken me from there," he spoke humbly, "then I am as I come from there. Apparently, you need me like this at this moment."[33] As he later explained: "It was not simply the summons of an individual, but of the entire Church to with he had belonged since birth; indirectly, it was also a call to his nation."[34] Hence, the Pope projected his own calling onto his nation, and even broader on the whole Slavic family of nations. He tried to penetrate the inscrutable decree of Providence and understand what the world needed the Slavs for at that moment.

---

28. John Paul II, *Return to Poland*, 43, 45, 84. For other instances missing in English translation, see Jan Paweł II, *Pielgrzymki do Ojczyzny*, 47, 48, 204.

29. John Paul II, *Return to Poland*, 43, 53. See also Jan Paweł II, *Pielgrzymki do Ojczyzny*, 38, 159, 191, 204

30. Słowacki, "Our Slavic Pope."

31. See Burghardt "Historia tekstów młodzieńczych"; Dziedzic, *Romantyk Boży*, 220–27.

32. John Paul II, *Return to Poland*, 16, 24, 42, 54, 59, 62, 92, 112, 115.

33. Jan Paweł II, *Pielgrzymki do Ojczyzny*, 73.

34. John Paul II, *Memory and Identity*, 160.

In the homily on Lech's Hill, quoted at the beginning of this chapter, the Pope consistently developed the vision of the providential vocation of Poland and of Slavdom. First, he indicated his roots in Polish and Slavic culture: "Pope John Paul II, a Slav, a son of the Polish nation, feels how deeply fixed in the ground of history are the roots of his origin."[35] Then he tried to understand what consequences for Poland and Slavdom would arise from the fact that a Pole, and a Slav, had become Pope for the first time in history:

> Perhaps that is why Christ has chosen him, perhaps that is why the Holy Spirit has led him—in order that he might introduce into the communion of the Church the understanding of the words and of the languages. . . . He comes here to speak before the whole Church, before Europe and the world, of those often forgotten nations and peoples. He comes here to cry "with a loud voice." . . . He comes here to embrace all these peoples, together with his own nation, and to hold them close to the heart of the Church.[36]

Therefore, the choice of John Paul II as Pope indicates a special mission of Poland and the whole of Eastern Europe. The Pope said:

> Have we not the right . . . to think that Poland has become now-adays the land of a particularly responsible witness? The right to think that from here . . . that it is to proclaim Christ with singular humility but also with conviction? The right to think that one must come to this very place, to this land, on this route, to read again the witness of his Cross and his Resurrection? But if we accept all that I have dared to affirm in this moment, how many great duties and obligations arise? Are we capable of them?[37]

It is clear that this mission was mainly prophetic, since it was to concern the testimony of faith. Karol Wojtyła had previously indicated that the profession of faith by the people, alongside the teachings carried out by the Church hierarchy, is the participation in the prophetic mission of Christ.[38] Moreover, testimony of faith should not merely be of a private, but also a public character.[39] The "specially responsible testimony" to which Poles were called, was therefore in fact the participation in Christ's prophetic mission. Hence, for John Paul II his election as Pope was a special sign for Poland

---

35. John Paul II, *Return to Poland*, 45.
36. John Paul II, *Return to Poland*, 43, 45.
37. John Paul II, *Return to Poland*, 25.
38. Wojtyła, *Sources of Renewal*, 94.
39. Wojtyła, *Sign of Contradiction*, 121.

and Slavdom, indicating the tasks ahead for them. As Father Kowlaczyk showed, the Pope apparently believed that he "inaugurated a new era of the Church: the Slavic era, the era of the Church of Slavs, the era of the history of redemption on Slavic lands in full swing."[40]

In order to comprehend what this Slavic era meant for John Paul II, one has to have a look at his early poems. For it seems that the cardinals, by their choice of a Pole as Pope, confirmed the onetime intuition of Karol Wojtyła that it was Slavdom that had some special role to play in the realization of Christianity in the world. Wojtyła finished his *Slavic Book* "on the day of St. John 1939," and sent it in the autumn to his friend Mieczysław Kotlarczyk for review.[41] Some of these poems must have been brought to Krakow from Wadowice. Presumably, these were the works that he read to his comrades at a military training camp for young people and then declaimed at his first artistic soiree in Krakow. Danuta Michałowska, who heard them before the war, recalled: "I must state that they were extraordinary. Not only for their exceptional maturity and intellectual horizons of the eighteen-year-old author, but primarily for some audacious prophetic tone."[42] This tone was not, however, the catastrophic prophetism of many poets of the generation, but it was clearly messianistic. According to Stanisław Dziedzic, Wojtyła's poems "though written shortly before the outbreak of war, do not herald the coming armed conflict . . . however, there is the anticipation of a breakthrough, the fulfilment of times in Christ, the rebirth of the Christian epoch."[43]

The fundamental theme of *Slavic Book* is precisely the anticipation of the regeneration of the world. "I believe," confessed the young Wojtyła, "in materialization of united will: in a progressing breakthrough."[44] The result of this breakthrough was to be the advent of the new "Era,"[45] the "Golden Age."[46] The new epoch was to be religious in character. Wojtyła described his own times as an epoch of "expecting the Spirit"[47] and "reaching out hands to Christ"[48]; the coming era was to "push darkness aside" and "bring God's love closer."[49] Wojtyła wrote that the New Era is to be a synthesis of the two

40. Kowalczyk, "Z teologii historii narodu," 259.

41. Wojtyła, "Listy," 308.

42. Michałowska, "Karol Wojtyła," 90.

43. Dziedzic, *Romantyk Boży*, 175.

44. Wojtyła, *Poezje, dramaty, szkice*, 33.

45. Wojtyła, *Poezje, dramaty, szkice*, 32.

46. Wojtyła, *Poezje, dramaty, szkice*, 30.

47. Wojtyła, *Poezje, dramaty, szkice*, 38.

48. Wojtyła, *Poezje, dramaty, szkice*, 45.

49. Wojtyła, *Poezje, dramaty, szkice*, 33.

previous periods: "the soul of the coming age is gothic and renaissance."[50]
In an extended note to *Psalter* he explained that the gothic was based on the
commandment of love of God, and the renaissance on that of man. These
rules, taken separately, had led to many disasters in history:

> Gothic and renaissance separately taken are exclusiveness; to-
> gether, they harmony make. Gothic has a soaring and narrow
> path. . . . Down it we may fall in servility, in subjugation of soul.
> Against this I revolt! Let us now look at renaissance. Its way is
> rather wide, its way is vast. . . . Coming down this path, we reach
> slackening and negation of harmony.[51]

The new epoch should harmoniously integrate the two principles of
the gothic love of God and the renaissance love of man. "In this coalescence
richness is great. . . . The gothic way leads upwards, renaissance sideways.
The two paths cross. The perfect form."[52]

Slavs were to play a special role in the advent of this new age. This
was to be so because, according to Wojtyła, the "Slavic soul" combines precisely the elements of the gothic and the renaissance, thanks to which it can
help the whole world develop this synthesis. He mentioned it directly in his
poem "Slavic Soul":

> There is within you freedom and frolicking of spruces, the for-
> est brawlers. there are coffered ceilings of cloud, there are green
> slopes of trees, and above this eternal freedom, there is the pious
> whiteness of mountain-peaks and there is the lofty reverie in the
> harmony of sharp-arched tones.[53]

Hence, the "Slavic soul" was to unite freedom and frolic on one hand,
and prayer, reverie and longing for God on the other. Therefore, it was a
synthesis of the "horizontal" renaissance love of other people and the whole
world and the "vertical" gothic reference to a transcendent God. The symbol
of the "Slavic soul" was, according to Wojtyła, Wawel Cathedral in Krakow,
amazingly uniting renaissance and gothic elements.[54] Hence, the "Slavic
soul" was the spirit of the "coming times," which endowed it with the special
mission of bringing this new era closer. Wojtyła wrote directly:

---

50. Wojtyła, *Poezje, dramaty, szkice*, 38.

51. Wojtyła, *Poezje, dramaty, szkice*, 49.

52. Wojtyła, *Poezje, dramaty, szkice*, 49.

53. Wojtyła, *Poezje, dramaty, szkice*, 34 (translation by Piotr Mizia, as cited by
Machniak, *God and Man*, 21).

54. Wojtyła, *Poezje, dramaty, szkice*, 35.

Lift, o Slavic soul, this Ark of Divine Revelations, descend upon the pining era and enlighten it with the brightness of the roadside crosses.[55]

The coming synthesis was to be realized precisely through the Slavs. It was they who were to undertake the task of transforming the world in the Christian spirit and satisfy the cravings of the modern era. Poland's Wawel Cathedral was to become a paradigm for the universal construction of an integral Christian civilization.

It is easy to find the two key ideas of Polish messianism: Christian millenarianism and Slavic missionism in Wojtyła's early poetry.[56] It did not, however, yet include the third element, passionism, which would appear shortly in Wojtyła's works written under Nazi German occupation. The vision of the coming Slavic era, which was to integrate previous epochs created by the Roman and German peoples, was a very popular motif in Polish and Russian messianism. In Poland, the most developed vision of this kind was presented by August Cieszkowski in *Prolegomena to Historiosophy* and by Zygmunt Krasiński in *The Position of Poland from the Divine and Human Points*.[57] The young Wojtyła merged this great vision with his beloved folk motifs, adding a lot of juvenile pathos to it. One of his friends recalled that when Wojtyła visited Wadowice before the war and read his poems to girls he had befriended, "we were so amused with the pathos that we in turns slipped off to the balcony to giggle."[58]

Between Wawel and Nowa Huta

Undoubtedly, Wojtyła spent his whole life developing and realizing the integral vision of "Slavic" Christianity he had expressed in his youth. On one hand, he wanted to encompass as much as possible of what is human, and on the other, to refer it all to the divine. For this reason, he tried in his ministry to combine ski excursions with common prayer, stressing in philosophical works the relation between love and responsibility, and writing in later encyclicals about the unity of truth and freedom. It seems that this integral vision is particularly visible in John Paul II's speeches during his first pilgrimage to Poland in 1979. The connection with his past Slavic poems is all the more striking because, as Pope, he spoke directly in his

55. Wojtyła, *Poezje, dramaty, szkice*, 38 (translation by Piotr Mizia, as cited by Machniak, *God and Man*, 23).

56. For a detailed analysis of Polish Messianism, see Rojek, *Liturgia dziejów*, 28–98.

57. Sokulski, "Stanowisko Polski."

58. Recorded by Zając, "Przewodnik po książkach," 315.

homilies about the role of Poland and Slavdom. Hence, his sermons of this period may be seen as a continuation, after forty years, of his juvenile vision from the *Slavic Book*.

First, I would like to draw attention to a speech delivered on June 4 to a group of monastic superiors at the Jasna Góra. The audience was very close to the Pope and his speech was, as he himself admitted, mostly improvised. "Let no one in the world," he joked, "no journalist, pick holes in papal words!"[59] But it is worth taking a look at what he said. John Paul II openly indicated that contemporary Polish Christianity had special significance for the whole world. He said:

> God has given us very hard experiences. But through these experiences, in a way thanks to them, we are reading the signs of the time differently. Differently, and probably more aptly. I do not want to be accused of local patriotism by anyone. I have to be very careful, especially since October 16 last year. But I judge a bit by the fruit. This is no apriorism. This is theological and pastoral aposteriorism. Or if someone prefers: empiricism. Anyway, that is how I see these things.[60]

As can be seen, the value of Polish Christianity resulted, according to the Pope, not from any special choice by God but simply from the coincidence of historical circumstances (which, anyway, could by their nature be providential). Poland was experiencing at that time a fundamental conflict between traditional religion and secular modernity. The conflict was particularly fierce because, on one side stood a strong Church, deeply rooted in the people and leading an ideological offensive, while on the other side were the powerful Communist authorities, greatly supported by the Soviet empire, who realized their program of the rapid modernization of Poland. This was a true spiritual, and often also physical, clash of giants. Poland's situation was exceptional, because in many other countries this struggle had either not begun or had already ended. Strong religion typically characterized backward or developing countries, especially in Third World, and modern Western states were already considerably secular. Poland in 1979 could be seen as a real laboratory of modernity. One could see there the possibility of an alternative form of modernity transformed by religion.

I think the message of John Paul II can be grasped best in his homily delivered in Nowa Huta, a separate industrial part of Krakow, on June 9. The sermon had a very personal tone, because it followed from previous

59. Jan Paweł II, *Pielgrzymki do Ojczyzny*, 58. That whole speech is missing in English edition.

60. Jan Paweł II, *Pielgrzymki do Ojczyzny*, 57.

experiences of the Pope, who, as Archbishop of Krakow, had actively participated in the ultimately victorious struggle to build a church in Nowa
Huta. The inhabitants of that district, mainly workers at the local steel mill,
rebelled against the Communist vision of the new secular community and
bravely defended a cross raised in the place where they planned to erect
a church. The essential motif of the exquisite homily of John Paul II was
the vision of the construction of Nowa Huta at the foundation of the cross.
The Pope wanted to show in this way that it is possible and necessary to
combine industrial civilization with traditional religion, and that, thanks to
the mutual engagement of workers and members of the clergy, a true city of
the future was to emerge:

> I am thankful to God's Providence that I could build Nowa
> Huta on the foundation of Christ's cross with you, along with
> the entire new regime. . . . In the spirit of fraternal solidarity, I
> built it together with you: the directors, the engineers, the met-
> allurgists, the workers, the ministers! I built it with you on the
> foundation of Christ's cross![61]

With this mighty gesture, John Paul II included Communist industri-
alization in the task of building God's kingdom on earth. This gesture could
be compared only to the proposal of Bogdan Wielkopolski, a forgotten Polish émigré messianist, who suggested that a statue of the Holy Virgin Mary
be erected on top of the Joseph Stalin Palace of Culture in Warsaw after
victory over the Communists.[62] The Pope showed that the confrontation
between religion and modernity should lead to religion encompassing and
permeating all positive worldly realities. The Pope wanted Poland to remain
"Catholic,"[63] but at the same time to become "powerful through its work."[64]
This fresh combination of religion and modernity was to be the most semi-
nal truth encountered by the Polish experience. In Poland, churches were
built in new socialist class quarters, workers at industrial plants participated
in religious practices on a mass scale, and communist modernization became the chance for a new Christianization. In this way, there emerged a
unique synthesis of the human and the divine. Such was the essence of the
Polish experience, which could serve as a model for the whole world: "From
the Cross of Nowa Huta," said the Pope, "began the new evangelization, the
evangelization of the second Millennium."[65]

61. Jan Paweł II, *Pielgrzymki do Ojczyzny*, 191.
62. See Chojnacki, "Mesjanizm," 75.
63. John Paul II, *Return to Poland*, 77.
64. Jan Paweł II, *Pielgrzymki do Ojczyzny*, 136.
65. John Paul II, *Return to Poland*, 158.

It was this moving vision, so vividly expressed by John Paul II in Nowa Huta, that became the ideological foundation of the Solidarity movement less than a year after his homily. Besides, the Pope wished that his pilgrimage "be continued in Poland,"[66] not only in individual souls but also in society and nation. "I think," the Pope said, "that the desire of Christ, which awakens, which has already awakened so much, must pass through a great test, through a *social test*, so that it can meet some providential intentions of God himself."[67] John Paul II clearly have expected that his vision would somehow be materialized by the Poles on a mass scale. Yet, it is unlikely that anybody could have envisaged what actually happened. The Solidarity movement, may be understood as precisely an attempt at the realization of John Paul II's great idea.[68] Solidarity tried to combine traditional religion with the modern world on a mass scale. Holy masses held at workplaces during strikes, which will be discussed later, were a great symbol of this synthesis. In 1987, in Gdańsk, the Pope spoke about the experience of Solidarity:

> They were surprised at various places that it could be so. That there is a bond between the world of work and the cross of Christ, that there is a bond between human work and mass. . . . Many were surprised. Or maybe they discovered something at the same time? They discovered the forgotten dimension of the whole "social question." . . . Work and Christ? Work and Eucharist? And yet it was like this here. And rightly.[69]

The shipyard workers on the Polish coast hence embraced the same idea presented by the Pope to the steelworkers in Nowa Huta. The whole of Poland thus became for many years the laboratory for an amazing socio-theological experiment, the effects of which were to influence the whole world.

It seems that the vision of combining religion and modernity presented by John Paul II during the confrontation of the Church with the Communist regime, and then undertaken on a mass scale by the Solidarity movement, corresponds to the vision of the Slavic soul formulated by him many years earlier in his juvenile poems. The Slavs, according to the young Wojtyła, were to unite the gothic orientation to God with the renaissance interest in the world. Likewise, Poles were for John Paul II to unite traditional religiosity with modern civilization. Thus, after many years, the

---

66. Jan Paweł II, *Pielgrzymki do Ojczyzny*, 195.
67. Jan Paweł II, *Pielgrzymki do Ojczyzny*, 131 (emphasis mine).
68. See Rojek, *Liturgia dziejów*, 199–279.
69. Jan Paweł II, *Pielgrzymki do Ojczyzny*, 494–5.

old Slavic soul was incarnated in Polish workers. It is apparent how long the evolution of the idea was: from the rustic images of the young Wojtyła to the industrial vision of John Paul II. The thatched cottages inhabited by hospitable Slavs gave way to contemporary blocks of flats. The idea, however, remained the same. In this way, the Polish experience of traditional Catholicism encountering Communist modernization and led to a religious synthesis. If the old Wawel Cathedral was the symbol of the Slavic soul for the young Wojtyła, the new Ark of the Lord church in Nowa Huta symbolized the new era for Pope John Paul II.

Bibliography

Bartnik, Czesław Stanisław. *Idea polskości.* Radom: Polskie Wydawnictwo Encyklopedyczne, 2001.

———. "Problematyka teologii narodu." In *Polska teologia narodu,* edited by Czesław Stanisław Bartnik, 9–42. Lublin: TN KUL, 1986.

———. "Sakrament pojednania narodu w nauczaniu Jana Pawła II w Polsce w 1983 roku." In *Polska teologia narodu,* edited by Czesław Stanisław Bartnik, 309–27. Lublin: TN KUL, 1986.

———. *Teologia narodu.* Częstochowa: Tygodnik Katolicki Niedziela, 1999.

Bobrownicka, Maria. *Narkotyk mitu. Szkice o świadomości narodowej i kulturowej Słowian Zachodnich i Południowych.* Krakow: Universitas, 1995.

Buczek, Jerzy. *Teologia narodu w ujęciu wybranych polskich teologów.* Rzeszów: Bonus Liber, 2014.

Burghardt, Marta. "Historia tekstów młodzieńczych poezji Karola Wojtyły." In *Przestrzeń Słowa. Twórczość literacka Karola Wojtyły—Jana Pawła II,* edited by Zofia Zarębianka and Jan Machniak, 51–60. Krakow: Wydawnictwo św. Stanisława, 2006.

Chojnacki, Paweł. "Mesjanizm Drugiej Wielkiej Emigracji. Wielkopolski, Dzieduszycki i Nałęcz." *Pressje* 30–31 (2012) 72–86.

Dziedzic, Stanisław. *Romantyk Boży.* Krakow: Wydawnictwo M, 2014.

Gałkowski, Juliusz. "Naród i Objawienie. Spór o status teologii narodu." In *Społeczeństwo teologiczne. Polska teologia narodu 966–2016,* edited by Paweł Rojek, 175–94. Krakow: Klub Jagielloński, Wydawnictwo M, 2016.

John Paul II. "Laborem Exercens." Encyclical letter. September 14, 1981. http://w2.vatican.va/content/john-paul-ii/en/encyclicals/documents/hf_jp-ii_enc_14091981_laborem-exercens.html.

———. *Memory and Identity. Personal Reflections.* London: Weidenfeld & Nicolson, 2005.

———. *Pielgrzymki do Ojczyzny. Przemówienia i homilie.* Krakow: Znak, 2012.

———. *Return to Poland. The Collected Speeches of John Paul II.* London: Collins, 1979.

———. "Slavorum Apostoli." Encyclical letter. June 2, 1985. http://w2.vatican.va/content/john-paul-ii/en/encyclicals/documents/hf_jp-ii_enc_19850602_slavorum-apostoli.html.

Kowalczyk, Mirosław. "Z teologii historii narodu Jana Pawła II." In *Polska teologia narodu,* edited by Czesław Stanisław Bartnik, 243–72. Lublin: TN KUL, 1986,

Llywelyn, Dorian. *Toward a Catholic Theology of Nationality*. Lanham: Lexington, 2010.

Machniak, Jan. *God and Man in the Poetry of Karol Wojtyła—John Paul II*. Translated by Piotr Mizia. Krakow: Wydawnictwo św. Stanisława, 2008.

Michałowska, Danuta. "Karol Wojtyła—czy można przestać być poetą?" *Więź* 3 (1999) 89–96.

Popiołek, Piotr. "Polska szkoła teologii narodu. Stefan Wyszyński, Jan Paweł II i Czesław Bartnik." In *Społeczeństwo teologiczne. Polska teologia narodu 966–2016*, edited by Paweł Rojek, 153–74. Krakow: Klub Jagielloński, Wydawnictwo M, 2016.

———. "Poza narodem nie ma zbawienia?" *Pressje* 38 (2014) 35–46.

Przebinda, Grzegorz. *Większa Europa. Papież wobec Rosji i Ukrainy*. Krakow: Znak, 2001.

Pshebinda, Gzhegozh. *Mezhdu Krakovom, Rimom i Moskvoy. Russkaya ideya v novoy Pol'she*. Moscow: Izdatel'stvo RGGU, 2013.

Rojek, Paweł. *Liturgia dziejów. Jan Paweł II i polski mesjanizm*. Krakow: Klub Jagielloński, Wydawnictwo M, 2016.

———. "Społeczeństwo teologiczne." In *Społeczeństwo teologiczne. Polska teologia narodu 966–2016*, edited by Paweł Rojek, 9–20. Krakow: Klub Jagielloński, Wydawnictwo M, 2016.

Słowacki, Juliusz. "Our Slavic Pope." In *Bear Now My Soul: Polish Verse in English Translation*, edited by Noel Clark, 88–89. Wroclaw: Ossolineum, 1997.

Sokulski, Michał. 2016. "Stanowisko Polski z Bożych względów. Romantyczna teologia narodu Zygmunta Krasińskiego." In *Społeczeństwo teologiczne. Polska teologia narodu 966–2016*, edited by Paweł Rojek, 89–108. Krakow: Klub Jagielloński, Wydawnictwo M, 2016.

Strzelczyk, Grzegorz. "Kłopoty z teologią narodu." *Więź* 1 (2016) 34–42.

Valitskiy, Andzhey. *Rossiya, katolichestvo i pol'skiy vopros*, translated by Elena S. Tverdislova. Moscow: Izdatel'stvo Moskovskogo Universiteta, 2012.

Wojtyła, Karol. *Katolicka etyka społeczna*. Lublin: Wydawnictwo KUL, 2018.

———. "Listy Karola Wojtyły do Mieczysława Kotlarczyka." In *O Teatrze Rapsodycznym. sześćdziesięciolecie powstania Teatru Rapsodycznego*, by Mieczysław Kotlarczyk and Karol Wojtyła, 297–335. Krakow: Państwowa Wyższa Szkoła Teatralna im. Ludwika Solskiego w Krakowie, 2001.

———. *Poezje, dramaty, szkice. Tryptyk rzymski*. Krakow: Znak, 2004.

———. "Przemówienie inauguracyjne." In *Współcześni Słowianie wobec własnych tradycji i mitów. Sympozjum w Castel Gandolfo, 19–20 sierpnia 1996*, edited by Maria Bobrownicka, et al., 9–13. Krakow: Universitas, 1997.

———. *Sign of Contradiction*. Translated by Mary Smith. Middlegreen: St. Paul, 1979.

———. *Sources of Renewal. The Implementation of the Second Vatican Council*. Translated by P. S. Falla. San Francisco: Harper and Row, 1980.

Zając, Marek. "Przewodnik po książkach o Janie Pawle II." *Teologia Polityczna* 3 (2006) 313–21.